ROUTLEDGE LIBRARY EDITIONS: COMPARATIVE EDUCATION

Volume 2

EDUCATION IN CENTRAL AMERICA AND THE CARIBBEAN

EDUCATION IN CENTRAL AMERICA AND THE CARIBBEAN

Edited by
COLIN BROCK AND
DONALD CLARKSON

Routledge
Taylor & Francis Group
LONDON AND NEW YORK

First published in 1990 by Routledge

This edition first published in 2018
by Routledge
2 Park Square, Milton Park, Abingdon, Oxon OX14 4RN

and by Routledge
711 Third Avenue, New York, NY 10017

Routledge is an imprint of the Taylor & Francis Group, an informa business

British Library Cataloguing in Publication Data
A catalogue record for this book is available from the British Library

ISBN: 978-1-138-54113-9 (Set)
ISBN: 978-1-351-00358-2 (Set) (ebk)
ISBN: 978-1-138-54400-0 (Volume 2) (hbk)
ISBN: 978-1-138-54453-6 (Volume 2) (pbk)
ISBN: 978-1-351-00522-7 (Volume 2) (ebk)

Publisher's Note
The publisher has gone to great lengths to ensure the quality of this reprint but points out that some imperfections in the original copies may be apparent.

Disclaimer
The publisher has made every effort to trace copyright holders and would welcome correspondence from those they have been unable to trace.

Education in Central America and the Caribbean

The Caribbean basin is an extremely diverse area in geographical, ethnic and cultural terms. Its educational systems, too, are remarkably varied, reflecting colonial and religious traditions as well as those of a broad range of post-independence movements. Even these show a pronounced merging of the home-grown and the foreign, with the influence of the superpowers never far away.

This book comprises a number of case studies ranging across the Caribbean region. The contributors focus in particular on Puerto Rico, Cuba, Jamaica, the British Virgin Islands, Mexico City, Central America, Costa Rica and Venezuela. By assembling studies from diverse cultural and political traditions and networks, the book gives a more comprehensive Caribbean perspective on education than has hitherto been available.

The Editors

Colin Brock is Senior Lecturer in Education, and Chairman of the International Education Unit at the University of Hull. Donald Clarkson is Professor of Education at the University of Bridgeport, Connecticut.

Education in Central America and the Caribbean

Edited by Colin Brock and Donald Clarkson

Routledge
London and New York

First published 1990 by Routledge
11 New Fetter Lane, London EC4P 4EE

Simultaneously published in the USA and Canada
by Routledge
a division of Routledge, Chapman and Hall, Inc.
29 West 35th Street, New York, NY 10001

Printed and bound in Great Britain by
Biddles Ltd, Guildford and King's Lynn

British Library Cataloguing in Publication Data

Education in Central America and the
Caribbean
1. Caribbean region. Education
I. Brock, Colin, *1939–* II. Clarkson,
Donald
370'.9182'1

ISBN 0-415-03885-5

Library of Congress Cataloging in Publication Data
is available

CONTENTS

FIGURES

TABLES

THE CONTRIBUTORS

COLIN BROCK is Senior Lecturer in Education and Chairman of the International Education Unit, University of Hull, England.

DONALD CLARKSON is Professor of Education and Chairman of the Division of Education at the University of Bridgeport, Connecticut, USA.

. . . .

PILAR AGUILAR is a Research Student at the University of Hull, England.

LILIA BORRERO is Head of the Statistics Section of the Ministry of Education, Venezuela.

LUPITA GONZALEZ-PAREDES is a Research Student at King's College, University of London, England.

EYRA JIMENEZ is an Educational Planner at the Ministry of Education, Venezuela.

ERROL MILLER is Professor of Teacher Education at the University of the West Indies, Mona, Jamaica.

GONZALO RETAMAL is Education Officer, Technical Support Service, United Nations Commission for Refugees, Geneva, Switzerland.

MARK RICHMOND is Senior Lecturer in Sociology in the School of Social and Professional Studies at Humberside College of Higher Education, Hull, England

DAVID SMAWFIELD is Lecturer in Education at the University of Hull, England.

DAVID TURNER is Senior Lecturer in the School for Independent Study, Polytechnic of East London, England.

ACKNOWLEDGEMENTS

The editors would like to express their gratitude to all the other contributors to this volume for their forbearance during the process of production from the response to our invitation to the eventual date of publication.

We are also most grateful for the diligence and professionalism of Shirley Brock in respect of proof-reading and the compilation of an index, and Lupita and David Turner for undertaking the task of word-processing the camera ready copy for publication.

Chapter One

EDITORIAL INTRODUCTION:

THE CARIBBEAN BASIN - A REALISTIC REGIONAL CONCEPT?

Colin Brock

Due to the formative influences of politics and language on the development of education systems, their evolution and related stocks of literature tend often to appear relatively discrete. In the Caribbean region this is illustrated by the several legacies of the colonial powers in respect of education, there being Hispanic, Francophone and Anglophone sets of countries and traditions which have been interrelated or disconnected at different times over the past five hundred years. Furthermore, pre-Columban educational developments were present in some form in all the indigenous Amerindian communities of the Caribbean basin, and reached very high levels in the case of the Mayan civilizations of Central America. Because of the plural nature of colonial influences in this part of the world, the 'Caribbean Basin' has not normally been perceived as a region from the outside, except of course from the perspective of the USA as regularized in one of the most recent of its backyard campaigns, the 'Caribbean Basin Initiative'. Florida, of course, forms part of the northern rim of the basin and Miami is arguably the chief central place in systematic terms, even though being peripheral in physical location.

At the height of the Spanish Empire in the New World, the majority of the basin was under Iberian control, and the fact that their principal convoy routes for imports and exports in respect of the whole of Spanish South and Central America focused on the south and east littorals of the Caribbean Sea provided a veneer of cultural cohesion, but that was to crack under the strain of repeated incursions by other empire-building powers, especially in the West Indian islands. Indeed, even today the bulk of the Central and South American states that comprise the western and southern rims of the basin remain Hispanic in language and tradition, the only exception being Belize, as the Guyanas are physically outside - though in cultural terms undoubtedly 'Caribbean'. The islands that collectively comprise the West Indies in general remained colonies longer than the mainland states. Though the majority are now independent of their European metropoles, at least in respect of direct political control, some are still colonies of the United Kingdom, others form a joint Kingdom with The Netherlands, while Guadaloupe, Guyane and Martinique are an integral part of France. Among the larger islands of the greater Antilles, two - Cuba and Puerto Rico - have attracted the interest of the superpowers who have taken on the mantle of metropolitan policemen. In addition to Cuba and Puerto Rico, Haiti and the Dominican Republic have also experienced the tutelage of the USA in the past, while more recently the Windward Island state Grenada was the centre of Cuban and Soviet attention before being invaded by the USA in 1983 and returned to the western fold. So the active interest of external forces which led to the Caribbean political geography of the mid- twentieth century is still occurring, albeit with new agencies to the fore.

This not only testifies to the strategic sensitivity of the Caribbean region but also carries educational implications. Perhaps of all colonial legacies, that of education is the most enduring, and in the case of the island states of the West Indies even more influential in that, as Naipaul puts it, these countries and communities are 'the creations of empire'. Whereas in the mainland states of the Americas and elsewhere there was an indigenous population that survived in different degrees and contributed to the hybrid culture, in the islands, where Amerindians were exterminated or expelled, an entirely derived society was created. Throughout the Caribbean region, numerous Christian denominations vied with each other to convert both indigenous and imported populations to their beliefs, and inevitably education had to be involved in the work of these missions if they were to achieve their objectives. Where slavery formed the basis of the economic order, that is to say in the non-Hispanic colonies, schooling was not permitted until emancipation. Consequently in the Latin Caribbean, schooling has a longer record of existence and is predominantly Catholic in tradition. Early in their colonization, the Spanish established seminaries and universities as the formative phase of what were to become highly selective and academic systems typical of their legacy throughout Latin America. They lent themselves to the servicing of the elite, conservative agencies ensuring cultural and social reproduction. However, another strand of the Catholic tradition in the Latin Caribbean has long supported the underprivileged, working with rural communities, spreading literacy and awareness. Within the region in recent times the most notable inputs of this kind have been in Nicaragua, where they inevitably conflict with the conservatism of American patronage. In Cuba, the Catholic educational tradition conflicts ideologically with the doctrine of the secular state, but in that case the state itself has rendered educational opportunity universally accessible since the revolution of 1959.

In the non-Hispanic West Indian Islands and Belize, denominationalism has created a kaleidoscopic quilt, the composition of which contributes strongly to the idiosyncracy of both island society and the schooling that helps to regulate it. Insularity, smallness of scale and remoteness of location combine in different degrees, island by island, to further promote locale-specific educational situations, the problems associated with them being less amenable to resolution through theories and methods developed from the experience of larger industrialized nations. Nonetheless, received conventional wisdom whereby salvation - economic as well as spiritual - derives from education seems undiminished.

Even in the larger states of the region, the economies remain dependent on the old or new metropolitan markets. From the fruit company plantations of Central America to the sugar plantations of Cuba to the yacht havens of the Virgin Islands and the oil industry of Trinidad, metropolitan capital is in control and, except in the most sophisticated states such as

Mexico and Venezuela, the relatively concentrated nature of these economies poses problems for relating a general education to the occupational structure. In general, the smaller the country, the greater the discrepancy; even affluent tax havens like the Cayman Islands rely on externally generated wealth.

In the era of European colonialism, groups of metropolitan-related Caribbean and Central American states, while being dependent, did belong to networks of culturally related political systems and their attendant educational philosophies and provisions. This was paternalistic and formative, greatly affecting attitudes and assumptions about schooling that have been resistant to change. So while in Cuba and Puerto Rico the relatively recent influence of the respective superpower ideologies and systems is strong, a continuum of Spanish-derived individuality is still a significant part of the culture of education. As Donald Clarkson shows in his historical narrative of American influence on Puerto Rican education, despite the firm association with the USA and freedom of movement between the Commonwealth of Puerto Rico and the mainland states of the Union, adherence to certain cultural traits, and especially the Spanish language, in education is enduring.

Both islands are significant influences at the regional level, and Mark Richmond takes up this theme in relation to Cuba in particular. New networks are developing, interconnecting and overlapping with the remnants of the old. Jamaica and the British Virgin Islands represent the core and the periphery of the former 'British West Indies'. Now, as Errol Miller illustrates, the question of marginality is a key concern in the former, while the latter finds itself in a symbiotic relationship with a powerful and proximate neighbour that even extends to being within the $US zone. Nonetheless, David Smawfield is able to highlight the educational idiosyncracies that derive not only from extreme smallness of scale, but also from a degree of colonial cultural inertia as far as compulsory schooling is concerned.

The politics of Central America, so internationally visible in recent decades, inevitably make their mark on educational policy and provision. In such a context, adult educational policy represents the front line of the advancement of awareness. Without this thrust and the extension of adult literacy, any significant amelioration of chronic legacies of curricular irrelevance, wastage and underachievement at school level is almost impossible to achieve. Yet the political implications of adult educational advance are problematic for existing systems of social regulation in many of the national units in the area. In his contribution to this volume, Gonzalo Retamal is able to catalogue the resulting tension in a wide-ranging review of the mixed fortunes of this sector in Central America.

What can be achieved when educational access and opportunity are encouraged is well illustrated by Pilar Aguilar in the celebrated and distinctive case of Costa Rica. In Venezuela, too, recent educational reform - as described by Lilia Borrero and Eyra Jimenez - has been attempting to utilize some of the 'fortunes of oil' to support a human resource development that will meet the diversified needs of a post-petroleum economy. Indeed, in places where educational reform has become endemic, such as Mexico, innovations tend not to be thoroughly carried through. Pressurizing the reformist momentum established more than half a century ago by the Mexican Revolution, there are now the educational demands of unprecedented urbanization. Mexico City is arguably the world's largest, and the educational problems and policies attached to such relentless expansion are examined here by Guadalupe Gonzalez-Paredes and David Turner.

That we have within the Caribbean basin a remarkable range of educational contexts, in an area that was once colonially homogeneous and is relatively modest in scale in global terms, is undeniable. There is also no doubt that in physical terms we are looking at a distinctive region. Whether it is realistic to view it as such in educational terms is obviously less clear, but it would seem that developing educational networks, such as the Association of Caribbean Universities, and more strongly, the role of education in the extension and maintenance of American influence, make a focus on the basin from this viewpoint a legitimate one. While a volume of essays such as this cannot pretend to take an integrated view, it is hoped that, if only by assembling studies from various cultural and political traditions and networks of the area within one set, a more comprehensive Caribbean perspective than that normally obtaining will have been encouraged in the field of international education. The region is rich in potential comparative studies of manageable proportions, but the educational literature relating to it is culture-specific and minimal.

These are just cases, but their juxtaposition is a first step on the way to a more regional perception of the Caribbean Basin in educational terms, and hopefully an encouragement to further studies.

Chapter Two

FORMATIVE INFLUENCES IN PUERTO RICAN EDUCATION

Donald Clarkson

INTRODUCTION

This chapter is concerned mainly with the impact of American influence on the development, structure and style of Puerto Rican education. Needless to say, the influence of American educational practices in the Caribbean has been linked with political actions taken during the twentieth century. The principal areas effected include Cuba, Haiti, the Dominican Republic (located on the island of Hispaniola), the United States Virgin Islands and the island of Puerto Rico. In general, American educational policy in the Caribbean was formulated by responsible American officials. In time, local officials supported and eventually assumed control of the educational programmes in their schools. This chapter will examine American influence in the Commonwealth of Puerto Rico through the historical phases of military territorial government, civil territorial government, and under the present Commonwealth status up to the achievement of educational autonomy in 1947.

THE BEGINNINGS

When the United States acquired Puerto Rico from Spain, under the provisions of the Treaty of Paris (1898), about one million people were added to the American population. Their culture was, and is, basically Hispanic with liberal cultural infusions from Africa, Europe and the Americas. Five hundred years of Spanish colonialism had developed strong emotional feelings of the need for self-rule and perhaps independence. Puerto Ricans were a people who identified themselves as Borinquenos (an old Indian name for the inland dwellers), inhabiting their own piece of earth. They had developed a feeling of political pride and governmental competence, having been granted autonomous internal self-rule from Spain in 1897. Their political thought processes concerning autonomy were their own, having developed through interaction with peninsula laissez-faire authority under the Crown, thus briefly exhibiting self-rule under the Spanish Republic; then in open conflict with the tightening of control by the peninsula government after the Restoration; finally through legitimate internal self-rule under an Autonomous Constitution. They had been loyal to the mother country, not because they were satisfied, but because the Puerto Rican is usually a constitutional fighter, not a revolutionary. After scarcely a year of self-rule their world changed. Conflict between the United States and Spain over Cuba led to war. Martial law was enforced in Puerto Rico, and then as a result of the Treaty of Paris the Borinquenos found themselves a United States colonial possession.

The United States accepted responsibility for the future development of the Borinquenos. American policy was directed by the belief that the inhabitants of Puerto Rico could be remade into Americans, as had been the case with Hispanic and French inhabitants of territories acquired in the westward expansion of the United States during the nineteenth century.

The institution selected to assimilate the Puerto Rican into American life was the school. This was in keeping with the belief that the school was the institution that Americanized the immigrants already coming to the USA from southern and eastern Europe. 'Americanized' in terms of aculturation generally meant the assimilated western European culture, and in particular, the English language. The tasks of American educational policy were threefold. First, it should build itself into as widespread an institution as possible. Second, it should make the people loyal to the United States: that is, the people of Puerto Rico would give up their nationalistic feeling as Borinquenos and transfer national feeling to the American flag. Third, English should be taught to everybody.

In order to provide as complete a picture as possible of the economic, social and political influence of the United States on the development of educational programmes of Puerto Rico in the twentieth century, this chapter contains background information of the economic, political and social support inherent in the development of educational programmes while Puerto Rico was first a Spanish colony and later a province (with full representation in the Cortes of the nation of Spain).

AN HISTORICAL BACKGROUND OF PUERTO RICO

The island of Puerto Rico, called Borinquen by the Arawak Indian inhabitants, was 'discovered' by Christopher Columbus on 16 November 1493. Early Spanish colonization centred on neighbouring Hispaniola, so that colonization of Puerto Rico did not take place until the sixteenth century. Ponce de Leon, the first governor of the island, entered San Juan harbour in 1508. He found the peaceful Arawak Indians, who called themselves Borinquenos, inhabiting the western end of the island, and the more warlike Caribs in control of the east. Various estimates of the number of Indians range from 5,500 to 600,000. The better studies seem to indicate a population of between 30,000 and 50,000, but within fifty years the Amerindians had either been eliminated by a combination of war, disease, enslavement and starvation (an artifact of Spanish colonization in the Caribbean) or assimilated by the growing Hispanic and Black population (Haas, 1940). Black slaves were introduced as a replacement population. In 1511, the present capital, San Juan, was founded by Ponce de Leon, and a thin stream of Spanish settlers began to arrive, but even as late as 1673, San Juan was populated by only 365 free men (white and black) plus their slaves and families. Puerto Rico was a disappointment to the Spanish. It did not yield the riches found in Hispaniola, Cuba and the continental Americas. The Spanish thought of Puerto Rico purely as a strategic military post, being in a good location from which to protect Hispaniola and the north-eastern coast of South America from the lesser Antilles, then controlled mainly by Britain, France and the Netherlands, all traditional enemies of Spain. Between 1595 and 1703, eight major foreign attacks were made on the island. Because of these attacks Puerto Rico would not attract large numbers of settlers until the nineteenth century and would not be viewed as an important colonial possession reaping economic benefits until that time.

Population growth was brought about by the arrival of prisoners from Spain, exiles from the Black revolution in Haiti, and refugees from the wars of independence of other Caribbean and South American colonies. Adding to the cultural mixture were marriages between the Spanish soldiers and mulattoes ('daughters of the land'), immigrants from the Canary Islands, deserters from the Spanish fleet and foreign Catholics who were allowed to cultivate sugar cane (Blanco, 1943). Table 2.1 shows the population growth of Puerto Rico from 1799 to 1899.

An additional spur to the growth of the diverse population of Puerto Rico was the change in Spanish policy as a result of the revolutions in South America and the growth of the Liberalism in Spain. In 1815, freedom to trade with foreign countries was granted, and a system of landholding was established, based on the ability to cultivate the soil. With the end of slavery the number of small landowners increased. Loyalist immigrants arrived from Venezuela and other former Spanish possessions. These settlers helped to establish municipal governments, law, and a merchant class.

EDUCATION IN PUERTO RICO UNDER SPAIN

The Early Period (1500-1820)

The Roman Catholic Church controlled education in Spain and so in 1511 King Ferdinand ordered the establishment of a monastery in Puerto Rico under the auspices of Franciscan monks. They were to care for the material and spiritual welfare of the Indians and their children. As in the mother country the places of worship were also used for school purposes.

Those desiring to prepare for the priesthood studied in the monasteries while the parish church served as an educational centre for children. Here they were taught the catechism, prayers, and also to read and write. During the sixteenth, seventeenth and eighteenth centuries several governors issued proclamations for the establishment of schools, or at least employed a person of good repute to teach catechism, reading, writing and ciphering, with the teacher's salary to be paid for by collections from the parents and donations from the civic minded (Ferrer Hernandez, 1885). This was the beginning of private and possibly public education in Puerto Rico. The controlling organization was still the Church.

Table 2.1

Population Growth of Puerto Rico: 1779-1899

Year	Population
1779	70,000
1786	96,000
1796	133,000
1800	155,426
1860	583,000
1899	953,243

Support for public education first appeared during the Napoleonic Wars, when many of Spain's colonies, including Puerto Rico, refused to acknowledge the French regime in Spain. In Puerto Rico an insular government was formed, not to break away from the mother country but to rule themselves. The first sign of governmental intervention in education in Puerto Rico occurred at this time when the colony was left to govern itself. On 22 July 1809, Governor Salvador Melendez ordered the municipality of San Juan to appoint an inspector of elementary schools (Ferrer Hernandez, 1885). The following year he ordered that there should be distributed to the schools writing copybooks, primers, a book of moral readings, catechisms, and paper. He further decreed that there should be annual examinations in all schools. These actions seem to imply that there were schools supported by public funds or private schools aided by public funds. The official ordering of annual examinations indicated a degree of public control over education in Puerto Rico, but there are no records of school enrolment or expenditures to support this assumption (Tapia y Rivera, 1854).

Education under the Control of Educational Societies (1820-1865)

Education in Puerto Rico as an insular movement begins in 1820 under the influence of the Liberal regime in Spain. Public elementary schools were established and administered by royal decrees. The development of public elementary education was much slower than that of private elementary and secondary schools in Puerto Rico. The Economic Society first in 1820 and again in 1822 tried to establish a free elementary school in San Juan. There are no records indicating that either was successfully established.

The first clear-cut evidence of publicly supported elementary education is found in the year 1830 in a report of the Crown. Some twenty-nine elementary schools, with the salaries of teachers partly paid by city councils, are listed as operational (de Cordoba, 1838). The interest in public education at the elementary level is manifested by Governor Don Juan de la Pezuela's 1850 order setting up three classes or districts of schools. He also established rules for school furnishings and the selection of teachers. This ordinance provided for schools in 66 municipalities. No provision was made for teacher salaries, but it is well known that each pupil paid a fee and the municipality paid for the poor (Macho Moreno, 1895).

La Real Academia de Buenas Letras was created in 1851 to administer education on the island as ordered by the Crown in a plan for educational programmes for Cuba and Puerto Rico. The duties of the Academy were all inclusive, creating in form a centralized school system. The Academy was empowered to issue certificates to teachers after examination, inspect all schools, appoint and dismiss teachers, report to the government on the conditions and needs of the schools, supervise all of the public institutions of the island, make such provisions as seemed advisable for public instruction, and encourage by all means possible the development of culture in general and the fine arts in particular (Macho Moreno, 1895).

The Academy established schedules for teacher salaries and examinations for promotions. It also encouraged schools for girls, and the establishment of schools in rural areas (the first such actions recorded in Puerto Rico). It also established rules for the attendance of poor children at school. The Academy mandated a curriculum that included reading, grammar, arithmetic, writing, religion and morals. Textbooks written in catechism form were generally used. The child learned the answer to questions, and 'recitation' consisted of repeating the answer when questioned. In large schools the older pupils were used as instructors, in keeping with the Lancasterian monitorial method. One problem area that the Academy did not address was the preparation of teachers. This would prove to be a major roadblock in the quantitative as well as qualitative development of public education in Puerto Rico.

Nevertheless, some progress was made. Interest in and support of public education was increasing, and some provisions for poor children were made; in fact their numbers had to be limited to provide room for paying students. Schools were established for girls, with their own curriculum. Rural education was under study. The census of 1860 reports 459 teachers. This must have included both public and private schools at the elementary and secondary levels (US War Department, 1899). The school census of 1864 reports the following for elementary education: 88 male teachers, 54 female teachers; 74 public schools for boys and 48 for girls; 2,396 boys attending of which 1,315 were poor, and 1,092 girls attending of which 695 were poor (US War Department, 1899).

Revolution in Spain, Political Unrest in Puerto Rico, and the Politicizing of Public Education (1865-1898)

The Crown's *Decreto Organico de 10 Junio de 1865* was seen as an attempt to use public education as a tool to carry out the aims of the Spanish colonial government. The Decree sought to further centralize public education in terms of administration, curriculum, teacher preparation and qualifications. Governor General Messina's own words point to the aim of the Decree:

> Not only that the intellectual program of these loyal and docile inhabitants may correspond to the material progress of the island which is

> developing rapidly, but also that they may be prepared to carry out the plan of studies for the Island of Cuba, when it will please Her Majesty to apply it to this Island [Puerto Rico]. (ibid)

One must remember that Cuba was in revolution at this time and the leadership of Puerto Rico gave full moral support to the Cuban attempt for independence. Between 1865 and 1868 strong political opposition to Messina's attempt to strengthen Spanish control of local government was voiced by Liberal leaders in local town governments. The Decree's aim was seen as another form of control, extending the power of the Spanish colonial government and diminishing local control. Messina was seen as a suppressor of Liberal political ideas, persecuting the Liberal leaders. Messina's plan for public education would manufacture cultural submissiveness to the policies of the mother country and make Puerto Ricans loyal subjects of Spain.

The rise of the Liberals in Spain, which led to the Revolution of 1868, was mirrored by the political leadership in Puerto Rico. There was significant criticism of Spain's attempt to retake Santo Domingo during the American Civil War. With the abolition of slavery in the United States, the leadership in Puerto Rico was demanding the same for their island. These two issues were linked with the opposition to Messina's plan for public education. Education became a prime political issue, remained so under United States control, and has continued as such under Commonwealth status.

Dissatisfaction with the Spanish government was brought to a climax by the Insurrection of Lares, 17 September 1868. The revolution in Spain brought about changes of the government in Puerto Rico. The island was made a province of Spain and given representation in the Spanish Cortes, and slavery was abolished in 1873. With the Republic established in Spain, public education was decentralized. Each municipality was given local control. In Puerto Rico the number of students attending public elementary schools decreased by 20 per cent. With the Restoration in 1874, royal reforms called for the centralization of public education in Spain and all its provinces, including Puerto Rico. Again education would become a tool of government. As such it would become the prime topic of Puerto Rican Liberals, who were demanding greater local control without suffering the death and desolation of their Caribbean brothers, the Cubans. A sense of the attempted control through education is seen in the following quote from an official directive to teachers:

> ...that all teachers in that province, in their respective spheres, support, and promote the policies of the government, and you place and maintain in office teachers... who are able to inspire and implant deeply in the souls of the young the satisfaction that results from exact execution of duty, from respect for the principals of authority and especially the authority of the fatherland, 'Patria'. You will see that under no pretext whatsoever do teachers stimulate the spirit of dissention, nor encourage the vertigo.

Then the mission of the teacher was dictated by subscribing unconditionally to the orders of the government. Liberal teachers were removed and replaced by conservative teachers. This was done legally by dismissing teachers who had been appointed by the municipalities during the Republic and replacing them with teachers who had been appointed under the *Decreto Organico de 10 Junio de 1865*, prior to the revolution. In addition, a programme of importing Spanish teachers for the public schools of Puerto Rico was initiated. The colonial government took action to discredit and dismiss Puerto Rican teachers. Two brief quotes firmly focus Governor Sanz's motivation in the above. The first is to the government in Madrid:

> It would be convenient to have a sufficient number of well trained teachers, who are completely Spanish in sentiment, to inculcate in the pupils the most healthy Christian and moral maxims, specially to teach them to love the fatherland so that they may grow to be loyal subjects of Spain.... As there are not in

> the Island all the teachers needed,... the opportunity be brought before the Spanish teachers, who have the qualifications,... [and] would like to be transferred to the Island, where many schools will be left vacant.

Two and one-half months later the Puerto Rican teachers had been dismissed and another communication went to the home government:

> Most of the teachers, some on account of their radical and autonomistic views, some of whom are affiliated with various secret societies and, because of their hostile sentiment to the Spaniards, which they unfortunately transmit to their pupils, are sowing a seed pernicious to the future welfare of the province and the fatherland, the bitter fruits of which are already being reaped in the sister Antilla [Cuba]. I have therefore directed as a political measure of the highest importance that all teachers be removed from the schools upon ground that their... reprehensible conduct renders them unworthy of the noble and lofty mission entrusted to them, especially when, with rare exception none of them have entered into the service by competitive examination, or by legal procedures as required by existing laws. I have already called your attention to the urgent need of teachers... we can put in charge of most of the schools that will remain vacant. That union [Spain and Puerto Rico] depends principally on the teaching given in the schools, as out of them will come good or bad Spaniards, according to the doctrine taught to the young by the teachers.

Clearly, public education was seen as a controlling mechanism by Governor Sanz. The main concern up to 1880 was appointment, transfer and resignation of teachers to provide the kind of political control to prevent another Lares incident or a general revolution as seen in Cuba. Sanz's administration may be seen as a continuation of the *Decreto Organico de 10 Junio de 1865,* emphasizing who should teach rather than what should be taught. The reaction to this policy touched all levels. Even the most conservative in the island who supported the government began to feel that the measures taken by Governor Sanz were too severe. Liberals in particular were outraged.

At first the Spanish government hesitated, but the schools were closed and something had to be done. Spanish teachers were appointed, but few actually arrived in Puerto Rico. During the entire school year 1874-75 most of the public schools remained closed. The few schools open were operated by political appointees recommended by the Conservative Party. Most of these appointments were temporary. This was in direct violation of Spanish laws which regarded teachers as government officials, permanently appointed, and only removable from their positions by due process of law. Very few Spanish teachers arrived in Puerto Rico, and those that did had difficulty with the climate, often leaving the island before the end of the school year. The use of substitutes and political appointees became the main source of teacher supply. The situation worsened when, in 1878, the new Governor General, Eulogio Despujols, came to Puerto Rico. The municipalities were ordered to ensure that boys and girls between six and fourteen were in school. The report issued indicated some 12,144 children in school, roughly four times the number reported in the 1864 census, but far from being in compliance with the *Decreto Organico de 10 Junio de 1865.* General Despujols concerned himself with the reorganization and stabilization of public elementary education. One of his first actions was to have the teachers assured of their positions, securing permanent appointments for all worthy teachers who had only temporary appointments. He also protected teachers who were doing satisfactory work from being replaced by teachers from Spain. He appropriated monies for supplies for the first time in fifteen years and laid the foundation for the expansion of public elementary education on the island.

In summary, there was little progress in elementary education after the Restoration, due to the intense political feeling entering school matters. Educational conditions in general were the same as in the year 1865, perhaps even worse. The attention given to the teacher was not moved by professional concern but by political aims. The teacher was the tool of the Governor. Little attention was given to curriculum and its effect upon the development of the peoples of Puerto Rico. The major problems of the period were not looked at from an educational viewpoint, but rather from a purely political position. In spite of such conditions, and minimal educational progress, the concept that education was a function of the state had been clearly defined, and education in Puerto Rico would in future be viewed as a tool of the state to carry out its political aims.

The Reorganization of Elementary Education - Decreto Organico of 1880 - and the Political Development of the Puerto Rican Republic

To understand the development of elementary education under the *Decreto Organico de 1880* one must first understand the political development of Puerto Rico during the Republic. The Puerto Ricans, both Liberal and Conservative, enjoyed almost complete self-rule during this period. As self-rule was suppressed after the Restoration, many Puerto Ricans planned and worked for its reinstatement. The Conservative Party, composed of Spaniards born on the peninsula and wealthier Puerto Ricans, sided with the Spanish government, running insular affairs by means of 'caciquismo' or 'boss rule'. They were opposed by the Liberal Puerto Ricans who wanted to return to self-rule.

After ten years of meetings and confrontations with the colonial government the Liberals united to form a new political group, Popular Liberal, representatives of which met at Ponce in 1887 under the leadership of Don Roman Balsorioty de Castro. They formed a new political party, 'El Partido Autonomista' (Autonomous Party), and demanded the right to regulate all internal affairs of the island, while accepting political and judicial ties with Spain and recognizing her sovereignty over the island. At the same time a secret society was organized with the aim of protecting its members from Spanish business interests on Puerto Rico.

Governor General Don Rummualdo Palacios identified El Partido Autonomista as being one and the same as the secret society. He charged the Autonomous Party with conspiracy against the national integrity and instituted what was known on the island as 'Los Compontes'. As the name implied, this meant persecution and torture for individuals suspected of conspiracy against the government. The 'Guardia Civil', or state police, were used to enforce 'Los Compontes'. The leaders of the Autonomous Party were tortured and imprisoned. The Governor would not allow any communication with Spain. After many attempts a small group of Autonomists secretly left the island and presented their grievance to the home government at Madrid. General Palacios was removed and replaced by Don Juan Contereras, who put an end to 'Los Compontes' and granted the membership of the Autonomous Party the right to assemble and participate in local political activities.

The Autonomists continued their struggle against the Conservative Party and the colonial government for self- rule. During the period 1891-1897 minor concessions were granted in respect of self-rule. Relations between Spain and Cuba worsened to the point of open rebellion. Again the Puerto Ricans gave vocal moral support to the Cuban people, while they demanded complete internal self-rule themselves, with the implied threat of revolution. Finally, in 1897, as a result of the Sagasta Pact, autonomy was granted to both islands. It was inaugurated in Puerto Rico on 11 February 1898. The new government consisted of the Governor General with his Cabinet and a representative assembly elected by the people. This new government had hardly begun to function when strained relations between the United States and Spain erupted into the Spanish-American War.

The *Decreto Organico de 1880*, implemented during a period of political unrest described above was concerned with the organization and curriculum of public elementary education unlike, the *Decreto Organico de 10 Junio de 1865*, which was concerned with who would teach. However the concern over who would teach persisted, due to the political conditions of that period. The *Decreto Organico de 1880* replaced the local control established under the Republic with a centralized school system. Local responsibility remained, but local initiative gave way to centralized decision-making.

The organization and curriculum of public education was

divided into elementary and superior. The elementary curriculum included catechism and elements of sacred history, reading, writing, elements of Spanish grammar, elements of arithmetic with legal weights, measures and money, elements of geography and an outline of agriculture, industry and commerce. Superior instruction included extension of all of the elementary content, plus the history and geography of Spain, geometry (with mechanical drawing and surveying), and an elementary outline of physics and natural history. The curriculum in the girls' schools included elementary drawing, designing, needlework, an elementary course in hygiene (replacing the geometry with mechanical drawing and surveying, and the elementary outline of physics and natural history found in the boys' curriculum).

Public schools were those supported wholly by the towns or those supported by charitable funds. Towns were required to include in their school budgets the teachers' salaries, rent for schools and teachers' residences, and school supplies. In summary, the budgeted funds of elementary education would come from local taxation and tuition. No funds came from Spain to support basic elementary schooling. The peninsula government mandated by decree. It was up to each local town government to meet the terms of the decrees and somehow fund its operation, with elementary instruction being compulsory from age six to twelve years, and the decree provided various kinds of punishment. In reality, there were not enough elementary schools in operation to make compulsory education possible, and only those who could prove they were poor were entitled to free public education. If parents had the money and a concern for education they either hired private tutors or sent their children to the private or Church-supported schools.

The general method of instruction remained the Lancasterian monitorial method. There was much concern about the quality of instruction, including the issue of rote learning. The following is a critical description of its implementation:

> Just as I have called attention to the progress made in education, I also must say that in most schools the teaching of moral and religious education is only a routine. Outside of the

> memory, exercised to repeat automatically the literal answer to questions, there is nothing. (Infiesta, 1886)

Punishment in the schools was provided by the teacher. The law allowed for a number of routine punishments, and although corporal and other unusual punishment was forbidden by the *Decreto Organico de 1880*, it was common practice for male teachers to use the 'palmeta' or strap.

The *Decreto Organico de 1880*, provided regulations for teacher qualifications, the establishment of 'normal schools', teacher certification and competitive examinations for appointment. Generally the criteria established were adhered to, except in the case of the rural school where exemptions were made in response to staffing difficulties.

As far as school buildings were concerned, none were erected during the period 1880-1898. Some municipalities bought other buildings for school purposes. The majority of the municipalities rented buildings for schools as well as for teachers' residences. The classroom or *La Sala* was often in practice the largest room of the teacher's residence. As such, these buildings were not really suitable for school purposes. The building problem in rural schools was much worse. The following quote gives a vivid description of the problem of school buildings in rural areas:

> The huts set aside as places to instruct the young look more like miserable hog pens than institutions of learning, many of them with yagua and palma floors, narrow and small, without light, without a place to hang a chart or a blackboard... the children crowded like bundles in a house used for storage. The teachers have not enough room to divide the school into sections, nor any opportunity to develop any sort of method. (Infiesta, 1886)

In 1888 the government requested the municipalities to make appropriations for school buildings, and in the same year prepared and issued three plans for school houses. In the event, nothing was done either by the municipalities or by the insular government. However, even though school buildings were inadequate, at least they existed. This was not the case with school equipment and supplies. Many of the schools lacked the basic furniture:

> The schools are in urgent need of furniture; many do not have a chair for the teacher, nor a crucifix, nor chart, nor shelves, nor tables and benches needed nor a book-case... (Infiesta, 1886)

EDUCATION UNDER THE AUTONOMOUS GOVERNMENT

The *Decreto Organico de 1880* was in force until 11 February 1898, when the Autonomous Constitution went into effect, which declared *inter alia* that Puerto Rico had full authority to establish its own system of education. A Department of Education was established, and replacing the Provincial Junta was the Council of Public Instruction, a body of thirty-six members. However, dissension soon arose among government officials, former members of the Provincial Junta and the membership of the newly created Council of Public Instruction. Finally the membership of the Council of Public Instruction resigned on 22 July 1898. By this time the Spanish-American War was being conducted and education as well as all other government functions was operating under martial law.

The educational system which the Americans found on taking over had developed as a result of the *Decreto Organico de 10 Junio de 1865*, the local efforts under the Republic, and the *Decreto Organico de 1880*. The growth of a centralized public elementary school system is reflected in statistics concerning total population of the island and school enrolment for the years 1865-1898 (Table 2.2).

THE EFFECT OF PUERTO RICAN - AMERICAN RELATIONS ON EDUCATIONAL DEVELOPMENT

Before the American influence upon the development of a centralized system of public education in Puerto Rico is examined, it will be helpful to consider the political relations between the United States and the Territory of Puerto Rico.

These relations set the stage for a unilateral interpretation of what the educational programmes would contain from 1899 to 1947.

The Puerto Ricans overwhelmingly welcomed American troops which to them meant 'freedom' under American leadership. A great majority of the *jibaros*, the peasant class under Spanish rule, knew little of the United States, but these Americans did not exhibit the elitism or *dignidad* of the Spaniards who had oppressed them for centuries. Most of the cosmopolitan Puerto Ricans accepted American rule because of the ideals associated with the Declaration of Independence, the fame of such men as George Washington, and the material success of the American people. The promise of freedom and self-rule seemed clear in the words of General Miles, the first military Governor:

> We have not come to make war upon the people of a country that for centuries has been oppressed but on the contrary to bring you protection... to promote your prosperity, and to bestow upon you the immunities and blessings of the liberal institutions of our government. (Aitkin, 1964)

In contrast, revisionist historian C. Hauberge offers the following interpretation:

> Unfortunately, the knight-errant, Sir Galahad image of the United States was soon tarnished and the Puerto Rican high hopes were to be dashed on the rocks of despair - at least for a time.
>
> Possibly the best explanation for this is to be found in a type of blind and bland arrogance that come with power and affluence; the arrogance of Puritan thrift and self-assurance began to replace the Spanish dignidad and the conquistador. Unwilling or unable to face its new responsibility openly and reluctant to be classed as imperialistic, the United States caused Puerto Rico to be termed an 'unincorporated'

> rather than an 'incorporated territory', because the latter implied that the territory would eventually become an American State. Thus, after the Foraker Act of 1900 was passed, the beautiful little island had a Flag without a constitution and citizenship without suffrage; also it became a 'state' without representation. Spanish rule had been autocratic; American democratic rule, despite its glowing heritage, was also autocratic. (Hauberge, 1974)

Table 2.2

School Census of Puerto Rico: 1864-1898

Year	Enrolment
1864	3,488
1867	9,472
1869	8,129
1878	11,097
1880	15,218
1881	24,120
1886	27,480
1898	44,861

(US War Department, 1899)

The Era of Broken Pledges (1898-1930)

Revisionist historians, in their zeal to tell the true story, often paint a landscape full of negative and perilous images. However, the potential to rule autocratically was strengthened by the 'Insular Cases' decisions by the United States Supreme Court. These rulings involved cases in which the prime question was: Does the Constitution follow the flag? The answer was a resounding 'No'! Puerto Ricans learned that they were denied certain fundamental constitutional rights, such as the grand jury indictment process, trial by jury and the usual limitation of federal taxation.

The first US government of the island was military. This was set up by General Miles and lasted until 1900. Under military leadership reforms were begun which were appreciated by the Puerto Ricans. Military-directed reform included a postal system, a police force, the right to trial by jury and Habeas Corpus, as well as free public schools.

The Foraker Act of 1900 replaced the military government with a civilian one and created the political entity termed the 'People of Puerto Rico', neither citizens of the United States nor of any independent state. Puerto Rico had become an American colony. This act provided for a Governor to be appointed by the President, an Executive Council also appointed, including a Commissioner of Education. In addition the Foraker Act stipulated that Puerto Rico should have a thirty-five-member elected House of Delegates. The laws passed by the House of Delegates were subject to the Governor's and Congressional veto. For direct contact with Congress the Foraker Act provided for an elected Resident Commissioner to represent the territory in the United States Congress. He could speak, but had no vote. This was less than the Sagasta Pact, which provided the Autonomous Government of Puerto Rico full membership and the right to vote in the Spanish Cortes, negotiate commercial treaties and the most important right to have veto power on proposed amendments to the Pact by the Cortes. One can understand the consternation of the political leadership of Puerto Rico. As noted, the Foraker Act did not provide for voting representation in the United States Congress, and the United States Congress retained sovereignty in the areas of treaties as well as amendments to the Foraker Act. Finally, there was no provision in the Act for plebicites or any statement about Puerto Rico's future status. Clearly, Puerto Rico was a colony of a 'closet' imperialistic nation, the United

States. This then would be the political position of Puerto Rico until 1917 (Lewis, 1963). The politics on the island during this period ranged from the acceptance of secondary status with the patience to work and hope for a positive change, to the formation of the Unionist Party whose membership demanded independence.

It is interesting to note that the first significant change in the political relationship with the United States came under duress, much the same as Spain was forced to agree to the Sagasta Pact. It was 1917 and the United States would surely be drawn into World War I. For strategic military reasons the United States purchased the Danish Virgin Islands and passed the Jones-Shaforth Act, commonly called the Jones Act. It extended the rights and powers of the Puerto Ricans, granting United States citizenship to the 'people of Puerto Rico'. United States citizenship was opposed by the Unionist Party, because it was inconsistent with their demand for independence. Other important changes were made in the organization of the island government, in particular the establishment of an elective senate. However executive power continued to have an ultimate veto over the elected legislature, and the most important officers of the Governor's Council, the Attorney General and the Commissioner of Education, were still to be appointed by the President of the United States.

During the 1920s the political parties tried to enlarge the powers of two popularly elected chambers, unfortunately within a framework designed to curb expansion. In frustration the political parties tended to cooperate with the Governor in 'stonewalling' popularist movements for reform. It should also be noted that the Governors appointed by the President for Puerto Rico did not understand the 'Puerto Rican situation'. Most were retired military men or former Congressmen, and arrived knowing little or nothing of the island's problems. Theodore Roosevelt Jr, who held the office from 1929 to 1931, was one Governor who tried to understand the problems of Puerto Rico and bring about meaningful reform, but he was thwarted by the Depression and the national concern for solving the problems 'at home'.

Nature further complicated the problems of the island with two disastrous hurricanes; one in 1899 destroyed the coffee plantations of Puerto Rico, which were never rebuilt. Instead the economy was shifted to sugar cane and citrus fruit production by absentee landlords, major United States corporations. The sugar industry typifies the effect of the shift from general agriculture to specialized agriculture, with the consequences of the *coloni* (farmer) being forced to sell his small-holding to a one-crop organization, thus cutting the production of staple foods to the point where the island was no longer self-sufficient. This caused the large-scale importation of basic food staples with their attendant import taxes. According to the Diffie study published in 1931, the tariff on principal Puerto Rican foodstuffs raised the total price by $9,000,000 or 30 per cent annually. Basic foodstuffs imported included flour, rice, lard, dairy products, beans, meats, potatoes, peas, and cornmeal, all essential to the traditional Puerto Rican diet.

This meant that the average worker who earned 60 cents a day received in buying value 42 cents a day, compared with 97 cents in Hawaii, $1.26 in Cuba and $1.95 in the Bahamas (Diffie and Diffie, 1931). The following statement by United States Secretary of the Interior Ickes in 1935 describes the plight of the Puerto Rican worker:

> Puerto Rico has been the victim of the laissez-faire economy which has developed of the great absentee-owned sugar corporations, which have absorbed much land formerly belonging to small independent growers and who in consequence have been reduced to virtual economic serfdom. (Lewis, 1963)

In the area of direct taxation the powerful absentee owners were able to secure very low assessments on their properties often passing on to the island people. Even though Puerto Rico was not completely a 'sugar island' like Cuba, it was sufficiently so to prove that sugar production based upon absentee ownership and the exclusion of staple crops does not make a happy colony or make the people more economically secure.

In the areas of banking and public utilities the story was much the same. Interest and utility rates were double that of the United States mainland. The excuse offered was the potential for revolution. This did not apply to Puerto Rico, there being no threat of revolution or violence as was being experienced in the countries of Central America, the Dominican Republic or Haiti (Lewis, 1963).

An already bad situation worsened when another destructive hurricane hit the island in 1928, and forever put an end to large-scale coffee production on the island. More important in the long run was the disaster relief report prepared for the United States Congress which highlighted the poverty of the island. One investigator's 'unofficial' comment ran as follows:

> As a result of American colonialism coupled with natural disasters, Puerto Rico by 1930 was on the edge of socio-economic disaster. Even casual visitors could not help but note the pitious spectacle of poverty and the bite-the-fingernail misery of the island people. Malodorous, filthy habitations surrounded the more prosperous areas. Possibly some 35,000 suffered from tuberculosis, some 200,000 from malaria and some 600,000 from hookworm. (Diffie and Diffie, 1931)

Another observation gives a more personalized view of the condition of the proud but poor Puerto Rican:

> The family secured permission to pick up the garbage can of a wealthy upper-class family to fatten the family's sow. Finally the rich family took an interest in the family sow and investigated. But there was no sow on display. There never had been a real sow! The garbage pickings had been used to fill the mouths of growing children. (Mathews, 1960)

Three events profoundly affected the life of Puerto Rico during the 1930s. Two would be felt immediately, the third was more latent, but would have a lasting effect. The first was the worldwide depression whose devastating economic effect created increased political activity over the issues of independence and the use of English as the medium of instruction in the public schools. The second was San Cipriano, another severe hurricane in which over 200 persons died, property damage was set at $30 million and 100,000 were left homeless. The third was the 'New Deal', which in the longer term was to bring prosperity and new problems to the island. This New Deal brought together two men, one a Puerto Rican and the other a mainland American. Together they would mend many of the 'broken pledges'.

During the early 1930s the political situation in Puerto Rico continued to boil. Strong negative feelings came to the surface over 'Americanization' which became linked to the question of the use of English in the public schools. Dr Jose Padin, appointed Commissioner of Education by President Hoover in 1930 and retained by President Roosevelt, set the charge for the 1930s:

> Thirty years of vacillation and suffering have gone by without any certainty as to the end for which we are preparing our country. I assert that Porto Rico must be prepared to live its own life, because Porto Rico has a sense of self, because its personality is clearly formed. (Padin, 1945)

Dr Padin was speaking specifically of the issue of English as a medium of instruction in the island's public schools and generally about the political position of Puerto Rico. He clearly wanted to take the issue of English language out of the political arena, and proposed and carried through a series of educational experiments that would establish a basic mode of bilingualism for the public schools of Puerto Rico. In the end Puerto Ricans would mould the American school system into their own distinctive institution, but for this to develop and prosper a period of economic and political stability was necessary.

The Era of Munoz Marin

In 1932 Munoz Marin won a seat in the Senate. He was

an example of the *Independentista* maturing into a moderate. He was not a blend of two cultures but rather the first generation of a new breed. His view of the political structure for Puerto Rico was 'between statehood on the one hand and independence or autonomy on the other'. He felt that total independence would be disadvantageous to the economy of the island. Economic and social justice could be achieved by some connection with the United States. In his view, Puerto Rico did not have the diversity of natural resources and was not large enough to survive without some connection with the United States.

Between 1932 and 1940, Munoz Marin worked to secure a political base to insure stability in economic reform. He would ride out into the rural areas to talk to the *jibaros*. It was common for the *jibaros* to sell their votes for $2 (three days wages). He tried to convince them to vote for him and not take the bribe. He promised reforms that would help the *jibaros* and their families, especially the prospects for their children. Munoz became almost legendary and hacienda owners, fearing his growing influence, began to forbid their *jibaros* from attendance at his meetings. Nonetheless, Munoz's Populares won the election of 1940, and he sent a letter to President Roosevelt pledging his cooperation. In part he said, 'Help us Mr President so that the democracy discovered in... our unhappy people may be of the fullest use to themselves' (Mathews, 1960).

The President sent Rexford Guy Tugwell as the new Governor of Puerto Rico. Tugwell, a Liberal and a trained economist, believed that progress could be made by cooperative planning between government and business. He was well aware of many of Puerto Rico's problems. As a representative of the Department of Agriculture he had toured Puerto Rico in the early 1930s. Both Tugwell and Roosevelt knew two immediate problems that had to be addressed: first, the slums and squatter dwellings which were unsafe and unhealthy; second, the unsanitary, impure, disease-bearing water system. Tugwell, working with Munoz, accomplished this during the first two years of the new decade. This two-man team continued to work together towards improving the political, economic and social conditions in Puerto Rico. They reached agreements, such as the elimination of the Terna, a list of political appointees the

Governor was obliged to choose from for political reasons. Appointees would henceforth be chosen on their qualifications to meet specific position requirements. Discrimination against Puerto Ricans was eliminated, but this aggrieved others with vested interests.

During World War II, to provide much needed manufactured goods, factories were built cooperatively by the Puerto Rico and USA governments. At the end of the war these were sold to private enterprises. At this point 'Operation Bootstrap', or the industrialization of Puerto Rico, went into 'top gear'. With Tugwell in charge of the planning and Munoz working with the politicians things went relatively smoothly. Tax incentives were offered to mainland corporations to attract and secure additional investments in Puerto Rico. With increased revenues, and some support from the federal government, low-income housing projects started to develop in urban areas. Once again, Tugwell's planning skills supported Munoz's political skills.

In 1946, President Truman appointed the first Puerto Rican as Governor, Jesus Pinero, to replace Tugwell, and in 1947 the Jones Act was amended by the Elective Government Act of 1947, thus paving the way for the election of Munoz Marin (by a margin of four to one) as the first elected Governor in 1948.

Governor Munoz Marin proposed the establishment of *Estado Libre Asociado* or 'Commonwealth status'. In March of 1949, the Resident Commissioner proposed a bill to the United States Congress, which would authorize the people of Puerto Rico 'to organize a government pursuant to a constitution of their own adoption', to become effective if approved by the people of Puerto Rico as well as by Congress. In a referendum in 1951, the concept of *Estado Libre Asociado* was approved by a four-to-one margin, and a constitutional convention was called. The constitution was approved on 25 July 1952, also by a four-to-one margin. This was the fifty-fourth anniversary of the United States' occupation of Puerto Rico.

Now after thirty years of Commonwealth status, Puerto Rico has the highest standard of living in the Caribbean, is a major centre for manufacturing and banking, but still has many problems to solve. With the political background of the island for the first half of the twentieth century now outlined, the discussion of the development of educational provision can be resumed.

AMERICAN INTERVENTION AND THE DEVELOPMENT OF CENTRALIZED PUBLIC EDUCATION (1898-1947)

Education under the American Military Government

As soon as the American military government was set up, it began to concern itself with the Americanization of Puerto Rico. Its principal vehicle was education, historically the institution identified to be in charge of this process for the millions of immigrants who came to America's shores.

Dr John Eaton and Dr Victor S. Clark, both mainland educators, were put in charge of the reorganization of the Puerto Rican schools. As reported above, there had been a public elementary school system developed under the Spanish regime. In 1898 this consisted of 380 schools for boys, 148 schools for girls and one school for adults. In addition there were 26 private schools. Although the education system seemed meagre by American standards, Puerto Rico was in fact as well off educationally as the mother country overall. Nonetheless, Dr Clark was not impressed with the level of education he found. In his report to the Secretary of War he wrote:

> Only from the very small intellectual minority in Puerto Rico, trained in Europe, and imbued with European ideas of education and government, have we to anticipate active resistance to the introduction of the American school system and the English language. (Great Britain Board of Education, 1900)

Dr Clark stated clearly and succinctly the cardinal principle of American education in Puerto Rico, which was that the school system was to be a typical American one; it would Americanize; the language medium was to be English. Even if there had been opposition to Americanization, it is doubtful if there would have been much variation in American thinking and policy development. The United States was in Puerto Rico to stay. The occupation of Cuba was temporary, until she was ready for independence. Puerto Rico was a permanent possession to be assimilated, just as the previously Hispanic south-western mainland territories had been in their turn.

Dr Clark seems to have felt the need to denigrate the existing culture and language of the people, perhaps to strengthen his educational reasons for the assimilation process. In minimizing Spanish as the language of instruction, he was quoted as saying:

> There does not seem to be among the masses the same devotion to their native tongue or to any national ideal that animates the Frenchman, for instance, in Canada or the Rhine provinces. Another important fact that must not be overlooked is that a majority of the people of this island do not speak pure Spanish. The language is a patois almost unintelligible to the natives of Barcelona and Madrid. It possesses no literature and has little value as an intellectual medium. There is a bare possibility that it will be nearly as easy to educate this people out of their patois into English as it will be to educate them into the elegant tongue of Castille. (Osuna, 1949)

Many Puerto Ricans have felt that Dr Clark was in no position to determine their feelings about Spanish. All people cling to their vernacular long after everything else has been lost. Pure Spanish is as much of a fiction as pure English. In any case, Puerto Ricans did not speak a Spanish patois any more than Americans spoke an English patois. The reference to Barcelona was unfortunate since the Barcelonan spoke Catalan, not Spanish. As far as a literature was concerned, there was, and is, available to Puerto Ricans one of the richest in the world, that of the Spanish-speaking peoples.

Throughout this survey of American educational policy for Puerto Rico (and it is true of the larger Caribbean educational policy) emphasis has been placed on the fact that American educators had a justifiable pride in the achievements of public education. On the other hand it is clear that such pride sometimes defeated the purposes of education in dealing with the Spanish-speaking Puerto Rican. All too often the culture was ignored in the press to get the educational job done quickly.

The first school laws were compiled by Dr Clark early in 1899. They provided for elective school boards, free public schools and a course of study. Local boards were not required to open schools; they were allowed to, but the law did not make it mandatory. On 9 May 1899 Brigadier General George M. Davis became Military Governor. He appointed a committee of Puerto Rican teachers with the charge of reviewing the laws. Apparently General Davis was concerned about Clark's imposition of law concerning educational programmes without having the input of those who were going to be governed. As a result the law was amended to remove authority from local school boards if they did not use it to appoint teachers. The President of the Insular Board of Education was authorized to name new teachers when the local boards neglected to do so.

In 1900, the school system was made more centralized by dividing the island into six school districts, with one representative for each district serving on the new centralized board of education. The view from the central board was that the local boards were not interested in public education, paralleling the view of the central board of the Autonomous Provincial Government under Spain and in keeping with the military mentality for the chain of command concept. Authority passed more and more into the hands of the central office in San Juan. By the time the Organic Act for the establishment of a civil government went into effect, the idea of a centralized school system was an accepted fact. It is of course a matter of conjecture as to whether one concludes that the centralized school system was arrived at only from the traditions of educational programmes under Spanish control or as a result of United States military rule. But it must be pointed out that centralization of authority is not an American tradition of the early twentieth century. Rather, local control was a jealously guarded right at the local board level. Education was deemed by the Constitutional Fathers as a power reserved to the states and the people. Americans were afraid of centralizing anything, and as such granted centralized authority only when there was no other way to do what needed to be done.

During the nineteen months of military control, the American elementary school was well established. Great emphasis was placed on the learning of English, and on patriotism. It was believed that patriotic exercises would Americanize the children. The school was to be used to convert former Spanish subjects into loyal American citizens as quickly as possible. Little attention was given to those factors of local culture which might have facilitated the achievement of the goals set down for the schools. For example, coeducation existed in the United States; so, it was introduced in Puerto Rico. That this step was revolutionary in an Hispanic culture did not occur to anyone in the United States team of supervising educators. Further, the team failed to see, as reported by Osuna (1949), that discrepancy between the elementary school enrolment under the provincial autonomous education programme and the military might have been caused by coeducation. In 1898, the number of elementary school students was reported as 44,861 (War Department Census, 1899). In 1899 enrolment was reported to be 24,392 in municipal schools: a net decrease of 45 per cent! Some of this discrepancy can be ascribed to the aftermath of the war, but certainly not on this massive scale. One might speculate the effect of the Americanization effort with English and the use of army volunteers for English instruction and patriotism exercises upon Spanish-speaking parents of the children. In any event the public schools were operational with 24,392 children of whom 96 per cent were in the first three grades. About three thousand children were taught by American mainland teachers and about one-third of the children received instruction from English-speaking teachers (records are not available on the number of Puerto Rican teachers fluent enough in English to teach it and a second group of army volunteers who gave English instruction in the public schools). In any case, the American Army was not long in control. On 1 May 1900 a civil government was established.

Education under the American Civil Government (1900-1947)

Educational policy under civil government was determined chiefly by the Commissioner of Education, a political appointee of the President under the terms of the Foraker Act of 1900 and the Jones Act of 1917. The first six Commissioners were from the mainland. After 1921 and until Commonwealth status, three Commissioners of Education were Puerto Rican.

Education under Mainland Commissioners of Education (1901-1921)

The first Organic Act which provided civil government for Puerto Rico was the aforementioned Foraker Act of 1900, which in respect of education provided:

> That the Commissioner of Education shall superintend public instruction throughout Porto Rico [Puerto Rico], and all disbursements on account thereof must be approved by him, and he shall perform such other duties as may be prescribed by law, and make such reports through the governor as may be required by the Commissioner of Education for the United States which shall annually be transmitted to Congress. (United States War Department, 1909)

The Commissioner of Education was appointed for a four-year term by the President of the United States. He exercised almost absolute power over the educational programme, appointing all of the subordinate officials, school administrators and teachers.

The first Commissioner of Education was Dr M. G. Brumbaugh (1900-1902). He was appointed by President McKinley, and took office on 6 August 1900. He found the schools operating under laws set up by the United States Army. These laws were based on the Massachusetts school system. Often they were not adaptable to Puerto Rico, which had neither the experience nor the money (the public school operational budget until the 1930s would come exclusively from tax monies generated by import, property, and after 1917, income taxes) to develop such a system. The local school boards, not the Department of Education, would hire and have control over much of the teaching force. Dr Brumbaugh wrote:

> It gives the power to employ teachers, wholely

> to the local boards, unless they do not exercise their authority. This is fatal to the advancement of the schools. It is impossible to supervise education as required by the act of Congress... so long as the commissioner is absolutely helpless in the control of teachers.... There should be change here that make it impossible for incompetent teachers to hold a license, and that will protect good teachers from... pernicious interference of politicians..... Many of these boards are composed of good men, anxious to promote education, and to cooperate with the department but they confess their inability to do as they would like, because they have neither the power nor resource to do so. (United States War Department, 1901)

Dr Brumbaugh was looking to the American government as the final critic of Puerto Rican education, and felt that the Foraker Act called for a strong Commissioner. Otherwise he would have had faith in the local boards or in the President of the Insular Board. The resources at his disposal were the same as the local boards: locally collected Puerto Rican tax revenue. In any case, the Republican majority in the lower house legislature helped him achieve his aims, as did his holding a seat on the Executive Council. Apparently the Puerto Rican Republicans shared the Commissioner's lack of faith in locally controlled education. At least this move by the Commissioner melded with the political history of the island under Spanish colonial rule and the Autonomous government; that is to say, centralization of authority and control.

In 1901, Commissioner Brumbaugh secured a new school law, which centralized control in the hands of the Commissioner of Education: section 23 sets forth his duties and powers as follows:

> The Commissioner of Education, being required by act of Congress April 12, 1900 to supervise education in Porto Rico, he shall, to comply with said act, appoint from time to time supervisors, or superintendents of schools, who

> shall be subject to the commissioner in all respects; he shall prepare and promulgate all courses of study, conduct all examinations; prepare and issue all licenses or certificates to teachers; select and purchase all school books, supplies and equipment necessary for the proper conduct of education; approve all plans for public school buildings to be erected in Porto Rico. (United States War Department, 1901)

This legislation made school boards powerless. Centralization of public education was now supported by custom and law.

Dr Brumbaugh found that the military government had established sixteen supervisors of English, and these he continued. The school law stated that:

> Their duties shall be prescribed by the commissioner of education and their services may be dispensed with at any time he may deem it necessary for the good of the schools to do so. (United States War Department, 1901)

Supervisory authority and administrative authority had become identical.

Under Army rule, teacher licensing had been defined by law. A training school had been set up at Fajardo, a city on the south-eastern coast. Because of its location and poor administration it failed: again an example of cultural inertia, for most Latin Americans look to the capital for cultural leadership. The Commissioner moved the training school to Rio Piedras, near the capital, where it remained, later to become the University of Puerto Rico (United States War Department, 1901).

The policy of sending Puerto Rican teachers to study in the United States began in 1899, with the support of the military government. It was US policy to train Puerto Ricans to take over their own schools, a highly enlightened approach in 1899. Preparatory students were also sent to school in the United States under the supervision of the US Commissioner of Education. By 1901, 219 were studying in American schools and it was unfortunate that in some cases the schools chosen were inappropriate or considered 'second class'. Dr Osuna, an outstanding Puerto Rican educator, was sent to Carlisle, a school dedicated to the education of the American Indian. He liked to tell the story of the little *jibaro* (country peasant) who was uprooted from his rural mountainside and suddenly found himself among fierce North American Indians, who a short time before had been only a figment of his childhood imagination.

Dr Brumbaugh continued the policy of employing American teachers. The first American teachers had been army men, mule skinners and adventurers who knew no Spanish and perhaps little 'school' English, but gradually better teachers were hired.

Elementary education had been supported by the military government. In 1900, out of 322,393 children of legal school age (five to eighteen), 29,393 were in school, an increase of some 5,000 from 1899 but still 15,000 short of the 1898 enrolment figures. In 1901, the number of elementary school students increased to about 50,000 surpassing the enrolment of 1898 for the first time. Despite these advances, elementary education in the rural areas was particularly inadequate, and its expansion was delayed by poor roads and the lack of finance (Osuna, 1944). The elementary course of study was similar to that in the United States. It prepared students for high school but did little to prepare them for life. Reviewing the curriculum mandated by the Spanish *Decreto Organico de 1880*, it would seem more practical for the majority of students, who in this period would terminate their formal education after three or four years, to have entered the world of work.

High school education was not mandated at this early date of American public education in Puerto Rico. Secondary education was in the province of the private and church-affiliated school sector in Puerto Rico. However, Dr Brumbaugh supported the expansion into secondary education. By 1 November 1900 a high school was opened in San Juan, and the following year Ponce High School was opened.

Adult education was provided for in night schools. By the school year 1901-1902 there were 2,767 adult students in attendance (United States War Department, 1903).

By 1901, Puerto Rico had the foundations of an American

school system: the elementary school, the high school, and the beginnings of a university in the normal school at Rio Piedras. Dr Brumbaugh left Puerto Rico in 1902, to be succeeded by Commissioner Lindsay.

Dr Samuel McCune Lindsay took over a system of some 55,000 students in the schools of Puerto Rico, or 5.4 per cent of the total population. The new Commissioner felt that the schools in Puerto Rico should attempt to match the enrolment percentage seen in the United States. At this time there were about 1,000 teachers in the system of whom 125 were Americans (Lindsay, 1902).

What seems to have interested Dr Lindsay was a new departure in Puerto Rico for American education. He was impressed by the high degree of centralization; he wrote:

> In Porto Rico education is a serious business of the government. The work is conducted by one of six great departments and is carried on not by municipal authorities alone, but at the expense of the insular government itself. This is quite unlike anything in the administration of public schools in the States, where school management and support are left largely to the town or local government.... This government aspect of education is one of the many wise provisions of the Foraker law. (Lindsay, 1902)

The European concept of education as a department of government had been established. Most American educators tried to develop some sort of local control, but the tendency towards centralization continued. The reasons for this development are many, but tradition and inertia are powerful forces in any society. Government under Spain, first as a colony, then in republican form and finally as an incorporated province, had been a centralized sequence. The concept of local control never took root under American civil territorial rule, nor under Commonwealth status.

Lindsay pointed out that the Americans had not solved the educational problems of the island. Out of 1,000 schools, 490 were one-room rural schools, and most of the teachers were poorly trained. In rural areas only twelve regular agricultural schools had been established. Lindsay acted swiftly. The following year, twenty-five were in operation with the mornings devoted to regular elementary education, and the afternoons to agriculture; most of the agriculture teachers were American.

There were 345 town-graded schools by 1902, and as far as possible, an American was assigned to teach English in each school. On the professional level, improvement had been made at the Normal School in Rio Piedras where a new building was constructed so the school system was growing, and by December 1902, there were 1,200 public schools with an enrolment over 60,000. Of the teachers, 1,100 were Puerto Rican and 150 were American, the latter group still mostly engaged in teaching English. Additionally, 58 adult schools were in operation (Lindsay, 1902).

The growth of public education was mostly at the expense of the Puerto Rican people. About one quarter of insular revenues went to public education. The legislature that appropriated the funds had very little to say about their actual use. Lack of sufficient resources made it impossible for the schools to meet the growing demand for public education. All schools had long waiting lists of pupils who could not be accommodated. Malpractices developed, as principals selected pupils for first grade by personal preference. Interest in education was universal, but the island did not have the fiscal resources to provide facilities for all the children and adults who desired the perceived benefits of education.

The United States federal government was approached for assistance, but the response that came was specifically designated for teacher training for Puerto Ricans, and for teacher recruitment to identify Americans to take teaching positions in Puerto Rico. Also President McKinley authorized the return of $200,000 which had been collected by the federal government in custom duties on Puerto Rican goods entering the United States before the Foraker Law, which had established free trade between Puerto Rico and the United States, went into effect. This money was earmarked for roads and schools (Miller, 1921). More specifically, Dr Lindsay asked Wahington for direct financial aid for expansion of the instructional programme. But the United States government was unwilling to 'underwrite a larger insular system'. The

Commissioner therefore increased the number of Puerto Ricans studying in the United States from 219 to 451. They were funded at the expense of the insular government for preparatory and professional training (Lindsay, 1902). To provide for the future advanced education of Puerto Ricans, the legislature on 12 March 1903 established the University of Puerto Rico. It was situated on the campus of the Normal School at Rio Piedras. This meant that more young people would be able to undertake tertiary level studies and training without leaving the island.

In general, Commissioner Lindsay carried on the policies which had been started by Dr Brumbaugh. There was a gradual expansion of the public school system. Relations with the insular legislature were generally positive.

Dr Lindsay was succeeded by the *third* Commissioner, Roland F. Falkner in 1905. Commissioner Falkner's main concern was with extending and expanding the use of English as the language of instruction. He believed the political situation in Puerto Rico made it necessary, in particular the revivial of the Federalist Party under the banner of the Union Party. They had gained several seats in the House of Delegates, mainly supported by small farmers who had lost their land to the growing absentee-owned sugar plantations. The Unionists were in favour of independence. Commissioner Falkner thought the Americanization process was losing the battle to assimilate the young into the American culture. In discussing his own attitude in terms of the utility of English as the medium of instruction he stated:

> It was obvious that the political conditions had brought a new factor into the school situation, namely the English language. A place must be created for it in the school system. No one dreamed of displacing the Spanish language, in the schools or in the life of the people.... Yet the new relations with the United States... made it highly desirable that the educated classes should use both languages. If these results can be obtained, it must be largely through the schools.... It [English] has also the function in a humble and more practical way of

> coordinating school instruction in Porto Rico with the institutions of higher learning in the United States. Colleges and professional schools do not exist in Porto Rico. (Falkner, 1909)

During the administration of the first two Commissioners, English as the medium of instruction had been introduced at the high school level and met little resistance. The private secondary school in Puerto Rico did much the same, yet Commissioner Falkner's idea of introducing English as the medium of instruction at the elementary or graded school level was considered revolutionary by the membership of the Unionist Party.

Reaction in the schools was mixed, the vast majority of Puerto Rican teachers began to prepare themselves to use English partly as the medium of instruction. There was some resistance to the importation of American mainland teachers.

> The people believe that more than enough ability exists here to direct these schools, and they do not wish the department of education to import ability that we here can export. (Cebollero, 1945)

At the same time apprehension and conflict were building about the importation of teachers on the island, critics of the government policies in Puerto Rico were publishing articles carrying such titles as *Our Failure in Porto Rico* (Stone, 1905), and *What Our Youngest Child Wants* (Abbott, 1906).

The difference in perception is seen in the following quotes:

> We have given them probably the best government.... They have American Protection without American taxation... our government and our people have bestowed liberal relief and assistance in a time of affliction... education and sanitation are well provided for.... They have been literally and actually 'killed with kindness'. (Stone, 1905)

> The Congress ought to give aid to public education in Porto Rico. We may well let the higher education wait on the broader education. But, with all the economy practiced, with the small amounts expended for buildings and the comparatively small salaries paid and the large proportion of the income of the island devoted to education... (Abbott, 1906)

Not everybody was in accord with this outcry for federal aid, but it is interesting to note that a sense of obligation to give aid was growing. The attitude seemed to be that if English was to be taught to all, if assimilation were to be attempted, and if the principle of universal education were to be supported, then the federal government must pay part of the cost. As federal aid was not forthcoming, Falkner had to do what he could with local funds.

During Falkner's administration rural schools were increased to 614 in total. Urban graded schools, well organized and increasing the use of English as the medium of instruction in the later grades, enrolled 29,904 (40.6 per cent of the available urban population). Night school saw a significant increase in the eight to fifteen span, but adult attendance dropped drastically (Osuna, 1949).

In 1908, The United States extended the Morrill-Hatch Act to Puerto Rico. The insular legislature appropriated money to buy land and construct a building for an agricultural school at Mayaguez. This was the beginnings of the College of Agriculture and Mechanical Arts of the University of Puerto Rico, which opened in 1912.

Edward G. Baxter succeeded Falkner as Commissioner for Education in 1909, and under his guidance expansion continued, extending right through from elementary school to university. Graduates of the San Juan and Mayaguez High Schools found no difficulty in entering any college or university in the United States (Lindsay, 1912). American culture, while not replacing Spanish culture, was modifying the culture of Puerto Rico through the educational system. It would be inaccurate to think that protest was not developing. Baxter's aim for the island's educational system is best summed up by the following quote:

> ...to provide instruction in the branches comprising the common school education to all children of school age in the island, this education to be both in English and Spanish. (United States War Department, 1912)

Baxter, in his zeal, almost replaced Spanish with English in the urban graded elementary schools during his tenure. Not surprisingly, a split was developing between the Commissioner and the island staff; and this inevitably spread into the political arena. The House of Delegates tried to get complete control of all departments through its power to appropriate money under the Foraker Act. In 1909, it refused to pass a budget, but the United States Congress amended the Foraker Act to allow the government to function on the amount of the previous year's budget (Diffie and Diffie, 1931).

By 1910, the school-age population was 390,640 and only 121,453 were enrolled. When Dr Baxter resigned in 1912, the public school enrolled 160,657. The goal Baxter set himself may have been over optimistic, but his achievement was nonetheless significant.

Edward W. Bainter took office as Commissioner in 1912, and inherited a developing quarrel over language in the schools. The Teachers' Association, founded in 1911, was concerned about language policy. In 1913 it requested that arithmetic be taught in Spanish on all grade levels. In 1914, the Association requested that Spanish be used as the medium of instruction in the first four grades (Fife and Herschel, 1951). By August, 1913 the discussion of the language to be used by the schools was taken up by the legislature.

That the language question was based on the fear of American cultural penetration is revealed by the personality of the man who led the fight against English, Jose de Diego. He had been an early supporter of preserving Spanish culture and was a well-known poet in his own right, a not infrequent quality of national leaders in Latin America. In Puerto Rico they have tended to be practical politicians. The language debate revolved around the opening of 600 new schools. A rider had been attached to the bill appropriating money for the new schools, which stipulated that all subjects should be taught in Spanish. Mr Huyke, who was to become the first Puerto

Rican Commissioner of Education, defended the use of English as the medium of instruction. It is perhaps interesting that one of Bainter's severest critics felt that Bainter himself favoured a more liberal language policy (Cebollero, 1945). The language question was made a political issue which the Unionist Party would continue to exploit in the House of Delegates.

Bitterness towards American language policy developed as the public school system expanded. By 1914 enrolment had reached 207,101, the highest figure to date in the history of Puerto Rico, and representing over 50 per cent of the school age population. This was a phenomenal rise from the 1910 figure of 31 per cent. The American ideal of a common school education for all was approaching reality, provided the pace could be maintained (United States War Department, 1915).

Paul G. Miller became Commissioner in 1915, and the Head of the Department of Education. He was a product of the Puerto Rican school system, having been a teacher, supervisor of schools and Director of the Normal Training School (Fife and Herschel, 1951). Commissioner Miller's administration would be influenced by two world crises, the worldwide depression of 1914 and World War I. In 1917, as a result of the Jones Act, all Puerto Ricans became United States citizens and a general democratization of the insular government was mandated. All three events would influence the development of the public school system.

Under the Jones Act the Executive Council was replaced by an elective Senate. All Cabinet appointments were to be made by the Governor and approved by the Puerto Rican Senate. Two significant exceptions were made. The appointments of the Attorney General and Commissioner of Education continued to be appointed by the President of the United States and approved by the United States Senate (Fife and Herschel, 1951).

Of the nature and extent of his powers, Commissioner Miller wrote:

> Under the terms of the organic act the commissioner of education is given ample power and wide responsibilities.... It has been sometimes charged that this centralization scheme of administration lends itself to

> abuses.... It is largely through this centralization that the progress attained in education during the past two decades has been accomplished. (Miller, 1921)

A major effect of centralization was the abolition of local school boards in 1919. The American concept of local control through local non-political school boards did not fit the thinking of a people who regarded education as a direct function of government. Education with centralization was and would continue to be a keen political issue in Puerto Rico.

The Depression of 1914 caused a shortfall in revenue to the insular government thereby cutting funding of public education and a slight decrease in enrolment. By 1920, only 45 per cent of the school-age children were enrolled (Miller, 1921). In 1921, out of 436,747 children of legal school age, only 193,369 were in schools supported by public funds (Teachers' Association, 1921). In 1914, Puerto Rico spent $2,698,263 for education; by 1920, the school budget was $3,150,761 for a smaller enrolment (Osuna, 1949). The cost of education had risen and the enrolment was not being maintained at the 50 per cent level. Commissioner Miller realized that the Puerto Rican people were doing as much as they could. He declared:

> The people of Porto Rico are doing reasonably well in the matter of providing educational facilities for the children of school age, who constitute one-third of the population. It is true that the appropriations made by the insular legislature and municipalities have been and are today far from adequate, but it is also true that the budget for education has been uniformly larger than that of any department. Furthermore, in making comparisons, one should bear in mind that the per capita wealth of Porto Rico is only $204.00, or about one-tenth of the people of the United States. (Miller, 1921)

He made the usual plea in favour of federal aid to public education:

> In all matters of federal legislation on education, Porto Rico should be included. Porto Ricans are American citizens. As such they deserve attention. The federal Vocational Education Act should be made applicable to Porto Rico, where vocational education is a great need. Any pending legislation looking toward federal aid to the States should apply to Porto Rico as well. This is a matter in which Uncle Sam can afford to be generous. (Miller, 1921)

Progress had been made, but federal aid would have stimulated a reversal of declining enrolment. The illiteracy rate was declining. Of people over ten years of age in 1899, 79.6 per cent had been illiterates. In 1910, the rate was 66.5 per cent, and by 1920 it was down to 55 per cent, still high but dropping (Miller, 1921).

In the area of language instruction Commissioner Miller felt bilingualism to be essential. In an article published in the *Review of Reviews*, he wrote:

> Since Porto Ricans were made American Citizens by virtue of the Jones Act of 1917, the study of English is essential. Because of the geographical location, the ancestry and the traditions of the people, from the standpoint of business and particularly because of Pan-american relations of the United States, there is every reason for continuing the study of Spanish in the schools.
>
> In the course of events it is entirely reasonable to presume that Spanish will be the language of the Puerto Rican home a hundred years from today, but practically all persons who have had the advantages of education will be bilingual. The Porto Rican will continue to make love and say his prayers in Spanish, but his reading will be largely in English. (Miller, 1921)

Unlike many of his predecessors, Miller did not go overboard regarding the function of the school as being solely the teaching of English. Two reasons seem to account for this: first Miller was a product of the system as mentioned earlier, and second his review of a study conducted by General Superintendent Jose Padin, in which he pointed out the fundamental weaknesses of the Falkner policy in the following terms:

> When a child reaches the third grade he has read in English, one primer, one reader and one language book, but he finds to his surprise that he has not learned enough English to do his arithmetic work. He is required to think in English, to reason out processes in English. His previous training in the language has not prepared him for this. He not only cannot think in English but the vocabulary in which the concrete problems of arithmetic are stated differs unfairly from what he is used to. (Cebollero, 1945)

As a result of the Padin Study Miller reformed the Falkner language policy, making Spanish the medium of instruction for the first four years of the graded school. Still it was with mixed feelings that he urged the continued importation of teachers from the mainland to teach English:

> Porto Rico needs many more well trained and devoted teachers from the continent. The proportion of American teachers from the United States to the total number of teachers has grown alarmingly in recent years. (Miller, 1921)

The continuing agitation by Puerto Rican politicians had maintained the language issue as a political matter. The two major political parties carried planks in their 1920 platforms regarding the language of instruction and English. The Unionist Party, favouring independence, declared:

> The Unionist Party favors the teaching of English as a subject in our schools... but is opposed to the use of any language that is not

> the language of the country as a medium of instruction. (La Revista Escolar, 1920)

The Republican Party, favouring statehood, held:

> We believe that the question of popular education, the primary education of children and adults, and the diffusion of English... is of first importance so that democratic doctrine may be understood and widely practiced by Porto Ricans.

When Commissioner Miller was about to leave Puerto Rico, he made a plea to the teachers for a separation of the schools from political development such as the quotes above. He exhorted:

> Keep the schools free from all banefull influences and false doctrines that exert harmful effects upon the minds of the young and thus maintain unsullied the good name of the best and greatest American institution in Puerto Rico, the American School. (La Revista Escolar, 1921)

Commissioner Miller was the last of the continental American Commissioners. By 1921 the school had become an integral part of Puerto Rican life. If it had not done so it would have failed. The Puerto Rican school system was mature enough to furnish its own leadership. In recognition of this fact, American educational policy shifted toward granting more control to the Puerto Ricans. For Dr Miller's successor, in 1921, the President of the United States appointed Juan B. Huyke as Commissioner, the first Puerto Rican educator to hold that post.

Education under Puerto Rican Commissioners of Education (1921-1947)

The Commissioner of Education is a powerful figure in Puerto Rican life. His great powers made the position eagerly sought, and highly political in nature. One must remember that Mr Huyke defended the use of English as the medium of instruction in the legislative hearings of 1915, which was also consistent with the Republican Party's plank in the election of 1920.

By 1921, the vast majority of the teachers were Puerto Rican (Osuna, 1949). The island had changed under American rule. The schools had contributed most to the change with their close contact with the North American culture. Yet, a contemporary writer who knew the island well declared:

> It does not become less Porto Rican or less Spanish-American, but it shows signs of becoming more cosmopolitan; and its leaders are discovering the value of being able to read and speak two great languages, each of which, in some important sense, belong to them, and of which has so great a practical value to stimulate their best efforts. (Shaw, 1921)

When two peoples come in contact, the result is the development of a third mode of behaviour distinct from the two originals. In not recognizing this process, American policy-makers in Puerto Rico failed to assimilate the Puerto Ricans. As Puerto Rico changed it changed in a Puerto Rican manner.

Many Americans felt that help should be given to island education, since Puerto Ricans had been able to do so well with so little. One such plea was for teacher education in the United States:

> It ought to be a fixed policy of the United States government... to assist Porto Rican Teachers to attend summer school in the United States.... It should also be made easy for teachers from the United States to come and go. Some use of Army transports in the past has shown that more might well be done in the future. (Shaw, 1921)

As in any policy looking toward the education of peoples from other cultures, one must look at the motivation. If the motivation is for the development of the young, for the welfare of their people, then well and good. However if the motivation is control, to create permanent, loyal friends for this country, the results may prove at the least doubtful. The friendly feelings of graduates who return to their homelands are likely to be conditioned by the effect of American policy on their own people. This is demonstrated by the fact that many of the Puerto Ricans educated in the United States became the severest critics of anything American. A representative of this type of intellectual was Coll y Cuchi, who wrote:

> The moment that my artificial student personality came into conflict with my true native personality, with the traditions of my race, as soon as I discovered that what I had learned in the United States was repudiated by the spontaneous sentiments of my heart, I realized that it was impossible to change that part of us which God has shaped with his own hands.... So we threw ourselves headlong into the battle to rescue our indestructable heritage and traditions, our race, our language, our religion. (Coll y Cuchi, 1922)

Many 'Americanized' Puerto Ricans very frequently were the most vociferous in opposing unpopular American policies. In education they felt that Americans took too much of the Puerto Rican effort for granted. Actually the schools system was developed with insular funds and mostly by Puerto Ricans. Under Commissioner Huyke, a Puerto Rican but still not responsible to the people of the island, scant regard was given to local wishes. In this period American writers still stressed the importance of the help given by the United States in education. A more accurate point of view follows:

> General education in Porto Rico was resuscitated twenty-five years ago by help from the United States. Now, already Porto Rico is making an important offering in return. By reason of its position central to the Americas and of its cultural inheritance from Spain, the

> West Indian dependency of the United States is ambitious to become the converging point of Pan-American economic and scientific development and the meeting place of Spanish and English culture....
> The educational history of Porto Rico since the island was severed from Spain has been exemplary. With no financial aid from the United States and with 33.6 per cent of its budget at present devoted to schools, Porto Rico is developing an educational system that the International Institute of Teachers College has recently found comparable to that of New York and Massachusetts. During the past twenty-five years illiteracy has been reduced from 85 per cent to 45 per cent, the number of schools has been increased from 545 to 2,943 and the enrollment has grown from 44,681 to 233,425. (Abbott, 1923)

Puerto Ricans were responsible for this growth. There were however 200,000 children not in school and 84 per cent of those who were did not reach beyond the third grade. At this same time, the majority of mainland Americans did not get beyond the sixth grade (Abbott, 1923). Puerto Rico was willing to spend money for education, but there just was not enough money to enrol all 200,000 children.

Commissioner Huyke was still faced with the division of his own system on the language medium issue. Publicly he favoured English with the modification instituted by Commissioner Miller. He also faced the independence-minded majority in the legislature. The Unionist Party under the leadership of Antonio Barcelo favoured complete separation from the United States, and the exclusive use of Spanish as the medium of instruction. When Monty Reilly was sent to Puerto Rico as Governor by President Harding, he threatened to remove 'independentistas' from the government. He was apparently unaware of the political situation on the island.

> He went to the island resolved to be the strong man who would check the 'seditious' activities

> of the Unionist politicians. He... declared no advocate of independence would hold any office in his appointive power, and he was going to work to make 'the language of Washington, Lincoln and Harding' the official language of the schools. The latter shows how ignorant he was of Porto Rico affairs since English has been the language taught in the schools for some time. (Munoz Rivera, 1922)

Reilly was a politician who did not investigate carefully to discover the truth. Antagonism between the Governor and the legislature was a foregone conclusion. Huyke was regarded as a puppet who did the bidding of his chiefs. His tenure was full of stress and tension. Nonetheless improvements were made in the school system. The legislature increased funds to education, and the annual budget for education represented between 30 and 35 per cent of the insular budget. At the end of his tenure 221,000 out of 530,148 children of school age, in other words 42 per cent of those of school age, were enrolled (Osuna, 1949).

The legislature was increasingly interested in children, and was willing to use the facilities of the schools to promote their welfare. Many public school children lived near starvation. To help them, the legislature appropriated $10,000 in 1919-1920 for a school lunch programme. The amount was increased to $60,000 by 1930, a small amount considering the problem, but a start in the right direction.

Secondary and higher education were becoming increasingly important. In 1921, the high schools produced 367 graduates; by 1931, the figure had risen to 969. In 1923, the University of Puerto Rico was reorganized. The office of Chancellor, separate from that of the Commissioner of Education, was created. This action paralleled similar actions by state-supported universities on the east coast of the United States. In 1924, the School of Tropical Medicine was established at the University of Puerto Rico, with technical assistance from Columbia University. For rural education, Huyke received an appropriation of $250,000 in 1928. He established six rural consolidated schools. These schools were both traditional and vocational in character. They became models for replication in other rural areas of Puerto Rico.

In 1930, Dr Jose Padin replaced Hüyke as Commissioner of Education. The world Depression was beginning and difficult times were ahead. During the years 1930 to 1936, Dr Padin followed the policy of expanding enrolment, building schools, and trying to solve the language question. In 1930-1931, 226,215 children were enrolled out of 530,955 of legal school age. By 1936, enrolment figures had reached 256,352 out of 566,321 children of school age. Padin faced a restricted budget during the Depression years. In 1930, the insular and municipal budgets amounted to $5,408,748, but in 1936 they had declined to $4,897,855 although insular revenues had increased by some $4,000,000 (Osuna, 1949).

Rising anti-Americanism coloured political thinking in the 1930s. The Nationalist Party's agitation against the United States reached levels of open violence and possible revolution in 1922, and this was carried into the 1930s. The Nationalists had declared that:

> Spanish should be the official language of Porto Rico and that the use of any other in the schools is an attack on the Porto Rican personality and belittling to our civilisation. (Diffie and Diffie, 1931)

The Americanization policy of the schools was facing sharp resistance. There were signs that assimilation was slowly passing out of the educational scene. The over-emphasis of English was becoming a thing of the past under Commissioner Padin. Anti-imperialist American writers were attacking American educational policy. Often these attacks were well-intentioned, but were composed of half-truths. Usually, criticisms were made by people who were not educators. One of the most effective and detailed attacks on American administration in Puerto Rico was that of Diffie and Diffie:

> Hundreds of American teachers have gone to Porto Rico to teach English but they were paid in Porto Rican dollars.... Their salaries, along with other expenses attached to English instruction, have been a crushing burden on the

> slender resources of the island. Why spend millions of dollars to teach them English when they are ragged, hungry, unskilled and might better have learned a trade or been taught something of scientific agriculture?... And to the teaching of English the American government has never contributed a penny. The progress made in insular education is something of which to be proud. Almost our sole contribution has been the unnecessary and almost useless financial outlay imposed on the people of Porto Rico.... The struggle to educate the people would have been difficult enough with help and without obstacles; it has been impossible without help and with obstacles. (Diffie and Diffie, 1931)

American education in Puerto Rico has achieved far more, of course, than just the teaching of English. It is important to emphasize that Puerto Ricans had paid most of their education bill themselves. But more important they had made out of the American school, established for assimilation, a Puerto Rican institution.

Dr Padin's administration concerned itself with the teaching of English. He introduced experimental methods trying to solve the problem. First, to set the record straight, he stated that the problem was an educational one and not a political one. Since Padin's approach was publicly known and he had been appointed by President Hoover, he declared his position regarding education:

> Thirty years of vacillation and suffering have gone by without any certainty as to the end for which we are preparing our country. I assert that Porto Rico must be prepared to live its own life, because Porto Rico has a sense of self, because its personality is clearly formed. (Padin, 1945)

A more liberal policy toward Puerto Rican education seemed to be in the making. Nobody would say that the

Hoover administration was famous for its liberalism, but it seemed willing to allow Puerto Ricans some room to adapt.

In keeping with his pledge to approach the language problem scientifically, Padin did not make a change until a series of studies made between 1931 and 1934 had been completed. In 1934, the Commissioner issued a circular letter making Spanish the language of instruction in the eight grades of the elementary school. English was taught as a subject from the first grade through high school. In the high schools English was to be the medium of instruction in all subjects except Spanish. Additional time was allotted for English in grades seven and eight (Cebollero, 1945). To improve the teaching of English under this new policy, in 1936 the legislature allowed funds for employing 100 additional teachers of English to intensify the work in the upper grades of the elementary schools. The Governor of Puerto Rico, Blanton Winship, supported the addition to the continental staff. In 1935 and 1936, the Governor called attention to the importance of English for Puerto Ricans who migrate to the United States. However, the Governor expressed dissatisfaction with the Padin policy and dwelt on the political importance of English for Puerto Ricans (Fife and Herschel, 1951).

In 1936 the activities of the Nationalist Party made it difficult for educators favouring the use of English as a medium of instruction. They tended to be looked upon as anti-American and subversive. In the same year, Padin resigned to enter an educational career in the United States (Fife and Herschel, 1951).

Dr Jose M. Gallardo succeeded Padin and arrived in Puerto Rico as a relative unknown in education. He continued the policies of Americanization, emphasis on English, and expansion of the school system. The public school system continued to grow. The enrolment in 1945-1946 was 360,635 by which time the school-age population had reached 663,376. A detailed breakdown of the 360,635 by level is shown in Table 2.3.

According to these statistics, 54.36 per cent of the school-age population were in attendance. Puerto Rican illiteracy had already been reduced to 31.5 per cent by 1940, and continued to decline, and enrolment at the University of Puerto Rico was 7,321. Compared to the neighbouring

Dominican Republic, much larger and of greater wealth, Puerto Rico had progressed far in education. The total enrolment in Dominican normal and secondary schools was then 2,300, with 750 students attending university.

As federal control of education in Puerto Rico neared its end, United States aid to education increased. After 1942, the United States Treasury was authorized to return to Puerto Rico the beverage tax on insular liquors, mostly rum, collected in the United States. Three per cent of the insular and federal tax was assigned to the University of Puerto Rico. By 1945, this amounted to $1,315,111. In 1946-1947, $2,700,758 was granted to aid the school lunch programme, and in 1949-1950 funds for the same purpose amounted to $4,087,919.

Table 2.3

Enrolment in Puerto Rican Schools: 1945-1946

Level	No. in school	% in school
Elementary (6-12)	251,628	66.78
Junior High (13-15)	78,892	52.52
Senior High (16-18)	30,115	22.08

THE ACHIEVEMENT OF EDUCATIONAL AUTONOMY

On 5 August 1947, the Congress of the United States approved an amendment to the Organic Act to allow Puerto Ricans to elect their own Governor. He in turn has the authority to appoint the Commissioner of Education. For the first time, responsibility for Puerto Rican education was entirely in Puerto Rican hands. Fifty years of American direction were over. In those fifty years of American leadership, illiteracy had been greatly reduced. By 1948, it stood at 23.6 per cent, and school enrolment figures showed 55 per cent of the children of school age in attendance.

During the first few years of Puerto Rican control of education excellent progress was made. For example, in 1950 the number of students attending public schools rose by some 24,000; a percentage increase of 5.8. But what of the language issue, the most controversial element in the development of the Puerto Rican public school system? The United States' need to Americanize led to imposition of instruction in English in several different ways. The answer is really quite simple. One of the first modifications made under Puerto Rican control was a revision of language policy to the use of Spanish, the vernacular, as the language of instruction. English is taught as a foreign language on all grade levels. It took 50 years to achieve what any capable educator would have recommended as being sound for education and for the learning of a foreign language. Such is the inertial effect of politics on educational provision!

. . . .

Since 1947 'educational tension' between the USA and Puerto Rico has eased considerably. Much cooperation and improvement has taken place. As of 1985, the enrolment rate exceeds 90 per cent, the high school drop-out rate is less than 50 per cent, and the United States contributes $150 million per annum to public education in Puerto Rico, no 'educational strings' attached.

BIBLIOGRAPHICAL REFERENCES

Abbott, L. (1906) What our youngest child wants, **The Outlook**, August

Abbott, L. (1923) Porto Rico as a center for Pan American Education, **The Outlook**, January

Aitkin, T. (1964) **Poet in the Fortress** (New York, New American Library)

Blanco, T. (1943) **Prontuario Historico de Puerto Rico** (Venezuela, E. Franklin & Co.)

Cebollero, P. (1945) **A School Language for Puerto Rico** (San Juan, Imprenta Baldrich)

Coll y Cuchi, C. (1922) American rule in Porto Rico, **The Living Age**, July

Cordoba, P. (1838) **Memoria Sobre todos los Ramos de Administracion de la Isla de Puerto** (Madrid, Rico Yenes)

Diffie, B. and Diffie, J.W. (1931) **Porto Rico: A Broken Pledge** (New York, Vanguard Press)

Falkner, R. (1909) The English Language in Puerto Rico, **The Forum**, March

Ferrer Hernandez, G. (1885) **La Instruccion Publica en Puerto Rico** (San Juan)

Fife, R. and Herschel, M. (1951) **The Teaching of English in Puerto Rico** (San Juan, Department of Education Press)

Great Britain, Board of Education (1900) **Special Reports on Educational Subjects** (London, Wyman & Sons Ltd)

Haas, W.H. (1940) **The American Empire** (Chicago, University of Chicago Press)

Hauberge, C. (1974) **Puerto Rico and the Puerto Ricans** (New York, Hippocrene Books)

Infiesta, A. (1886) **Inspector de Primera Ensenanza del Distro Sud: Memoria con los cuadros de ensenanza y estadisticos correspondientes** (San Juan, Tip. El Comercio)

Lewis, G. (1963) **Puerto Rico: Freedom and Power in the Caribbean** (New York, M. R. Press)

Lindsay, S.M.(1902) Education in Puerto Rico, **Independent**

Lindsay, S.M.(1912) What we have done in Porto Rico?, **The American Review of Reviews**, May

Macho Moreno, J. (1895) **Compilacion Legislativa de Primera Ensenanza de la Isla de Puerto Rico y Formularios para Toda Clase de Servicios Relacionados con la Instruccion Primaria** (Madrid, Viuda de Hernando y Compania)

Mathews, T. (1960) **Puerto Rican Politics and the New Deal** (Gainsville, University of Florida Press)

Miller, P. (1921) Address to the teachers of Porto Rico, **La Revista Escolar Porto Rico**, February

Miller, P. (1921) Education in Puerto Rico, problems and progress, **The American Review of Reviews**, September

Munoz Riveria, L. (1922) A ninety-eight percent American in Porto Rico, **The New Republic**, January

Osuna, J. (1949) **A History of Education in Puerto Rico** (Rio Piedras, Puerto Rico, Editorial de la Universidad de Puerto Rico)

Osuna, J. (1956) **Puerto Rico, U.S.A.** (Washington DC, Office of the Commonwealth of Puerto Rico)

Padin, J. (1945) **Consideraciones en torno al Regimen Colonial** (Rio Piedras, Puerto Rico, Junta Editora de la Universidad de Puerto Rico)

Reid, C.F.(1929) **Overseas America** (New York, Foreign Policy Association)

Shaw, A. (1921) Porto Ricans as Citizens, **The American Review of Reviews**, May

Stone, R. (1905) Our Failure in Porto Rico, **The North American Review**, October

Tapia y Rivera, A. (1854) **Biblioteca Historica de Puerto Rico** (Puerto Rico, Imp. de Marquez)

Teachers Association (1920) **La Revista Escolar de Porto Rico**, October

Teachers Association (1921) **La Revista Escolar de Porto Rico**, September

United States War Department (1899) **Report on the Census of Porto Rico** (Washington DC, Government Printing Office)

United States War Department (1901) **Report of the Commissioner of Education** (Washington DC, Government Printing Office)

United States War Department (1909) **Report of the Commissioner of Education** (Washington DC, Government Printing Office)

United States War Department (1912) **Report of the Governor of Puerto Rico** (Washington DC, Government Printing Office)

United States War Department (1915) **Report of the Commissioner of Education** (Washington DC, Government Printing Office)

Chapter Three

THE CUBAN EDUCATIONAL MODEL AND ITS INFLUENCE IN THE CARIBBEAN REGION

Mark Richmond

INTRODUCTION

In early 1986, two events took place which reveal much about the way education in the Caribbean region is being pushed and pulled in contrary directions. Over three days at the end of January of that year, the *Pedagogy '86 International Congress* was held in Havana, attracting over 3,500 educationists from thirty-five countries, mostly Latin American and Caribbean. The 'Final Declaration' of this conference, unanimously approved by participants reflecting different national contexts and representing a variety of theoretical positions, stated that:

> the huge sums now devoted by our countries to attempts to pay the foreign debt should be destined in large measure to educational development. (*Granma Weekly Review*, 9.2.86:3)

The second event occurred on 20 February 1986, when President Reagan paid a one-day visit to Grenada to celebrate the victory of the US-led invasion of that island in October 1983. Responding to a request from the Grenadian Prime Minister, President Reagan announced that:

> Over this year and the next two we will roughly triple the funding for our training and

> educational programmes for the Caribbean. Our goal is to train 1,500 students from these islands each year. (*Latin America Weekly Report*, 28.2.86: 3)

Though rather modest, this gift of US government-funded scholarships has significance for illustrating how educational aid is currently a favoured form of international assistance in the Caribbean region.

In their different ways, these events show how education, as well as being an important area of domestic policy, can raise issues with far-reaching international implications or become embroiled in controversies which transcend national boundaries. As far as the Caribbean region is concerned, no clearer example can be found of the 'internationalization' of educational questions than the widely felt impact of Cuban educational ideas and achievements since the 1959 Revolution. While evaluations of the type, extent, and meaning of Cuba's educational changes vary considerably, and while recognition of Cuba's educational advances can range between grudging acknowledgement and uncritical enthusiasm, regional states have had to take their neighbour's record into account. The extreme position of rejecting or ignoring all evidence of positive educational progress in socialist Cuba plays no major role in current discussions. Some implacable anti-Castroists or anti-communists may subscribe to this viewpoint, perhaps on the grounds that education in Castro's Cuba is not education at all but merely Marxist-Leninist indoctrination, but the real debate lies elsewhere. Cuban education continues to arouse interest and controversy not because it has been a total failure but because it can lay serious claim to considerable success.

The Cuban government, of course, is in no doubt that the educational advances made since 1959 represent one of the major triumphs of the regime; indeed, Cuba's educational achievements are being used to advertise the Revolution as a whole. For Cuba's leaders, satisfaction will be mixed with no small measure of relief that the enormous investment of effort, scarce resources, and prestige has begun to pay off. From the beginning of the Castro regime, education was given a high priority not only for its own sake and as a popular item of social consumption but also as a means to pursue a variety of national and revolutionary goals. Since 1959, Cuban education has passed through several phases, each of which has tested the commitment of the revolutionary leadership to the effective solution of pressing educational problems (Richmond, 1985). As a reward for its handling of these challenges, Castro's government now feels able to point confidently to a record of educational success which offers a number of opportunities not only at home but also abroad. Indeed, this record of achievement has stimulated the idea that there is a Cuban educational model which, in whole or in part, may have wider relevance and applicability, especially in the Caribbean region. Before submitting the Cuban educational model and its influence to detailed examination, however, it may be helpful to give further consideration to the type and extent of the success which has been claimed for Cuba's educational system during the past two and a half decades.

AN EVALUATION OF CUBAN EDUCATION UNDER THE REVOLUTION

Evaluations of Cuban educational accomplishments since 1959 vary widely according to angle of approach, choice of criteria, and point of view. One common approach is to contrast the stagnation, inadequacy of provision, and elitist orientation of pre-revolutionary education with the later success-story of rapid expansion, democratization, and reform (Paulston, 1971). Alternatively, a comparative approach may be adopted which favourably contrasts current Cuban attainments with educational levels in the Third World and in much of the Caribbean region and Latin America (Blat, 1983). Another mode of analysis looks more to theory and practice, or promise and fulfilment, focusing upon the extent to which the Revolution's goals and targets regarding education are being realized (Bowles, 1971). These approaches make use of standard indicators of improvement in Cuban educational performance, such as higher literacy rates, lower pupil-teacher ratios, more schools and teachers, increased enrolments and school efficiency, and larger allocations to education in the State Budget. However, many important issues of evaluation cannot be resolved by reference to such indicators alone, not only because some official studies are unavailable or because conducting certain kinds of educational research in Cuba is very difficult, but also because questions of interpretation rest upon fundamentally different political, ideological, and moral viewpoints.

Several broad but distinguishable positions can be identified in the debate over Cuban education in recent years. If the extreme position mentioned earlier is excluded, all three major interpretative groupings acknowledge the reality of Cuban educational advances, although they differ markedly in their estimations of the extent and significance of these achievements. The first position is that adopted by many opponents and critics of Castro's regime who have brought themselves to accept the evidence of some improvement revealed by several, mostly quantitative, indicators of educational performance. However, the clear trend of argument is toward regarding these educational achievements as being fatally compromised by more serious failures.

These failures need not be specifically educational in nature. Theriot, for example, admits to Cuba's success in securing 'Near total elimination of illiteracy and a highly developed multilevel educational system' (Theriot, 1984: 69) but in his analysis these and companion advances in health care, nutrition, income redistribution, and popular consciousness are overshadowed and diminished by poor economic performance and excessive reliance upon the Soviet bloc. Other critical studies challenge Cuban education more squarely by contrasting its achievements with its failures, and by finding the latter more important. Thomas *et al* (1984: 41) for instance, find many statistical data concerning Cuba's educational performance 'impressive' but 'somewhat misleading' and in need of 'further analysis'. In order to downplay the much-publicized advances in mass education in Cuba, they give emphasis to elitist tendencies in higher education, communist indoctrination, and problems of internal efficiency, lack of resources, and cheating. Similarly, Montaner (1981) acknowledges some improvements in Cuban education but considers these outweighed by certain negative features. Among other criticisms, he castigates the combination of study with agricultural labour as an indulgence in Virgilian mythology. Some critics, however, find the work-study principle to be especially repugnant; Arthur Schlesinger Jr, for example, prefers to endow this pedagogical concept with the pejorative connotations of 'child labour' (Berube, 1984: 108).

From other points of view, however, such problems and trends within Cuban education are interpreted differently, with the result that they may appear less damaging or not damaging at all, and certainly do not negate the positive accomplishments secured since 1959. According to the second broad interpretative position, Cuba's educational transformation is found to be generally positive and praiseworthy, although criticisms, doubts, and anxieties of varying kinds and strengths form an integral part of the evaluation. Thus, the main themes of Cuban education (expansion at all levels; linking education with economic development, especially in rural areas; emphasis on science and technology; and the creation of the 'new man'), along with particular education reforms (for example, the Literacy Campaign, the schools to and in the countryside, and pre-school education) have attracted much sympathetic interest and widespread, though often qualified, approval and admiration (Casas, 1981; CEPAL, 1980). Leiner's approach illustrates the broad pattern of argumentation whereby praise, the dominant evaluation, is combined with criticism:

> Even while the record of educational progress is impressive in many ways, particularly in view of Cuba's developmental status, certain problems persist: a shortage of fully trained teachers, an emphasis on achievement testing as the gauge of progress, the problem of dropouts and holdovers, the emergence of special schools for scientifically and technically gifted students in a society dedicated to egalitarianism, and an apparent overemphasis on political considerations in the selection of educational leaders.(Leiner, 1985: 36)

Having voiced these criticisms, however, Leiner does not wish to end his analysis on a negative note, with Cuban education under a cloud; consequently, he adds a positive conclusion which reflects the overall trend of his evaluation.

There are, of course, many differences of emphasis, judgement, and interpretation amongst those who confirm the success of numerous aspects of Cuba's educational performance whilst also expressing various reservations and criticisms. As well as characterizing a range of progressive, left of centre ideological perspectives on Cuban education the second interpretative position is broadly typical of most analyses of Cuba's educational revolution conducted by specialists in education. Their approach, however, is distinguishable from the third broad position represented, on the one hand, by Cuban leaders and educationalists and, on the other hand, by foreign observers who either share a similar ideological perspective or identify very strongly with the educational revolution in Cuba (Kozol, 1978; Camper, 1979). It is a difference between those who are truly 'inside' the Revolution and those who are 'outside'. For the former, the revolutionary goals set for education are in the process of being achieved. While some setbacks and weaknesses may be admitted and occasional sharp criticisms applied, even by Fidel Castro himself (Waters, 1986a), there is an overwhelming sense of satisfaction with past and present achievements and an optimistic view of prospective educational performance. A close, dynamic relationship is held to exist between education and revolution, with the result that historical and comparative perspectives furnish strong contrasts (Bowles, 1971: 472). Attacks from opposed ideological perspectives do not threaten seriously. For example, the charge of indoctrination is dismissed on the grounds that all education, everywhere, serves the function of socio-cultural reproduction in conformity with particular power structures and value systems: Cuba is simply more open and forthright about ideological formation than, say, developed or dependent capitalist states. Finally, the success of Cuba's educational revolution is seen as an especially clear illustration of the success of the Cuban Revolution as a whole, which is regarded as a continuing, unfinished process.

This brief survey of the broad differences in

interpretation concerning Cuban education is admittedly incomplete but hopefully it shows how any evaluation of Cuba's 'success' needs to be handled with considerable care. Agreement is most widespread over various quantitative measurements of achievement and improvement; less agreement is evident over the evaluation of education's contribution to economic growth and socio-economic development, to the creation of a new socialist man and woman, or to the democratization of Cuba's social, economic, and political structures and processes. Thus, while it is widely recognized that there are more and healthier young people staying longer in more and better equipped schools staffed by more teachers, arguments continue to rage over what is taking place inside these schools, what types of educational institutions they are, and what effects this schooling is having. Before examining the overseas influence on Cuban educational theory and practice in the light of such interpretative differences, it will be necessary to identify the main features of what is increasingly seen as the Cuban educational model.

THE CUBAN EDUCATIONAL MODEL

This model may be characterized as a combination of distinctive educational features or, better still, as a distinctive combination of educational features some of which are themselves distinctive. By drawing upon selected aspects of their own culture, history, and traditions, and by borrowing from Soviet and East European educational experience and from an eclectic range of other sources, Cuban leaders and educators have fashioned an educational model which exhibits certain family resemblances and yet possesses originality and individuality. This model, furthermore, bears the marks of struggle: the lessons of practical experience are etched on its features.

The Cuban educational model is a representation at one and the same time of an educational system, a set of educational principles and practices, and a strategy of educational change. Inseparable from the model is the context within which it has been shaped and elaborated, a context which accounts for much of the model's significance. Cuba is a relatively poor, mainly rural and agricultural Caribbean country which, thanks to a decisive revolutionary break with the past, has committed itself to a rapid process of social transformation inspired by the egalitarian ideology of socialism, a revived sense of national identity, and strong sentiments of anti-imperialism. As an instrument of this process of socio-economic change and as an aspect of social life destined to be transformed by the dynamic forces released by the 1959 Revolution, education has been a central rather than a peripheral question.

Above all else, Cuba's educational model is one which proclaims not only the possibility of establishing mass education in a developing country but also, at the same time, the necessity to reform radically the educational process so that it becomes an effective contributor to national development, social welfare, and popular mobilization. In Cuba's case, the democratization of education has meant the provision of free, state schooling at the primary level and at succeeding levels, with strong support from the national leadership in the form of a large and growing budgetary allocation to the education sector and a clear ideological commitment to education as a basic right. Access to schooling has been improved by the removal of formal discriminatory barriers, by the fairer distribution of educational resources, and by broader egalitarian tendencies in society aimed at reducing impediments based on race, sex, location, and social class (Richmond, 1985). The total abolition of private schools in Cuba occurred in mid-1961; the buildings and facilities of private establishments were appropriated by government decree. Cuba has also witnessed the creation of a network of non-formal educational arrangements. Following an inspiring Literacy Campaign which mobilized large sections of the population in support of leadership goals as well as educational tasks, an extensive adult education system has been established which has been marked by flexibility, continuity, and opportunity. Though not examined in detail in his study, the Cuban Literacy Campaign would seem to meet most of the specification of Street's 'ideological' model of literacy (Street, 1984). With one-third of the population said to be enrolled upon some educational course or other, and with many thousands of adults trying to win their own personal battles for a sixth- or ninth-grade education, Cuba has paid much more than lip-service to the idea of lifelong learning and the concept of society as one big school.

The creation of a mass education system has required a large and rapid expansion of the teaching force, with the widespread use of under-trained teachers if necessary in order to guarantee access to education for all. According to one leading Cuban educator,

> Some people said that we should wait until the teachers could be properly trained. Others, myself included, felt it was important to make education accessible to everybody by whatever means we had at our disposal. This was a struggle of an ideological nature within the revolutionary process. (Martuza, 1981: 267)

The Cuban model may be said to recommend this policy despite the price, in the shape of lower standards, which had to be paid. Once the struggle for greater access was largely won, however, attention turned to the further professional training of teachers, especially in the handling of pedagogical methods expressing the ideological orientation of the regime.

Cuba's educational model, in fact, clearly demands that the traditional values and inherited orientations of education in such a developing country must be challenged and transformed if education is to serve the needs of national economic development. In mainly rural and agricultural societies such as Cuba, this means changing social attitudes towards manual labour, rural life, agricultural occupations, and the role of women. As agricultural diversification and industrialization processes gather momentum, the need for skilled workers, technicians, and professionals in a more complex economic environment requires that the curriculum turns more and more toward science and technology, which, with mathematics now constitutes about 40 per cent of the total (Cuba, Ministerio de Educacion, 1984). In Cuba, these changes in values, attitudes, and orientations were facilitated by the adoption of a strong solidarist ideology, socialism, reinforced by a new sense of national pride and by revolutionary symbolism. As well as furnishing an over-arching rationale and justification for many controversial policies and decisions, this ideological framework provided a powerful scheme of personal and social values which replaced traditional conceptions and offered an alternative to 'bourgeois ideology', the consumer society, and cultural imperialism. Thus, Cuban ideology came to stress revolutionary commitment, social justice, egalitarianism, personal self-sacrifice, internationalism, and solidarity, virtues which the 'new man' and the 'new woman' would partly absorb through formal and non-formal educational processes. Cuba's sharp break with the past made some such ideology of mobilization and regeneration an indispensable feature of the educational model. Offering a clearly politicized version of what education means, the Cuban educational model is based upon a radical vision of man's capacity for self-transformation through organized social change.

The model, of course, was not derived from a master-plan applied mechanically in 1959 and afterwards. Rather, it has evolved and changed through a process of development and innovation. The model itself may be seen to incorporate not only this evolutionary process, in conjunction with certain basic priorities and shifting emphases, but also the willingness to experiment and adapt. The importance of mass education, for example, is reflected in the sequence of educational change, for it was the main priority of the 196Os when primary schooling, literacy programmes, and adult education underwent a rapid, massive expansion. Other aspects of education such as secondary schooling, technical-vocational education, and university study were not totally neglected but the clear thrust of the strategy was towards educating the 'base' rather than training a narrow elite (Sahoy, 1978). While Cuba's leaders may now regret particular mistakes made in the 1960s, they are unlikely to question their choice of educational priority during that period. That choice is as much a part of the educational model as, say, the schools in the countryside; the same could be said of the decision to expand the other levels of the educational system in the 1970s and 1980s (partly due to the ongoing commitment to mass education and partly as a result of changes in development strategy demanding a greater output of skilled human resources). The educational model, in other words, is one which is flexible enough to respond to new phases in the process of educational change and socio-economic development.

This flexibility and responsiveness to change, furthermore, may involve not only the adoption or creation of new, distinctive educational forms but also their reform, modification, and even abandonment. The school to the countryside scheme, for example, was largely (though not completely) replaced by the school in the countryside programme. In recent years, important changes have occurred with the establishment of exact sciences high schools and exact sciences vocational high schools (Castro, 1986: 5). However, these changes and modifications can be seen to accord with the fundamental principles underlying the educational model.

By far the most important of these underlying principles is the idea of combining academic study and productive work. Applications of this principle can be found, in one form or another, in every type and level of education in Cuba, from the school gardens in many primary schools to integrated work placements for university students. Much, though not all, of the work is agricultural in character. The work-study principle is linked with many other precepts and practices in Cuban education, such as the principle of overcoming the division between manual and intellectual labour; the principle of education within the community; the need for schools and students to make a direct economic contribution, if possible; the school to and in the countryside schemes; the improvement of educational provision in rural areas; and the need to prepare young people for adult work roles. Prieto and Figueroa (1979) provide an overview of several of these principles and practices, while Richmond (1983) critically assesses Cuban policies in respect of transition from school to work.

Finally, the full flavour of the Cuban educational model would be lost without mentioning the active participation of the whole community in performing a broad, diverse range of educational tasks and duties. This participation is channelled through a number of political and mass organizations, including the Cuban Communist Party, the Young Communists, the Pioneers, student federations, trade unions, the Federation of Cuban Women, the School Councils, the Committees for the Defence of the Revolution, and the Local Organs of People's Power. This widespread, popular involvement is an essential aspect of the Cuban educational model, being a vital expression of the attempt to break down the barriers between school and society.

Clearly, the Cuban educational model is complex, dynamic, and multi-faceted, qualities which leave it open to a large number of diverse interpretations. Taking the model in its entirety, some observers may see it as a recipe for totalitarian education, while others may regard it as an integral part of a process of revolutionary change and national liberation. Alternatively, a particular facet of the model may be singled out for attention, perhaps eliciting a response which shapes the appreciation of other features. There is certainly no guarantee that perceptions of the Cuban educational model are accurate or fair. Indeed, those who borrow from Cuba's educational experience may be quite unwise, whereas those who ignore or reject the model may be missing a valuable opportunity. Much depends upon the observer's conception of what a model is and what it can be expected to do.

POSSIBLE APPLICATION OF THE CUBAN MODEL

Fernando Cardoso has raised many issues concerning the transfer of the Cuban revolutionary model which are relevant to our own particular discussion. Cardoso insists that 'the Cuban experience is more a symbol than a lesson' (Cardoso, 1973: 9). He is scathing towards those who would apply a model rigidly, regardless of historical conditions and national circumstances. If that is done, he maintains, the model becomes a straitjacket which deforms and constrains rather than a means of liberation. Condemning general, abstract analysis, 'imitation without creativity', and 'the lifeless transposition of formulas and methods', he argues that Cuba's chief value is as a symbol of hope; for him it represents the possibility of victory over dependency and the chance for a new version of socialist construction to emerge. By emphasizing the symbolic function of the Cuban model, Cardoso is anxious to deny that models offer definite answers or specific solutions which can be applied successfully in a mechanical, uncreative fashion. They are best seen as suggestive and indicative rather than prescriptive. It is in this sense that his statement 'Revolution cannot be exported' (Cardoso, 1973: 2) must be understood. As far as Cuba's educational model is concerned, Cardoso's remarks may serve as a warning to those who would 'export' or 'import' Cuban educational structures, programmes, and practices without carefully and creatively adapting them to local conditions. However, his analysis is itself historically situated and his strictures against 'revolutionary borrowing' may now seem excessively harsh in view of the changes in the Cuban model and the methods whereby it is projected abroad.

A sign of these changes occurred in 1986 in Havana, when Fidel Castro closed the Pedagogy '86 International Congress with the following parting message: 'What we have done would have been impossible without a revolution!' (Castro, 1986). Whilst hereby reaffirming the revolutionary path chosen by Cuba, Castro was careful to deny any suggestion that his remarks were intended to foment revolution or promote subversion elsewhere in the region. On the other hand, he clearly is not of the opinion that the Cuban revolutionary experience has importance only for Cuba and has no wider meaning or relevance. In that speech, Castro asked himself a rhetorical question: 'Can what you have done be done under the systems now prevailing in Latin America?' His answer expressed no shred of doubt: current regimes, unchanged, could not possibly spawn educational advances comparable to those achieved by Cuba since 1959. Suitable political change, in other words, is the indispensable precondition of significant educational progress; equally as important is the implication that the type of political change will determine the level of educational progress which is attainable. Thus, if the political change is not revolutionary in character, educational achievements will be commensurately modest; only revolution, not reform, can secure an educational transformation of Cuban proportions.

In the case of both revolution and reform, however,

The Cuban Model

Castro clearly believes that the Cuban educational model has much to offer to other countries. Selective borrowing from, and partial imitation of, Cuba's educational achievements promise benefits to a broad range of states. On the other hand, should revolutionary change break out in the region, any new radical regime could do no better than to look to Cuba for a working model of successful educational transformation. It is debatable, however, whether Castro seriously anticipates, or indeed recommends, the adoption of the whole educational model even by a revolutionary regime. Implicit in the following contrast between the Cuban and Nicaraguan revolutionary experiences is a recognition of constraints which can be expected to affect the transfer of the Cuban model, including the educational model:

> They themselves [the *Sandinistas*] will by no means say that the two revolutions are exactly alike. They are both profound revolutions, alike in many ways and in many ways different, as all true revolutions must be.... Each country has its own road, its own problems, its own style, methods, and objectives. We have our own; they have theirs. We did things one way, our way: they will do things their way. (Castro, 1979: 2)

Nevertheless, Cuba's leaders are convinced that the educational model has considerable relevance for the situations facing many neighbouring states; as we shall see, the Cuban government seeks to demonstrate this not only on the level of argument but also on the practical level of educational assistance programmes. Countries in the region, of course, respond differently to Cuba's educational offerings; some states find that they have more to gain than others. Much depends upon the continuing success of Cuba's educational system, upon the general performance of the Castro regime, and upon the interplay of various internal and external forces affecting the receptivity of individual countries and the Caribbean region to which they belong.

In a short analysis of the policy implications of Cuba's educational reforms for other developing countries, Carnoy and Werthein have raised a number of important issues and arguments. After noting the relevance of Cuba's manner of handling such educational problems as extending mass schooling to rural areas and matching educational output with manpower needs, the following question is asked:

> Can some of the educational reforms... be transferred to a society in which a radical ideological shift from capitalism to socialism has not taken place? (Carnoy and Werthein, 1983: 238)

After examining four of Cuba's educational reforms (rural boarding schools, the combination of work and study, adult literacy, and the development of an independent base for research and appropriate technology), Carnoy and Werthein conclude that

> While such educational reforms can perhaps be transferred to nonsocialist societies, in practice this transference is not likely to take place - not because of the malevolence of the parties involved, but because such transfer conflicts with the self-interest of dominant groups in a class- structured capitalist society. (Carnoy and Werthein, 1983: 240)

The work-study principle, for example, can be anticipated to be quite unpalatable to middle- and upper-class parents (and also unattractive to those lower-class parents who see schooling largely as a device for securing their children's upward social mobility). Similarly, the possibility of a Cuban-style literacy campaign being instigated in non-socialist or non-revolutionary developing countries looks extremely remote according to Carnoy and Werthein's analysis:

> It is unlikely that the urban bourgeoisie and middle class would permit the enormous investment of resources and time to reach poor illiterate peasants in far-off villages and

> teach them for nine months. (Carnoy and Werthein, 1983: 239)

In addition, there would probably be insuperable problems of mobilization since the purpose of large-scale literacy campaigns has to be linked with wider social goals and changes which a narrow focus on increasing the level of literacy would not provide:

> Any serious attempt to mobilise poor peasants in a dependent capitalist society dominated by urban businessmen, rural landowners, and multinational corporations cannot be implemented because there is nothing to mobilise them into. (Carnoy and Werthein, 1983: 240)

Since the great majority of states in the Caribbean region would fit into Carnoy and Werthein's broad category of dependent capitalist societies, the chances of a transfer of Cuban-style educational reforms seem slim indeed. However, the possibility is recognized that educational planners in such societies may learn from Cuba's experience; for one thing, they could avoid the mistake of undertaking a major rural literacy campaign. The costs of schooling might be reduced in both urban and rural schools by pupils engaging in productive work tasks for part of each school day. In the case of self-financing rural boarding schools and work-study arrangements, however, such reforms would be confined to schools attended by students from low-income backgrounds; even if these innovations proved to be viable, the middle classes in capitalist developing countries would want something different for their children. In any case, Carnoy and Werthein are convinced that such solutions would be inadequate in view of the enormity of the problems facing educational systems in most poor countries; these solutions, furthermore, are 'technical' in character, whereas the fundamental educational problems are overwhelmingly 'political'. Thus, 'political' solutions must be found. Without far-reaching ideological and socio-economic changes in capitalist developing countries, including those of the

Caribbean region, the prospects for the transfer or influence of Cuba's educational reforms appear slight.

The conclusions reached by Carnoy and Werthein must command broad agreement. However, certain aspects of their analysis may be questioned. First, more differentiation is needed within the category of 'capitalist developing countries' so that variations in receptivity to the Cuban educational model may be identified accurately and precisely. It surely makes some difference if the capitalist developing country in question is Trinidad and Tobago in the 1960s, Manley's Jamaica in the 1970s, or present-day Honduras. Second, class analysis needs to be supplemented in order that such factors as race, religion, language, and nationalism are given their due weight; this is clearly imperative in the case of the Caribbean region where these factors can be particularly significant. Third, the correspondence principle can create a somewhat misleading picture if it highlights 'outcome' at the expense of 'process'. Thus, Carnoy and Werthein's analysis tends to emphasize the typical educational outcome of class struggles within capitalist developing countries, namely, the preservation of the status quo. More attention needs to be paid to how the process of struggle is actually conducted within educational systems and schools, perhaps in such an accentuated form that an open antagonism emerges between 'education' and 'society'. This is not to suggest that schools can become the vanguard of revolutionary change in the absence of wider social and political upheavals; rather, it is to draw attention to circumstances in which educational reforms modelled upon, or similar to, Cuban theory and practice may become particularly attractive to, say, radicalized teachers and students. Analyses employing the correspondence principle perhaps do not say enough to those groups and individuals caught up in the everyday conflicts over educational policy and its implementation. To categorize their efforts as impractical liberal reformism may be neither accurate nor fair; to characterize their proposals as merely technical solutions (perhaps Cuban in derivation or flavour) may do scant justice to the felt educational needs of the great majority of people in developing countries where non-revolutionary instability and conflict are widespread.

Having said this, however, it is important to recognize

the good sense in what Carnoy and Werthein and others have argued regarding the danger of ignoring the correspondence principle. In the Caribbean region, for example, the Cuban educational model is likely to appeal most to those who share a similar ideological orientation. This orientation, however, may not be married to existing or prospective opportunities for revolutionary social change; even if a socialist party or a radical elite does obtain political power, the adoption of Cuban-style educational reforms will almost certainly fail if the wider society remains fundamentally unchanged. The experiences of several Latin American countries in the 1960s and 1970s may provide some valuable lessons for the Caribbean region:

> When political groups seeking to pattern social and educational change on the Cuban model have failed to take complete power, as in Chile, Bolivia, or Uruguay, externally supported repression has soon followed. Nor, on the other hand, is it sufficient for new elites, as in Peru, to dominate and intend to selectively adapt revolutionary educational programs. Recent Peruvian efforts to copy Cuban educational reform programs and approaches have, for example, largely failed because Peruvian schools cannot be radically changed within Peru's relatively static social situation, characterized by lack of participation and gross structured inequality. (Paulston, 1980: 173)

Thus, left-wing or progressive governments in the Caribbean region which are not presiding over a revolutionary, mobilized society may well find that, despite certain ideological sympathies and similarities, anything more than some modest borrowing from the Cuban educational model will be socially inappropriate or politically damaging. Reference need only be made to the hornets' nest which was stirred up in Jamaica in the mid-1970s when Manley's government, enjoying close relations with Havana, accepted some limited forms of technical aid and expressed interest in the Cuban model of socio-economic development (Jones, 1979). It needs to be re-emphasized, however, that the ideological orientations of the governments and dominant social forces of most of the Caribbean region are fundamentally hostile to Cuban socialism and, by extension, to Cuba's educational lessons.

Nevertheless, as has been noted already, ideology is not the only factor determining the receptivity of dependent capitalist states to the Cuban educational model. Various other factors may intervene either to reinforce or moderate the basic ideological orientations of governments, parties, and groups in the region, whether these orientations be hostile or friendly. These factors may or may not have any direct bearing upon the Cuban educational model as such, but their influence upon dispositions and attitudes toward Cuba may be considerable, affecting the ways in which Cuba's achievements in several fields (including education) may be perceived and evaluated.

Political factors are highly influential. Complex interactions between domestic and international politics are typical of the Caribbean region, and Cuba's establishment of formal diplomatic relations and conventional contacts with an ideologically diverse range of neighbouring states and governments has added further twists to this complexity. The end of Cuba's hemispheric isolation in the early 1970s owed much to four Commonwealth Caribbean states (Guyana, Jamaica, Trinidad and Tobago, and Barbados) whose multilateral act of recognition was later supplemented by further bilateral links of varying degrees of warmth and coolness. While, as Payne suggests, 'Cuba was perhaps more wooed than wooing, at least in the first instance' (Payne, 1984: 82), Cuba soon multiplied its own initiatives toward building more ties and closer relationships with countries in the region.

For its neighbours, Cuba simply could be ignored no longer; it had emerged as a powerful regional actor in its own right but, in addition, its association with the Soviet Union and the socialist bloc was of growing interest to several countries which were anxious to reduce their dependency on the United States and perhaps obtain new sources of credit, technology, and aid. Cuba's links with the

Third World and the Non-Aligned Movement were impressive to several developing countries in the Caribbean, while the successful military involvements in black Africa (especially Angola and Ethiopia) were widely, though not universally, applauded in the region. Cuba's anti-colonialism, anti-imperialism, anti-Americanism, and anti-apartheid stance won many friends, as did its championing of a New International Economic Order and a radical solution of the debt crisis. The abandonment of its aggressive foreign policy of the 1960s, that of 'exporting revolution' by supporting guerrilla forces in neighbouring states, not only eased diplomatic relations but also opened up the possibility of greater regional economic integration and cooperation.

The benefits of establishing and maintaining relations with Cuba, however, have had to be weighed against certain risks and possible disadvantages. At the international level, by far the greatest political constraint upon the spread of Cuban influence in the Caribbean region is the hostility of the US government and American interests generally. Many forms of pressure are exerted by Washington upon regional states in order to hinder, weaken, or destroy Cuba's efforts to establish good relations with its neighbours and thereby achieve a higher degree of security. Propaganda may be issued attacking the Cuban system and its supposed achievements, including those in the educational field; alternatively, diplomatic pressures may be applied to discourage the negotiation of trade and assistance agreements between Cuba and its neighbours. The US government, however, does not have things all its own way, for some regional states, if they are clever enough, may use the possibility of turning to Cuba and the Soviet bloc as a bargaining counter in order to extract more US aid and support.

Closer relations with Cuba, furthermore, may provide certain domestic political opportunities for some regional leaders. The Cuban connection may furnish 'a mantle of revolutionary legitimacy' (Maingot, 1983: 22) to essentially reformist regimes whose leaders might thereby undermine and out-manoeuvre their left-wing opposition at home; Forbes Burnham's tactics against Cheddi Jagan in Guyana offer a vivid example, with some embarrassment to Cuba. Not all regional leaders, of course, would welcome or seek Castro's embrace or feel comfortable sharing the same platform, but a surprisingly varied number have done so over the years.

The Cuban connection might provide domestic political advantage of another kind, in the shape of commercial and technical assistance agreements which might be popular with certain constituencies of support; in Jamaica, for example, Cuban aid was targeted at the social sectors which Manley's government had to satisfy:

> Much of the Cuban assistance to Jamaica has been highly visible, widely publicised, and aimed directly at problems faced by lower income groups.... The construction of the Jose Marti secondary school in Spanish Town by a joint Cuban-Jamaican work-force and Cuba's assignment of doctors to the Jamaican health service are two examples. The most striking instance of such direct efforts to promote social welfare is the Cuban sale of condensed milk to Jamaica. (Jones, 1979: 139)

Cuba's technical assistance programmes have varied from one country to another, largely depending upon the degree of Cuba's closeness with the regime and its leadership. Apart from their explicit purpose, such programmes have served Cuba's interests in several ways:

> Signing cultural, educational, medical, sports, and technical agreements with Caribbean countries helps build pride among the Cuban people in their revolution, while at the same time gaining diplomatic allies in a proximate and critical geopolitical region. (Duncan, 1979: 143)

Such agreements reinforce and exemplify the friendly, non-threatening, internationalist image Cuba has tried to cultivate. For our purposes, however, Cuba's overseas civilian assistance schemes in the Caribbean region are a vital means for publicizing and promoting the Cuban educational model and its benefits. Some of the aid is specifically 'educational' in nature (school buildings and furniture, reading materials, teachers, scholarships) while some represents the output of the Cuban educational system, that is, trained professionals and skilled workers with 'small island development skills... which may be suitable to other Caribbean countries' (Duncan, 1979: 146). More will be said shortly about these various types of educational aid; for the moment, it is important to recognize how Cuba's political relations with its neighbours have created opportunities for advertising the Cuban educational model in practical, highly visible ways. Such opportunities have, however, been sharply restricted in recent years by determined American opposition and by changing domestic and international political conditions affecting states in the Caribbean region. Manley's electoral defeat, for example, not only signalled the end of Cuba's influence in Jamaica for several years but also marked the loss of an important supporter of Cuba's regional role. Furthermore, the events surrounding the killing of Maurice Bishop and the invasion of Grenada have many and varied implications for the whole area, but especially for left-wing parties and movements (Thomas, 1985). In current circumstances, too close or premature a relationship with Cuba may prove to be counterproductive.

On the other hand, the maintenance of relations with Cuba, even by capitalist developing states which are not particularly friendly toward their socialist neighbour, may have some value as a sign of political independence. Such relations, therefore, may contain some element of defiance, some assertion of national sovereignty. In this way, showing interest in Cuba's achievements (for example, in education) and perhaps negotiating bilateral trade and technical assistance agreements with Cuba may have symbolic as well as practical significance. However, many states in the Caribbean region would not be persuaded by such considerations. In any case, their national pride would rule out the possibility of receiving Cuban aid or even of admitting they could learn anything from Cuba's experience. Ideological antipathy, feelings of cultural superiority, and belief in one's own level of national development as more advanced combine with nationalist sentiments to limit the influence of Cuban policies and achievements.

Clearly, different observers will evaluate the Cuban educational model and its features according to their special concerns. Societies in the Caribbean region are likely to be acutely sensitive to Cuba's handling of racial differences within its population and how the educational system deals with these differences, for example, in the multi-racial, co-educational secondary boarding schools in the countryside (Richmond, 1985 op cit: 29-31; and Berube, 1984: 86-88). While it is widely accepted that much has been done to eliminate racial discrimination in Cuban society and especially in Cuban schools, from day-care centres onwards, doubts have been raised about the effective eradication of racism and therefore about the policies and commitment of Cuba's leadership. Bland official denials of the persistence of racism have not silenced these doubts, which have been further stimulated by the reluctance to make statistical data available. Perhaps partly in response to outside criticisms regarding the race question in Cuba a change of policy has emerged recently. At the Third Congress of the Cuban Communist Party, held in Havana in early February 1986, for the first time an affirmative action policy was adopted with a view to the more rapid promotion of Blacks, mulattoes, and mestizos toward leadership positions in Cuban society (Waters, 1986b). It is, of course, too soon to tell what will be the external impact of this change of policy, although it is unlikely to damage Cuban prestige and may well remove many doubts concerning the validity of Cuban reforms and achievements, for example, in the field of education.

While Castro has tried to forge links with states in the region on the basis of a shared heritage and experience of slavery, racism, colonialism, and imperialism, certain broad cultural-historical differences have presented considerable obstacles to this effort. For example, the differences between the 'Anglo' and 'Latin' traditions and associated linguistic variations may serve to make the Cuban educational model seem alien to many neighbouring states. Such obstacles, however, are not insuperable, as is shown by the links established between Cuba and several Commonwealth Caribbean states in recent years. The number of scholarship students from non-Spanish-speaking countries in the Caribbean who are presently studying in Cuba suggests that cultural-linguistic differences are being overcome, especially, perhaps, if there is a foundation of ideological sympathy and similarity on which to build.

However, it would be a serious mistake to underestimate the strength of the cultural differences which persist. Many countries in the Caribbean region, for example, have powerful churches and strong religious traditions which heighten their sensitivity to Cuba's handling of, say, Church-State relations and religious toleration. Cuba's official, atheistic ideology and its pervasive influence throughout the educational system can be relied upon to attract opposition, suspicion, and close scrutiny, as can the state's monopoly of schooling. It should be noted, however, that Castro has deliberately opened up a dialogue with the Catholic Church in Latin America and the Caribbean, especially with representatives of Liberation Theology. Whatever may be the precise implications of this exchange of ideas for Cuban education, Castro may use this dialogue to deflect external criticism and perhaps to forge alliances with 'progressive' forces in the region (Morgan, 1986).

Despite the numerous differences (ideological, political, cultural) between themselves and Cuba, many capitalist developing states in the Caribbean region can admire Cuba for its sheer survival in the face of unrelenting American hostility and for its clear sense of national identity and collective purpose. Cuba may also be admired as a model of socio-economic development. While lively academic debates continue to rage over the nature of the Cuban economic model (or models), its transferability, the record on economic growth, and Cuba's 'dependence' on the Soviet Union,

> There is no denying the political fact that in many parts of the Caribbean Cuba is viewed favourably as a development model. This derives partly from an emotional sympathy with the break it has made from the Western world, but also reflects the unquestionable successes of the Castro regime in reducing inequality, eliminating open unemployment, virtually eradicating illiteracy, improving public health and building up the housing

> stock. These achievements are contrasted with the low levels of social welfare in most other Caribbean societies. (Payne, 1984: 82)

Cuban achievements in terms of 'equity' and 'basic needs' represent a massive indictment of neighbouring states which, with more abundant resources, have failed to solve certain fundamental social problems. For poor states in the region, and especially for the poor in these states, Cuba's success shows what can be done and raises the question of why that success has not been attained in their own countries. As one analyst, who is far from being a Cubaphile, has noted,

> Those Latin American states concerned about the expansion of Cuban influence in the region would do well to address the problem of the human condition as effectively and as directly as has Cuba. (Broadhurst, 1983: 163)

Thus, as long as the capitalist developing states of the Caribbean region fail to match the educational achievements of Cuba, and providing Cuba's record of educational success can withstand the severe battering being suffered by the economy, there is every chance that the Cuban educational model will continue to attract attention and interest.

If we now turn to the relevance of the Cuban educational model to socialist developing states, the analysis undertaken by Carnoy and Werthein may again serve as a point of departure. Asking the question, 'What can socialist planners learn from the Cubans?', they make certain basic distinctions. First, their emphasis is firmly placed on African and Asian states; the revolutionary experiences of such states as Nicaragua and Grenada are not examined. Second, they distinguish between socialist developing states which are predominantly agricultural and those which have made noticeably more industrial progress; the former are likely to find Cuba's educational reforms more useful:

> Those that are mainly agricultural should study Cuba's experience in developing a system of education that focuses on rural

> training and consciousness, even for urban children. (Carnoy and Werthein, 1983: 241-242)

Thus, the school in the countryside scheme is recommended, not only for its self-financing qualities but also because it offers a chance to reduce urban-rural disparities and to use urban children for solving rural labour shortages. Carnoy and Werthein also suggest that Cuba's experience of using moral incentives, with important support and reinforcement coming from the educational system, may be instructive for low-income socialist states with limited material resources but with hopes of transforming values and attitudes. In general, it is argued that specific educational reforms, Cuba's relatively small size, the particular socialist road which has been selected, and broad trends toward democratization combine to offer a model of democratic socialist development with more attractions for developing countries than East European or Chinese models. Whatever the full merits of these arguments, Carnoy and Werthein identify several important factors which will reappear in the following brief analysis of the Cuban educational model's influence upon two socialist developing states in the Caribbean region.

The extent of Cuban influence in Nicaragua is a highly charged subject. Enemies of the *Sandinistas* like to paint a Cuban-hand-in-Nicaraguan-glove picture, while Cuba and Nicaragua simultaneously distance themselves by emphasizing the uniqueness of each national revolution but also draw closer by stressing the fraternal, internationalist, and solidarist bonds between the two countries. In illustration of the latter position, Black and Bevan focus upon the eclecticism of Nicaragua's approach to educational reform. For example, in preparing the Literacy Crusade, Nicaragua not only examined Cuba's 1961 Literacy Campaign but also investigated other campaigns in Peru, Sao Tome, and Guinea Bissau; moreover consultations were held with several international experts, including Paulo Freire. At the same time, Black and Bevan (1980) show how supportive Cuba has been in various practical ways, in sharp contrast with the response of much richer countries.

If the Nicaraguan Literacy Crusade clearly was partially

based upon the earlier Cuban campaign, other examples of Cuban educational influence can also be cited:

> Cuba helped design and implement the educational system by providing scholarships for Nicaraguans to study in Cuba, supplying professors and primary school teachers, and providing advice in the design of programs.
>
> By July 1980 Nicaragua and Cuba had signed an educational cooperation agreement providing for the services of 1,000 Cuban primary school teachers, 40 university professors, and scholarships for 3,000 Nicaraguans to study in Cuba. As a result, the Minister of Education, Carlos Tunnerman, could announce that Nicaragua would develop educational programs based upon the Cuban model. (Schwab and Sims, 1985: 448)

Clearly, Cuba's educational influence has been extensive and, in some instances, detailed. Nicaragua's decision to borrow directly from Cuban experience has probably been conditioned by lack of time and resources, inexperience and uncertainty, and offers of aid which have been too tempting to resist. Above all, the ideological affinities between the two regimes have facilitated the 'fit' of particular educational borrowings and have encouraged the development of similar approaches to education in general.

Nicaragua, in fact, has adopted a Cuban-style educational reform, as revealed by Article 40 of the 'Statute of Rights' issued soon after the *Sandinistas'* victory (Black and Bevan, 1980: 70) and by a succession of educational changes. Particularly noticeable have been the immediate attack on illiteracy through a politicized Literacy Crusade and follow-up adult education programmes; the expansion of free schooling, at primary and secondary levels; the substantial revision of school textbooks and materials in order to reflect Sandinista values and Nicaraguan realities; the adoption of the work-study principle; the emphasis on improving rural educational services; and university reform, with a stress on agricultural studies. Unlike Cuba, however, Nicaragua has not abolished private schools, although the Sandinistas have insisted that such schools are non-profit-making and are subject to the firm control and scrutiny of the state.

An interesting aspect of Nicaragua's educational reform is that it has partly been made possible by the provision of educational aid from Cuba, the Soviet bloc, and other countries. This aid has relieved some of the pressure on Nicaraguan resources in such a way as to allow, for example, the rapid expansion of mass educational provision of both a formal and non-formal character. Thus, while Cuban volunteers staff remote rural schools, young Nicaraguan students can be released for study abroad, perhaps in Cuba itself. In this way, the adoption of Cuban-style educational reforms is made easier by the availability of Cuban and Soviet aid.

The Nicaraguan case, however, also illustrates some of the problems associated with the choice of a Cuban-style model or with the acceptance of Cuban assistance. For example, the presence of Cubans, even if they are 'civilian' volunteers, may be used for potentially damaging propaganda purposes by the enemies (internal and external) of a socialist regime in a developing country. In addition, Cuban aid may be unsuitable for cultural as well as ideological reasons:

> While their [i.e., Cuban] experience has been vital to the development of the new educational programmes of Nicaragua, there have been minor cultural problems precisely because they have of necessity been sent to the areas - above all the Atlantic Coast - where revolutionary consciousness is least developed. The influence of some Evangelical church groups remains strong in this area, and has, on occasion, damaged the relationship between the Cubans and the new students. (Black and Bevan, 1980: 44-45)

Despite such problems, however, Cuba's educational influence within Nicaragua remains strong, with many hundreds of Nicaraguans studying in Cuba. In 1984, for example, one particular brigade of 1,500 young Nicaraguans was provided by Cuba with a fourteen-week intensive teacher-training course prior to being sent to isolated rural postings (Daniel, 1986). According to Gonzalez (1985), there were at that time about 6,000 Cuban civilians, including many teachers, working inside Nicaragua.

The influence of Cuba's educational model was also felt in Grenada during the New Jewel Movement's four years of power. Whilst drawing upon a varied range of revolutionary experiences, the young Grenadian leaders were particularly impressed by the Cuban Revolution, which was praised by Maurice Bishop in the following terms in 1979:

> It is now the best example of what socialism can do in a small country for health, education, employment, for ending poverty, prostitution and disease. It is now the best example in the world of what a small country under socialism can achieve. This is what socialism is all about. (Payne, Sutton and Thorndike, 1984: 82)

While it is important to distinguish between rhetoric and performance in the Grenadian Revolution, evidence of Cuban influence in the educational field is not difficult to find. Practical educational assistance was offered: school-buildings and furniture, books and materials, scholarships, teachers, and expertise in educational administration. The educational reforms which were introduced conformed to many basic precepts of the Cuban educational model: the work- study principle; free primary and (by 1981) secondary schooling; the development of close links between the school and the community; the explicit politicization of education for purposes of ideological formation; literacy programmes and adult education, using some teaching materials 'based upon similar programmes in Cuba' (ibid: 27); a deliberate focus on rural-agricultural conditions; free milk and school meal services; day-care centres; post-school youth programmes; and the training of teachers in the values and attitudes required by the new regime. There was also a good deal of imitation of Cuban educational slogans and the designation of 'Years';

for example; 1983 was named the 'Year of Political and Academic Education'.

One of the most important implications of the Grenadian case was that it destroyed any simplistic notions of the impossibility of the 'Anglo' and 'Latin' states of the Caribbean region speaking seriously with one another. Differences in language and culture were not insurmountable; the fact that it was two revolutionary states which were engaged in deep conversation across the cultural-linguistic divide set off alarm-bells not only in Washington but also in several Caribbean capitals.

Grenada and Nicaragua offer the clearest illustrations of the influence of the Cuban educational model upon socialist developing states in the Caribbean region. However, the invasion of Grenada and the ongoing attempts, by military and other means, to bring down the *Sandinista* regime have exposed the limits of this influence and have revealed the enormous difficulties facing Cuba in its efforts to reduce its isolation and vulnerability and to spread its revolutionary message. In view of these constraints, Cuba has realized that it cannot afford to neglect its non-socialist and non-revolutionary neighbours. In reaching out to various states in the Caribbean region, however, Cuba must be careful not to alienate or offend potential friends by choosing the wrong methods of influence. For these reasons, Cuba has largely forsaken its former practice of giving military aid to guerrilla movements (in any case, a new strategy of revolutionary change has been formulated for application in Central America (Evans, 1984)). Instead, Cuba has cultivated conventional state-to-state relations and contacts which are designed to be non-threatening and helpful for building goodwill. Educational aid schemes and technical assistance programmes which utilize the success of Cuba's human resource development fulfil these requirements and offer additional advantages, such as the possibility of earning sorely needed foreign exchange (Eckstein, 1985) and providing a way of employing 'a growing surplus of young men and women, many with technical skills that could not be absorbed by the island's stagnant economy' (Gonzalez, 1985: 87). These schemes and programmes present a broad range of methods for 'exporting' the Cuban educational model.

There are, of course, several traditional methods for publicizing one's country's educational performance, many of which are often used by Cuba; for example, the inclusion of items on Cuban education in official journals, magazines, and newspapers; contributions of statistical data and reports to such agencies as UNESCO; participation in international cultural, sporting, and scientific events; holding or attending conferences on educational themes; and invitations to visiting dignitaries to see Cuban schools and institutes at first hand, such as the schools for foreign students on the Isle of Youth.

A particularly important form of Cuban educational aid, however, is the scholarship programme for foreign students. While the majority of the recipients of these scholarships tend to be African students, the growing importance of the Caribbean region to Cuba in recent years has been reflected in the distribution of scholarships to students from neighbouring states. According to data supplied to UNESCO, only 69 higher education students from the Caribbean region were studying in Cuba in 1976 (by contrast, there were 801 African students); by 1982, this figure had risen rapidly to 784 (the number of African students had grown to 1387) (UNESCO, 1984 and Richmond, 1986). Cuba's scholarships are free, covering all educational and living expenses, and generally are distributed to students from low income backgrounds whose educational opportunities would be quite restricted in their own countries.

The contrast with US scholarship programmes is dramatic, for these have tended to be small in scale and, if anything, to reward the children of the region's elite (especially in Central America). Several recent studies, including the Kissinger Commission Report, have recommended a considerable enlargement of the US scholarship programme for students from the Caribbean region. However, the Commission's proposals for counteracting Cuban and Soviet bloc influence in the area have been criticized as inadequate and unrealistic. According to Lowenthal (1985),

> The report's recommendations for promoting social change are limited, if not ironic. Its bold endorsements of a Literacy Corps to

> teach Central Americans to read and of a massive scholarship program are astonishing, if somewhat impractical, tributes to Cuban policy through the sincerest form of flattery.

Further criticisms of US scholarship programmes have come from the Caribbean region itself, where many states fear that these programmes merely accelerate the 'brain drain' to the US. By contrast, Cuba promises that its foreign students, thanks to the kinds of commitment and values which are encouraged in Cuban educational institutions, will invariably return to their country of origin, where they will apply their socially and economically useful skills and knowledge to productive effect.

In addition to the scholarship programmes for foreign students, Cuba also provides other forms of educational assistance: many thousands of young Cuban teachers, for example, have volunteered for internationalist duties abroad (several losing their lives in Nicaragua owing to 'contra' attacks); educational specialists have been seconded to foreign governments to help devise and implement schemes of educational reform; free or cheap books and teaching materials have been made available; and school-construction projects have been undertaken.

In ways such as these, through the scholarship programmes, and through the technical assistance agreements offering Cuba's skilled workers, technicians, and professionals, the meaning as well as some of the benefits of the Cuban educational model have been communicated to Cuba's neighbours. The Caribbean region presents Cuba with many obstacles but also opportunities; above all, it is the failure of other states to satisfy the educational needs of their populations which ensures the relevance of the Cuban educational model.

BIBLIOGRAPHICAL REFERENCES

Berube, M.R. (1984) **Education and Poverty: Effective Schooling in the United States and Cuba** (Westport, Greenwood Press)

Black, G. and Bevan, J. (1980) **The Loss of Fear: Education in Nicaragua before and after the Revolution** (Nicaragua Solidarity Campaign/World University Service)

Blat, J. (1983) **Education in Latin America and the Caribbean: Trends and Prospects, 1970-2000** (Paris, UNESCO)

Bowles, S. (1971) Cuban education and the revolutionary ideology, **Harvard Educational Review** 41, 4: 472-500

Broadhurst, A.I. (1983) Foreign policy and internationalism: the case of Cuba, in Whetten, L. L. (ed.) **The Present State of Communist Internationalism** (Lexington, Mass., Lexington Books)

Camper, N.K. (1979) **Cuba's Post-Revolutionary Work-Study Education: 1959-1975**, (Ph.D thesis, Boston College)

Cardoso, F. H. (1973) Cuba: lesson or symbol? (Module 267), in Barkin, D. P. and Manitzas, N. R. (eds) **Cuba: The Logic of the Revolution** (Andover, Mass., Warner Modular Publications)

Carnoy, M. and Werthein, J. (1983) Cuba: training and mobilization, in Simmons, J. (ed.) **Better Schools: International Lessons for Reform** (New York, Praeger)

Casas, J. (1981) Education et developpement a Cuba, **Revue Tiers-Monde** xxii, 85: 99-119

Castro, F. (1979) Speech on 26 July, **Granma Weekly Review**, 5 August: 2

Castro, F. (1986) Main report to the Third Congress of the Cuban Communist Party, **Granma Weekly Review**, 16 February: 5

CEPAL (1980) **Cuba: Estilo de Desarrollo y Politicas Sociales** (Mexico City, Siglo Veintiuno Editores)

Cuba, Ministerio de Educacion (1984), **Cuba, Organizacion de la Educacion 1981-83**, XXXIX Conferencia Internacional de Educacion, OIE Ginebra, Suiza

Daniel, P. (1986) Teachers become targets of counter-revolution, **The Times Educational Supplement**, 14 March (London)

Duncan, W. R. (1979) Soviet and Cuban interests in the Caribbean, in Millett, R. and Will, W. M. (eds) **The Restless Caribbean: Changing Patterns of International Relations**, (New York, Praeger)

Eckstein, S. (1985) Cuban internationalism, in Halebsky, S. and Kirk, J. M. (eds) **Cuba: Twenty-five Years of Revolution, 1959-1984** (New York, Praeger)

Evans, E. (1984) Revolutionary movements in Central America: The development of a new strategy, in Wiarda, H. J. (ed.) **Rift and Revolution: The Central American Imbroglio** (Washington, DC, American Enterprise Institute for Public Policy Research)

Gonzalez, E. (1985) The Cuban and Soviet challenge in the Caribbean Basin, **Orbis** 29, 1: 87-88

Granma Weekly Review (1986) 9 February

Jones, R. E. (1979) Cuba and the English-speaking Caribbean, in Blasier, C. and Mesa-Lago, C. (eds), **Cuba in the World**, (Pittsburgh, University of Pittsburgh Press)

Kozol, J. (1978) **Children of the Revolution**, (New York, Delacorte Press)

Latin America Weekly Report (1986) 28 February: 3

Leiner, M. (1985) Cuba's schools: 25 years later, in Halebsky, S. and Kirk, J. M. (eds) **Cuba: Twenty-five Years of Revolution, 1959-1984** (New York, Praeger)

Lowenthal, A.F. (1985) The United States and Central America: Reflections on the Kissinger Commission Report, in Coleman, K. M. and Herring, G. C. (eds) **The Central American Crisis: Sources of Conflict and the Failure of US Policy** (Wilmington, Scholarly Resources Inc.), p.208

Maingot, A. P. (1983) Cuba and the Commonwealth Caribbean: playing the Cuban card, in Levine, B. B. (ed.) **The New Cuban Presence in the Caribbean** (Boulder, Westview Press)

Martuza, V. (1981) A conversation with Abel Prieto, **Journal of Reading** 25, 3

Montaner, C. A. (1981) **Secret Report on the Cuban Revolution** (New Brunswick, Transaction Books)

Morgan, J. (1986) Mystic and Marxist, **Guardian** (Third World Review) 17 January

Paulston, R. G. (1971) Education, in Mesa-Lago, C. (ed.) **Revolutionary Change in Cuba** (Pittsburgh, University of Pittsburg Press)

Paulston, R. G. (1980) Problems of educational reform and rural development in Latin America: some lessons from Cuba, in Avery, W. P. et al. (eds), **Rural Change and Public Policy: Eastern Europe, Latin America and Australia** (New York, Pergamon)

Payne, A. (1984) **The International Crisis in the Caribbean** (London, Croom Helm)

Payne, A., Sutton, P., and Thorndike, T. (1984) **Grenada: Revolution and Invasion** (London, Croom Helm)

Prieto, A. and Figueroa, M. (1979) The combination of study and work in the Cuban educational system, in Morsy, Z. (ed.) **Learning and Working** (Paris, UNESCO)

Richmond, M. (1983) Preparation for the transition from school to work in socialist Cuba, in Watson, K. (ed.) **Youth, Education and Employment: International Perspectives** (London, Croom Helm)

Richmond, M. (1985) Education and revolution in socialist Cuba: The promise of democratisation, in Brock, C. and Lawlor, H. (eds) **Education in Latin America** (London, Croom Helm)

Richmond, M. (1986) Internationalism and international student flow: the case of Cuba, in Smawfield, D. (ed.) **International Academic Interchange and Cooperation in Higher Education** (Hull, British Comparative and International Education Society)

Sahoy, P. (1978) Cuban educational strategies, **Caribbean Journal of Education** 5, 3: 136-138

Schwab, T. and Sims, H. (1985) Relations with the communist states, in Walker, T. W. (ed.) **Nicaragua: The First Five Years** (New York, Praeger)

Street, B. V. (1984) **Literacy in Theory and Practice** (Cambridge, Cambridge University Press)

Theriot, L. H. (1984) Cuba faces the economic realities of the 1980s, in Horowitz, I. L. (ed.) **Cuban Communism** (New Brunswick, Transaction Books)

Thomas, C. Y. (1985) The Grenadian crisis and the Caribbean left, **IDS Bulletin** 16, 2: 34-39

Thomas, H. S. et al. (1984) **The Cuban Revolution: 25 Years Later** (Boulder, Westview Press)

UNESCO (1980-1984) **Statistical Yearbooks** (Paris, UNESCO)

Waters, M.-A. (1986a) Cuba: economic battle: a 'people's war', **Intercontinental Press** 24, 5

Waters, M.-A. (1986b) Cuba: reporter's notebook on CP Congress, **Intercontinental Press** 24, 6: 167-168

Chapter Four

CONTEMPORARY ISSUES IN JAMAICAN EDUCATION

Errol Miller

INTRODUCTION

Contemporary issues in Jamaican education are defined in terms of those issues that have arisen over the past decade. They are the items placed on the national educational agenda since the first oil crisis in the 1970s. Some existed before but the aftermath of the economic crisis brought them into sharp relief. This chapter will discuss these issues from the perspective of: those associated with the interrelation between education and the economy, the social structure, culture and the political system on the one hand; those related to the internal efficiency of the educational system itself on the other hand. Before identifying and discussing these issues, however, it is necessary to provide some background by briefly stating some relevant historical aspects of Jamaican education as well as outlining in a little greater detail post-war educational development in that country.

HISTORICAL BACKGROUND

Early Formative Influences

The British who came to Jamaica did not come to stay. They came to make a fortune and return to Britain. It was mostly men who came and they did not bring with them the infrastructure of community including family and school. Education began in Jamaica as a posthumous expression of concern in the bequests of wealthy persons who willed money for the establishment of schools for the children of Europeans who had failed to realize their fortune and were trapped in the colony (Gordon, 1963).

The genesis of education in Jamaica is rooted in the rescue and liberation of children whose parents were unfortunately trapped by depressing circumstances. It first performed this redemption role for poor whites in the slave society, then for the children of mulattoes and Jews in the early decades of the nineteenth century, and eventually for the children of the blacks after the emancipation of the slaves in 1834. The tap-root of Jamaican education runs deep into the idealist dreams and aspirations of parents for their children to achieve through schooling what they themselves have failed to accomplish. Aspiration for upward social mobility has been the major force for popular participation in the educational system (Miller, 1976; Kuper, 1976).

Traditionally the wealthiest in the society have sent their children abroad for education. Their view about Jamaican education for the poorer groups in the society is that it should prepare students for the economic opportunities in that society. Accordingly they have always argued in favour of vocational and technical education related especially to jobs in agriculture. They have been opposed to academic or 'bookish' education leading to 'white collar jobs' and the professions.

> The ruling class of the late Nineteenth Century felt that training in Agriculture should be confined to the Elementary Schools since the children of these were destined to be workers of the soil. (Whyte, 1977)

As such, their outlook on education has been the direct opposite of the rest of the society. The interesting point to note is that Jamaica does not really have a hereditary elite. Very few families have remained upper class for, say, 100 years. The practice of sending children abroad and the bias in favour of vocational education is often held by persons who owe part of their social success to educational opportunities of the 'bookish' type.

Jamaican culture is an amalgam and synthesis of several old world cultures. The chief components are British and West African, but the educational system has been the major means of transmitting the British variant which was the dominant culture for over 300 years although it was the parent culture of a small minority of the population. The basic socialization pattern for the vast majority of the population was to acquire British culture through education while abandoning the parent culture of their homes. Of course this was never fully achieved.

Post-war Developments in Education

The post-war period in Jamaican history is replete with major developments. Social unrest in the late 1930s was followed by political changes in the subsequent decades. First, there were constitutional changes in 1943 which established adult suffrage and the principle of one person one vote. This was followed by further constitutional changes in the 1950s leading to full internal self-government in 1957. In 1962 the political transformation was completed with the achievement of political independence from Britain.

Economic developments were no less dramatic. Jefferson (1972) points out that in the post-war period there were the emergence and growth of the bauxite and alumina industry as the major component of the mining sector, the growth of a manufacturing sector based mainly on import substitution, the significant expansion of the tourist industry, and the beneficial effects of the growth of these sectors on the construction and furniture industries. Jefferson reports that, 'real national income per capita increased at the rate of approximately 4.3 per cent per annum during period 1950 to 1968'. He also records that over the period Gross Domestic Product at factor cost at 1956 prices increased at an annual rate of 6.7 per cent. Until the oil crisis of the 1970s, the Jamaican economy recorded impressive growth in the post-war period.

It is in this context of substantial political changes and sustained economic growth that educational development has to be understood. The major educational trends in the period 1945-1978 can be summarized as follows:

1. More direct involvement of the state in the financing and administration of education resulting in the centralization and bureaucratization of its administration through the Ministry of Education.

2. The integration of the different levels and elements of schooling into a unified system.

3. The expansion of educational provisions at all levels: in 1945 there were 176,909 children enrolled in elementary schools. By 1978 the number enrolled had grown to 422,919. In 1945 there were 23 high schools with an enrolment of 4,267. By 1978 there were 46 high schools with an enrolment of 47,056 students (Ministry of Education, 1978/1979).

4. Qualitative improvements at all levels: all the indicators of quality show positive signs over the period under review. These include the academic and professional qualifications of teachers, number of students remaining in school to complete their course of studies, terminal examination performance, and the physical provisions in terms of buildings and equipment.

5. The move to co-education as the norm: traditionally, single-sex schools predominated in the educational system. In the post-war period almost all new schools were established as co-educational institutions, and some of the previous single-sex institutions were converted to co-education.

6. Jamaicanization of the curriculum of schools at all levels: the decolonization of the curriculum commenced in the 1950s but gathered momentum in the 1960s and 1970s, that is to say, in the post-independence period.

7. Diversification of secondary and tertiary education: prior to the 1940s, tertiary education was limited to Teachers' Colleges, the Agricultural School and Theological Colleges.

Tertiary options have since been expanded and diversified to include Community Colleges, the College of Arts, Science and Technology, the Schools of Art, Dance, Drama and Music, the University of the West Indies, and the Maritime Institute. Similarly, at the secondary level, in addition to Grammar Schools there are now Technical High Schools, Comprehensive Schools, and New Secondary Schools.

8. Democratization of access to Secondary and Tertiary Institutions: while it cannot be said that all social groups are represented in secondary and tertiary institutions in accordance with their numbers in the population, significant advancement has in fact been made in reversing the historic imbalances. The author is currently conducting a research study of the social background of students in High Schools and Colleges during the period 1940 to 1982. Preliminary results show substantial changes in favour of less privileged groups in the society.

So while education by 1978 still had serious defects, relatively speaking, the period 1945-1978 could be accurately described as the 'golden era' of Jamaican education. It surpasses all previous periods in terms of overall achievement, even though it fell far short of what could be considered ideal or even desirable.

CONTEMPORARY ISSUES

Contemporary issues will be examined from two perspectives: those regarding the external relations of education to the economy, social stratification, policies and culture; those related to internal efficiency of the educational system.

External Relations Issues

The position taken here is that in any society education is intricately interwoven with the economy, the social structure, politics, and culture and cannot be meaningfully understood or discussed without reference to these interrelationships. This section will address educational issues related to economic, social, political, and cultural factors operative in the society at the present time.

The full impact of the dramatic increase in the price of petroleum products by OPEC countries was not felt in Jamaican education until about 1978. This was largely because the then government had imposed a levy on bauxite exports which helped to meet the increased costs. The oil crisis has been followed by the interest rate crisis and recession in the industrialized countries, which has meant an almost uninterrupted period of crisis for the Jamaican economy. This has obtained despite a change in 1980 from a Democratic Socialist government to a Conservative government pursuing monetaristic policies. By 1978 economic decline as evidenced by negative growth had already set in and the government had turned to the International Monetary Fund for assistance. The basic precription of the IMF has been: devaluation of the Jamaican currency; reduction in public expenditure; increased exports.

Reduction in Public Expenditure:

Reduction in public expenditure has had direct implications and consequences for education. Devaluation has had indirect consequences. The particular mechanism used for the devaluation of the Jamaican currency is an auction system in which banks bid each week for the foreign exchange available from the Central Bank. In order to keep banks prudent in their bids their liquidity ratio has been raised to 50 per cent. Where this was seen to have limited effect, other measures have been used to reduce their liquidity even further. The end result has been a dramatic increase in interest rates with the prime lending rate at 30 per cent in 1986. The net results have been significant increases in the cost of living. As far as education is concerned this increases the cost of goods and services important to the education sector. The reduction in public expenditure has to be seen in conjunction with the impact of the devaluation strategy.

By the 1970s education had become the largest single item of public expenditure. A general policy of decreasing public expenditure therefore could not be implemented without expenditure cuts in education as well. Accordingly, over the last seven years educational expenditure in real terms has fallen. In order to appreciate fully the purpose of reducing public expenditure, it is important to note what has happened over the last three years. In 1983, government's expenditure on education stood at 19.8 per cent of the recurrent budget. In 1985-1986, the percentage of public expenditure on education declined to 15 per cent. From this one could conclude that the government had changed its priority concerning education, but a close examination of the budget reveals that all other areas except one had also suffered similar decreases. The single item in the budget that had increased over the three-year period was debt servicing. In other words, the reduction in public expenditure is operating to improve government's capabilities of servicing the national debt. Monies therefore that had previously gone to educational expenditure were now going to debt servicing.

Reduction in public expenditure on education has led to retrenchment and reduction in the provisions for education in a number of different areas. In the post-war period the teacher/pupil ratio in primary schools had been reduced from 1 to 58 to 1 to 39 by 1981. Since 1982, as a result of the financial crisis, government decided to increase the ratio to 1 to 55. By way of Caribbean comparisons it should be noted that the teacher/pupil ratios for primary schools in the rest of the Commonwealth Caribbean does not exceed 1 to 35.

Over the last two decades strenuous effort has been made to reduce overcrowding in classrooms in primary schools. One of the effects of increasing the teacher/pupil ratio to 1 to 55 has been to further entrench overcrowded classes at this level. Another effect has been to increase unemployment among qualified teachers. Jamaica, like Barbados and Trinidad, had been fast approaching the target of a fully trained teaching force at the primary level. The teacher supply had been calculated at a pupil/teacher ratio of 1 to 40; thus the increase to 1 to 55 immediately means that a situation of over-supply now exists. As a consequence, government has reduced the number of teachers in training.

In September 1985 government closed one teachers' college and a teacher education department of a community college. In addition, it instructed the existing colleges not to admit any new students for the academic year 1985-1986. Within a decade Jamaica has found itself moving from a situation of a shortage of teachers and imploring young people to enter the profession, to a situation of over-supply and unemployment of qualified teachers trained at public expense.

Since 1978, wage guidelines have existed for salary increases to employees in the public sector. This is related to the overall policy of reducing public expenditure. It is important to note the impact of such policies on teachers' salaries. Since 1973, the cost of living in Jamaica has increased by 680 per cent. On the other hand teachers' salaries have increased by 312 per cent. In other words, in little more than a decade the standard of living of teachers in Jamaica has been cut by more than a half. The implications of this for both retaining teachers within the system to their satisfaction and for attracting new recruits are enormous. It is not unfair to say that teachers' salaries represent a depressed area and that the prospects for the future are not hopeful.

High schools and colleges in Jamaica are financed by a system of government grants paid to the institutions based on an agreed budget between the schools and the Ministry of Education. Over the last five years these institutions have been under-budgeted. In addition, in many instances they have not been able to obtain the agreed budgets. As a result, many are operating with deficits. Their survival is remarkable since current public policy does not allow any public institution to carry overdrafts at the bank. By and large, these institutions have survived on the basis of unofficial fees as well as contributions from parent/teachers associations, past students' associations and other interested parties. In other words, government has not been meeting the financial requirements of secondary and tertiary institutions, has not made any arrangements for their operating deficits to be met, and has turned a blind eye to such practices of the school to raise money to meet that deficit which contravene stated policy. To a great degree, principals at all levels of the educational system have been spending more time in fund-raising and have been mobilizing the support of teachers and students in such ventures to a much greater degree than they probably feel comfortable with, or than they would consider desirable.

Government has recently re-introduced fees for University and the College of Arts, Science and Technology, reversing the policy of free education in this area. It is proposed that students should pay 30 per cent of the tuition cost at each institution. Since 1973, Jamaica had pursued a policy of free secondary and tertiary education. Government explains the re-introduction of fees in terms of its inability to continue to bear the full cost of tertiary education in the light of its own financial constraints.

The immediate impression given by the various measures that government has adopted to effect reduction in educational expenditure, is that government is abandoning certain targets and objectives that have guided public policy in education over the last thirty years. It appears as if government has abandoned the objective of providing sound basic education at the primary level; that it is no longer pursuing the target of a fully trained teaching force at the primary and secondary levels; that it can no longer ensure an acceptable standard of living for teachers; that it is in the process of abandoning the concept of free education at the tertiary level and possibly also at the secondary level.

The immediate response has been resistance from students, teachers, and parents. The announcement of the re-introduction of fees has been greeted by student demonstrations. Teachers have been in a year-long dispute with government over the issue of salary increases. Parents and teachers have engaged in protest action islandwide concerning the crisis situation that they perceive to exist in education and the threat of diluting educational quality. While it has taken the issue of teachers' salaries to bring out the support of parents, the concern of parents has been wider than teachers' salaries. It has been focused on conditions within the educational system. It would appear that parents are implicitly making a fundamental statement about reducing educational expenditure in order to facilitate national debt repayment. In brief it could be said that education in Jamaica in the mid-1980s has become the focus for social unrest.

It may be useful at this point to examine the

implications and underlying assumptions of the reduction in public expenditure on education. First, it may be assumed that Jamaica is living above its means. It is therefore necessary to reduce public expenditure, especially in social services, and increase earnings mainly through exports in order to achieve economic viability. The social services that have to bear the brunt of financial cutbacks are health and education.

To illustrate this argument, it is necessary to note that Jamaicans enjoy life expectancy similar to that of the industrialized countries. Life expectancy is currently 69 years for males and 73 years for females. That is to say, Jamaicans enjoy life expectancy similar to that of citizens of countries with much higher income levels. If one is to use the economic criterion of national per capita income as the basis of judgement, then Jamaicans are living longer than they can afford. The reduction of health services then becomes an appropriate measure to adjust this imbalance between per capita income and life expectancy. While Jamaica does not enjoy educational standards, such as literacy levels, as high as the industrialized countries, like the rest of the Commonwealth Caribbean they are well above Third World norms. Thus, the essence of the argument above still applies.

The essential aspect of the argument is that Jamaica is living above its earning capacity. But Jamaica does not set the price of its imports, nor of its exports. In each transaction, the powerful industrialized countries determine the terms of trade in their favour. This is the position taken by those advocating a New International Economic Order. From this position it is the terms of trade between Third World countries like Jamaica and the industrialized giants that need to be changed and not the health and educational services that need to be cut back. This debate is no longer an academic one for Jamaica. It has officially taken the 'living above our means' argument and has begun to reduce educational and health services. In consequence, several other far-reaching educational issues arise.

Jamaica does not have compulsory education. Any compulsory education law would need to compel the state to provide education for the children. Historically, the state has been delinquent in providing education. In a totally voluntary system, 98 per cent of the children of primary school age are enrolled in school. However, attendance is a problem. Regular attendance averages just over 70 per cent. But on the days that most children attend there is neither the space nor the furniture to accommodate them. Reduction in public expenditure only reverses efforts to remedy this situation. It is a backward step, raising serious questions about the future of a small country in the 1990s and beyond which has an uneducated labour force in which unskilled illiterates predominate.

Another set of related issues surrounds the economic feasibility of the cuts at various levels. If one assumes the success of increased export earnings for the future, the question arises about the cost of restoring the educational system at that time. Currently the physical plant in many schools is being neglected and will need major repairs at some time. If maintenance is not effected, then replacement costs will be even higher. In addition, the high pupil/teacher ratio and overcrowded classrooms are bound to lower further the efficiency of primary education in the teaching of the basic skills of literacy and numeracy. In more prosperous future times remedial education to rectify this situation is most likely to be much more expensive, even in relative terms, than it is now. The question therefore is whether any real savings are being effected by current cutbacks in education. Physical plant is being neglected, existing infrastructure is being underutilized and control quality reduced to a bare minimum. In such circumstances educational productivity is decreasing, and the future cost of remedying the situation is likely to be much higher than any present savings. The current cutbacks may well turn out to be very short sighted.

The human factor also seems to have been ignored in the policy to reduce public expenditure. In industrialized countries where there is a great wealth of human resources, personnel changes with the implementation of new ideas. In Third World countries the pool of talent is much smaller. Hence the same people tend to be called upon to do a wide variety of development tasks. The question is whether the effects of these cutbacks would become so demoralizing for the small pool of development-oriented educators that it would become virtually impossible for them to be inspired to give the same level of effort in the future.

Education and Employment:

Unemployment, especially of young people, has been a perennial problem of Jamaican society. Successive governments have tried unsuccessfully to solve this problem particularly in the post-independence period. The assumption has been made that education is a route to employment. In the light of the Jamaican experience to date, it is appropriate both to examine a number of assumptions as well as to identify essential issues that have been raised by the circumstances. Two observations whould first be made:

1. The nature of the economy at any given point in time appears to be a more crucial factor than education in determining both employment and the nature of the jobs obtained. This can best be illustrated by anecdotal references. Recently the author took two visitors to Jamaica rafting. While they were enjoying this experience he spoke to two men whose rafts were not at that time engaged. Both men had been to vocational schools where one had been trained as a plumber, the other as a welder. Neither could find jobs in the trades in which he had been trained. The recession in the mining and manufacturing sectors over the past five years accounted for the lack of employment in these two areas. However, both men found jobs in the tourist industry, the sector of the economy that has been growing. While little plumbing or welding is required to guide a bamboo raft down a river, these men had obtained those jobs because they were better educated than their colleagues. While many of the young people graduating from high schools and colleges in Jamaica are far better educated than their parents or siblings, they end up as unemployed, their unemployment not being related to any deficiency in their education but almost solely related to the lack of levels of job, as perceived suitable by the aspirants, available in the economy.

2. Education plays a dual role with respect to employment. The level of a young person's education is necessary both to

obtain the job as well as to do the job. In the current state of the Jamaican economy, it looks as if the level of education required to get the job is higher than that required to do the job. This point is emphasized, for example, if one compares the qualifications required for comparable posts and jobs in Jamaica and the Bahamas. The educational requirements in Jamaica are usually higher than in the Bahamas which has a much more buoyant economy and where employers have to compete to obtain the available talents.

Looking at the interrelationship between education and employment in Jamaica, at least two major issues should be exercising the minds of local decision-makers. One relates to the well-known issue of education and training and the appropriate points in the educational system and the life of the individual at which these should take place. The other is with respect to the entire question of the relationship between education and employment in this particular setting. It is necessary to elaborate on both these issues.

Given the difficulties of accurately forecasting the course of the Jamaican economy on the one hand and the time involved in educating children and adolescents on the other, at what point should education as opposed to training be offered in the schooling of children? One view is that vocational education for the less academically inclined children should begin almost immediately after primary schooling. A less extreme view is that at the end of secondary school adolescents should have marketable skills which would allow them to find employment in specific sectors for which they have been trained. A third view is that secondary education should not include vocational training but should give adolescents a good general education in which they are exposed to languages, the arts, sciences, aesthetic areas, technology and sports. By stressing education and not training, emphasis is placed on generic concepts and skills that have applicability in widely different areas. In this latter view a sound general education enables the individual to become as flexible and as versatile as possible since over a working lifetime there may be the need to adjust to major technological and other changes and therefore to switch vocational pursuits several times. Specific skill training should be scheduled to coincide with the time at which each individual is being selected for specific jobs in the job market. Currently Jamaica has schools that have practised virtually all three positions. There are schools at the secondary level in Jamaica totally devoted to vocational training such as agricultural schools, home economic schools or other types of trade training. There are technical high schools offering a higher level of education and in addition specific training opportunities to give their students marketable skills. While traditional high schools do have some vocational training, in the main the emphasis is still on general education.

Three years ago, the government established the Human Employment and Resource Training Trust (HEART). The basic concept of this organization is to provide school-leavers with job-related training relative to areas in which they may be employed. The question arises as to whether it is economically and educationally feasible to continue with this plurality of approaches to the question of education and training or whether or not detailed studies need to be done in order to determine the most effective strategies taking into consideration the economic realities. It would appear that a highly developed job training programme designed to give individuals specific skills related to employment opportunities existing when they have attained school leaving age, would work better with a secondary education programme that emphasized general education broadly defined. The existing situation would appear to be unnecessarily wasteful, given the fact that technical and vocational education is probably the most costly type of education to deliver on a mass basis, in terms of facilities, equipment and manpower.

In examining the relationship between education and employment in Jamaica, the following commonly held assumptions need to be investigated:

1. Education raises expectations concerning both the standard of living and occupations that young people would like to achieve.

2. Education should be related to the job opportunities offered by the Jamaican economy.

3. The loss of educated people from the Jamaican labour

force - brain-drain - has harmful effects on the Jamaican economy.

It would appear that education in Jamaica does not really raise expectations concerning standards of living or of occupational levels but rather is a legitimate means of achieving these ends. Jamaica's close proximity to the United States and Canada, together with the intimate contact that exists between Jamaica and these countries through the mass media, travel, and the tourist industry has resulted in the vast mass of the Jamaican population being aware of some of the highest standards of living in the world. Tens of thousands of Jamaican labourers go to the United States and Canada each year as farm workers. Thousands more visit the United States and Canada each year on vacation, an even larger number hear of the 'good life' in America from relatives returning from farm work or vacation. Television, whether through the local station or satellite transmission, is heavily North American oriented. The same is true of the film industry which is a popular source of entertainment nationwide. In addition, large numbers of Jamaicans interact with tourists annually.

Given these circumstances it would be virtually impossible for the educational system to lower expectations of the 'good life' generated by proximity and contact with North American standards. Indeed, it would seem to be a positive and constructive means by which that life and standard of living can be achieved. In these circumstances it would not appear that any manipulation of educational opportunities would make any significant change to the expectations and aspirations held generally in the population. On the contrary, such manipulation may lead the population to a sense of hopelessness or to illegitimate means to satisfy these expectations and aspirations.

Given the limited capability of the Jamaican economy, if educational opportunity is related solely to job opportunities provided by the local economy then of necessity, the vast majority of Jamaicans would be confined to a life of unemployment or under-employment. The question arises as to whether or not the limited capabilities of the Jamaican economy should set the limits for the provision of educational opportunity. This question has been debated in Jamaica for almost a century, the position of the vested economic interests in Jamaica is that the school system should supply persons who would fit into the economic niches locally available. Gordon, commenting on education in the period 1845-1865, states:

> The Jamaican Assembly for a time offered special grants to schools attempting agricultural instruction, and conducted for five years a Normal School of Industry to train schoolmasters for the purpose. This enterprise was much criticised, particularly by the Baptists, on the grounds that it was an attempt to keep people tied to the sugar estates as hired labourers in conditions little removed from slavery. (Gordon, 1963: 44)

The Kandel Report (1943) in paragraphs 81, and 91 to 94 advocated that secondary education should be linked to the economic opportunities available in Jamaica, and should have a more technical and vocational emphasis. Reid, however, in surveying expectations of students, parents and teachers in rural areas, found a low preference for technical and vocational subjects. He stated:

> Attempts at agriculture and other aspects of vocational education will only prove acceptable to students when they are convinced of the profitability and the overall social satisfaction they can afford. (Reid, 1981: 48)

The popular view has clearly been nearer to Reid than Kandel. In a nutshell it is that the individual should be given the best education possible and allowed to solve his economic difficulties in the best way he can, wherever he finds economic opportunity. This leads immediately to the question as to whether education should assist migration and the brain-drain. Many politicians have condemned this popular view as the 'visa mentality'. On the other hand, starting with the migration to build the Panama railroads and canal, Jamaicans have always looked overseas for economic opportunities. This explains the sizeable Jamaican communities that exist in New York, Boston, Toronto, London, Birmingham, Costa Rica, Cuba, and Panama.

The economic programmes that have been developed with the United States and Canada, namely the Caribbean Basin Initiative (CBI) and the Caribbean Canadian Agreement (CARIBCAN), have dealt with the issue of the free movement of goods and services between the Commonwealth Caribbean and the United States and Canada, but these agreements do not include any provisions for the movement of people. If the economies of Caribbean countries are to be intricately linked with those of the United States and Canada, given the history of the Caribbean and its shared language with these countries, it seems almost irrational to exclude the movement of people. Given the fact that neither Canadian nor US migration policies pay any attention to illiterate or unskilled persons, it would appear that the matter of the education of Jamaican people as this affects their migration possibilities, in order to find jobs not available locally, is bound to become an item on the political agenda of the governments of all the countries concerned.

The Political Issue of Control:

In the political arena, the most fundamental issue that appears to be emerging in contemporary Jamaica is that of control. While Jamaica may have won the battle for political independence in 1962, it appears to be losing the war of sovereignty. It has virtually lost the battle for sovereignty in economic decision-making and appears to be in a losing position with respect to the matter of sovereignty in educational decision-making. In order to appreciate the issue fully it is necessary to trace some background.

During the colonial era, and certainly for the first half of the twentieth century, education was a local matter financed from local revenue and therefore did not attract the attention or direction of the Imperial government in England. Secondary schools were administered by the Jamaica Schools Commission, which was virtually autonomous. Primary and teacher education were administered by the Department of

Education which was headed by a Director appointed by the Colonial Office. However, because the funding came from the local assembly, decision-making was done within the colony. Capital development came from revenue left over after recurrent costs had been met.

In the post-war period, with the move towards political independence, modest grants were made by the British government for education through the Colonial Development and Welfare Fund. The projects on which they were spent were determined as a result of consultation between local decision-makers and the colonial office. This, in fact, was a forerunner of what would happen in the post-independence period. During the colonial period, educational ideas had been borrowed, largely from England, but this was more the result of voluntary imitation rather than the following of prescriptions laid down by the Colonial Office.

Following independence, successive Jamaican governments have sought loan funding from bilateral and multilateral agencies to finance educational developments. Consequently, a new pattern has emerged. It is that of the sector survey or feasibility study done by UNESCO or some other agency which then provides the blue-print for funding from USAID, the Canadian International Development Agency, the World Bank or the Inter-American Development Bank. From the early 1970s no tax revenue has remained to finance educational developments. Hence, in general, capital development in education has come from external borrowing. While there is consultation with local educators and decision-makers, and agreements with Jamaican decision-makers concerning the content of loan programmes, there can be no gainsaying the fact that the loans granted have also had to meet the conditions and priorities of the agency from which they are borrowed. It is not unfair to say therefore that in the 1980s educational developments in Jamaica are determined largely by external sources.

With IMF conditions now determining recurrent expenditure in the public sector, both capital and recurrent expenditure in education are now under external control. There is now far less control of the educational system by Jamaicans, after twenty-four years of independence, than there was at any time previously in its colonial history. The ideas which now guide Jamaica's education come more often out of the World Bank, UNESCO, USAID and the Inter-American Development Bank, than from the Jamaican Ministry of Education or from Jamaican educators. Programme managers in these organizations as well as consultants they employ, exercise a far more crucial role in determining the future course of Jamaican education than do their counterparts in Jamaica.

There is an internal dimension to the issue of control in addition to the external dimension discussed above. In the post-war period, educational administration financing and decision-making have been centralized and bureaucratized in the form of a Ministry of Education controlled by the political directorate. During this period as well, a better academically and professionally qualified teaching force represented by a powerful teachers organization, the Jamaica Teachers Association (JTA), has emerged. Mainly under the auspices of the University of the West Indies, an educational research capacity with highly trained professionals has become an integral part of local education generating knowledge concerning Jamaican education. Over the last seven years communities, churches, and individuals have been called upon to supplement government's expenditure on education. In addition, there have been incidences of whimsical decision-making in education from the political directorate consequent upon changes of government or changes of Ministers of Education. These factors have combined to produce a strong call locally for a national council of education which would take decision-making concerning the educational system out of the partisan political arena and replace it within the context of broad-based national decision-making (Montieth, 1984).

It could well be that the current economic crisis may provide the opportunity for substantial rethinking concerning the control of Jamaican education and the exercise of sovereignty in this domain.

Social Issues in Education:

The current economic and financial crisis in education has highlighted a number of social issues. These could be listed as follows: education as an avenue of social mobility; education as an agent of social integration; education as an instrument of social justice. Each of these will be discussed in turn.

Education has always been the *major avenue of social mobility* in Jamaica. It has provided an opportunity for every ethnic or social group that has ever been disadvantaged. The major institutions performing this social broker role have been the high schools, and teachers' and theological colleges. These institutions have offered opportunities for social progress historically to poor whites, mulattoes, Jews, black peasants, Chinese, and Indians during times when the society was divided along ethnic lines. In more recent times, it has continued to perform its social mobility role in a society that perceives itself to be more divided according to class than to ethnicity.

Because of this long tradition of education as an avenue of hope, any cutbacks in education, especially at the secondary and tertiary levels, are immediately perceived by the broad mass of the population as a move to restrict opportunity and to frustrate hopes. Miller (1967) in studies to find out the values of Jamaican adolescents, discovered that education was highest in their list of values principally because of the possibilities it offered for social mobility.

Education has then become *an agent of social integration* by virtue of its role as an avenue of social mobility, especially through the high schools. The traditional pattern was that wealthy Jamaicans sent their children abroad to be educated, the middle classes sent their children to private primary schools - called preparatory schools - and to government-aided high schools, while the peasants and other lower classes sent their children to public primary schools and teachers' colleges. Over the past thirty-five years, this pattern has been changing. In general, the upper class has been sending their children to preparatory schools for their primary education and then to government high schools, although they have continued to send their children abroad for university education. A significant number of middle-class people are now sending their children to public primary schools, especially where these are located in predominantly middle-class neighbourhoods that have developed over the last twenty-five years. Greater numbers of lower-class children are now gaining access to high schools, especially in the rural areas.

This role of education as an instrument of social integration has often been overlooked in many Third World nations. Greater emphasis is usually placed on education as a means of economic development. The role of education as a mechanism of social integration is of great importance in many newly independent countries like Jamaica, in which the society is segmented into different social classes and ethnic groups. The process of nation-building requires the integration of these different groups. It requires social learning and experience by each group of the other. Schooling is an important phase in the process of inter-group interaction and learning. When it is recalled that one of the greatest social problems of Third World countries is the great disparities between the standards of living of the rich and the poor, then the role of education and schooling as a meeting place for children from different social and ethnic backgrounds to interact with each other in normal and human terms cannot be overestimated.

The economic and financial pressures have been leading to policies which could include the widespread use of fees, especially at the secondary and tertiary levels, as a means of financing education, as well as the privatization of tertiary institutions. In other words government could think of divesting particular institutions so that it is relieved of responsibilities for those institutions from the public purse. One of the possible repercussions of such developments would be the segregation of education at these levels with certain social classes or ethnic groups patronizing certain institutions as opposed to others. The social consequences of such developments could be far-reaching. The question to be asked is what is the price to be paid for social integration? Can the concern of a government in the fledgling nation of Jamaica be solely that of keeping costs low and spending as little as possible, or are there objectives and ideals such as social integration that warrant economic and financial investments over and beyond simple cost benefit in economic terms?

It could be argued that both the economic growth of the

1960s and early 1970s, and the economic decline of the late 1970s and 1980s to date, have polarized the society even more than it was during colonial times; that these developments have exaggerated and deepened the cleavages and inequities. That the Jamaican society is now more segregated physically, by the development of housing areas according to income groups, than it was ever before in its history is now a feature of its human geography. Any future reforms in education which result in schools being segregated along class and ethnic lines would only be reflecting in education what has been happening economically and socially in the immediate past.

Even if this argument were to be accepted, the issue to be addressed is still whether or not the economic and social segregation patterns of the immediate past ought to be institutionalized within the educational system. It is possible that: (a) these economic and social patterns emerging since independence are the unintended consequences associated with inexperience in economic and social planning and management; (b) that they in fact run exactly counter to the values and views of the vast majority of Jamaicans; (c) that they are temporary abrasions that should never become permanent; (d) that it is these social and economic patterns that need to be altered, not the educational system. The reforms that are needed in education are those that would make the social and economic systems far more effective instruments themselves in the building of an integrated nation.

The role of *education as an instrument of social justice* in a society with a history of slavery and colonialism and entrenched social disparities that have limited the life chances of different ethnic groups, cannot be gainsaid. The provision of educational opportunities for disadvantaged groups is not only to offer the possibilities of mobility but in fact to provide legitimate means by which past injustices can be corrected. Rhetoric along these lines is usually the stuff of political manifestos at election time.

Cutbacks in education indiscriminately done on the basis of financial constraints could, in effect, aggravate concerns related to social justice. Take, for example, the aforementioned policy of increasing the primary school teacher/pupil ratio to 1 to 55, closing teacher training institutions and not accepting any new students in teachers' colleges for the academic year 1985-1986. Historically primary school teachers in Jamaica have largely been drawn from the black population in rural areas, a feature which has continued to be the case up to the present time. The impact of these cutbacks is to restrict significantly opportunities available to black rural youth in Jamaica, who are among the most disadvantaged social groups in the country. Cutbacks of this nature are bound to produce social resentment and even social unrest from the affected groups.

Cultural Issues:

Since independence in 1962, the trend has been towards the Jamaicanization of education. This is evidenced by the Jamaicanization of the administration of education, both at the national and institutional level, of the teaching profession at all levels, of syllabi and curricula, and the Jamaicanization and Caribbeanization of examinations.

Given that there are two major components to Jamaican culture, what seems to have been achieved is that Jamaican education appears to have been Jamaicanized into the Anglo-Jamaican variety of Jamaican culture. This is as opposed to the Afro-Jamaican variety of Jamaican culture. Yet Jamaican identity is essentially defined in terms of the Afro- Jamaican variety, especially as this relates to language, music, dance, cuisine, attitudes and values. However, traditionally, Afro-Jamaican culture has been viewed as inferior, improper, vulgar and even uncivilized. The whole point of education and socialization in school was to eradicate this culture and replace it with the 'superior' European variety. As such, Afro-Jamaican culture had no place in the school. With the rise of nationalism in the 1930s and a granting of political independence in 1962, Afro-Jamaican culture has been officially re-evaluated and accorded pride of place in terms of defining Jamaican identity.

Nevertheless, the school system, including syllabi and curricula, has not fully come to terms with this re-evaluation of Afro-Jamaican culture. Miller (1969a) found that secondary school students preferred Caucasian physical features and that they negatively regarded typical Negroid features. There is no evidence to indicate that this approach to evaluating body image by Jamaican children has changed. Part of the reason lies in the fact that the imagery of text books and the majority of aids used by teachers, especially at the primary level, are derived from sources that convey a positive image of Caucasians but a less than positive and sometimes decidedly negative image of people of African ancestry. While there is no evidence to indicate that this is deliberate and arises from prejudice, it does appear that an economic factor is involved.

By and large the materials used in schools in terms of textbooks and other print material are easily available and are usually obtained from North America and England. Jamaica's national motto, 'Out Of Many One People', does not seem to have been translated into any planned strategy in Jamaican education which presents physical images of the different racial groups that make up the Jamaican society in the educational materials and books used in schools. In other words, there does not seem to be any consistency between the national motto and the educational practice in terms of the images projected in the materials presented to children in schools.

The music taught to students of music is mainly classical. Exponents of Jamaican folk music and reggae have had a difficult time getting native music accepted as being worthy of study. Reggae music, which has spread throughout the Caribbean, and indeed the world, has done so with little asistance from the Jamaican educational system. This further illustrates the dichotomy between the popular culture of the country and the prescribed culture of the school. To a significant degree the culture of the school is divorced from large segments of Jamaican reality.

The most systematic and deliberate attempts to integrate Afro-Jamaican culture in the school system have taken place in the area of language. This has happened mainly through the work of Craig (1969, 1971) and Wilson, Craig, and Campbell (1978). The work of Craig, Wilson and their colleagues has been to use the Jamaican Creole as the base in teaching standard English to children in the first and second grades of primary schools. While the approach by

Craig and Wilson is a significant step forward, in the sense that the Jamaican Creole is recognized as a language with its own morphology and syntax, it is a means to an end rather than an end in itself. It is part of the methodology of teaching Standard English.

Acceptance of the Jamaican Creole as a languaqe in its own right, studied by children at the primary and secondary level for its own sake, as the vehicle of internal communication within the Jamaican society, is still a far way off. The present situation is that the Jamaican Creole is to be studied only by professional linguists, used by dramatists in plays and advertisements, and in the case of teachers used only insofar as it assists in the instruction in the early stages of primary school, with the teaching of Standard English.

It should be noted that there are cultural nationalists who advocate that the Jamaican Creole should replace Standard English as the medium of instruction and that there are some university lecturers who have gone to the point of using it as the medium of instruction in their own classes. At the other extreme are those who continue to maintain the traditional approach that the Jamaican Creole has no place in the educational system and its introduction would only serve to undermine the learning of English and lower standards in education. There is an increasing number of people, however, who take the view that both the Jamaican dialect and Standard English have their place in school and in Jamaican society and should be developed as such. English is the language of officialdom, of international and external communication and should also be learned, taught and developed as such. The Creole is the language of intimacy and internal communication and should be preserved as such. The traditional approach appears to be the strongest, that of the cultural nationalists the weakest, but the latter view is probably the more realistic nonetheless, and may prevail in the longer term.

The essential point being made here is that Jamaican education is conducted largely within the Anglo-Jamaican tradition which is a minority tradition. If one takes the position of Ausubel (1968), that meaningful learning in the classroom begins with what the child already knows, his existing cognitive structure, then it would appear that especially in the early grades of primary education, except for language learning, the existing cognitive structure of the vast majority of Jamaican children is being ignored. In other words, the rich source of relevant anchoring ideas based on the material Afro-Jamaican culture of these children is not being sufficiently utilized in teaching the children the prescribed curricula. This is a pedagogic issue of considerable import that needs to exercise the minds of educational researchers, policy-makers and practitioners. Its resolution, however, is not merely a pedagogic matter since it is caught up in the cultural transformation that is taking place within the Jamaican society itself.

Jamaica is still grappling with the transition from the dominance of a minority European culture to the acceptance of the majority Afro-Jamaican culture. Twenty-four years of national sovereignty does not appear to be sufficient time for that transition to be made.

Internal Efficiency Issues

To this point, attention has been focused on the external relations of education in Jamaica. The writer takes the view that economic, social, political, and cultural factors have a far more pervasive effect on determining the structure, nature and content of education in Jamaica than do strictly pedagogical considerations. These external factors set the broad parameters within which issues of internal efficiency of the educational system arise. A comprehensive review of issues in education, from this point of view, accords internal efficiency concerns second place to issues arising from the external relations of education. However, they have their own significance and will be discussed under five headings: Planning; Performance; Innovation; Evaluation; and the Education of Boys.

Planning:

Over the past decade, Jamaica has been operating without a development plan for the educational system. In 1977 an effort was made to develop one, and after much discussion and involvement of educators from all sectors, the

Ministry of Education developed a draft plan for the period 1978-1983. This plan was never adopted or implemented. The principal reason for this was the decline in the general economy, with consequential cutbacks in the education sector.

It is fair to say that education has been managed on a crisis basis since 1978. The efforts of the administrators and managers have been directed towards damage limitation and control in the various areas in which cuts have been made. This essentially means that the budget savings cuts have not been made in any systematic way and have taken place in areas in which least damage or public outcry could be expected. These are sometimes crucial areas like teacher education, class material and pupil/teacher ratios.

Each year the hope has been that the economy will recover, thus relieving the pressure on educational expenditure. However, this recovery has not taken place to date. The overall result is uncertainty, uncoordinated and haphazard efforts, and poor communication between the Ministry and the schools. No one wishes to take responsibility for decisions that must be made. Currently, low morale, uncertainty and a certain amount of confusion exists at all levels of the educational system.

The present situation is both untenable and unhealthy. The challenge is for the Ministry, and other organizations vitally important to the delivery of education, to come together to work out some systematic and rational approach for the planning and management of the educational system in spite of the fiscal problems.

Performance:

At the same time that education is under siege financially there are grave concerns about performance at different levels of the educational system. The first area of concern is with the level of literacy and numeracy at age 12 - the end of primary schooling. Public commentators (McNight, 1983 ; Jennings-Wray, 1984) have been quoting a figure of 50 per cent functional illiteracy at the end of primary schooling. While one is not sure of the source of the percentage or the basis on which it was derived in terms of the definition of functional literacy, it is generally agreed that the level of achievement in reading among primary school leavers is below levels currently considered acceptable.

The Jamal Foundation was established in 1972 to eliminate adult illiteracy in Jamaica over a four-year period. At that time it was estimated that there were probably 400,000 adult illiterates. Since its inception Jamal has been able to make about 214,000 adults literate (Jamal Foundation, 1984). But the level of adult illiteracy in Jamaica may not have changed significantly over the period because of the number of persons coming out of the school system unable to read.

Secondary education has also been hampered by the number of students leaving primary schools who have not mastered the basic skills. Teachers and administrators at this level cite this factor as a contributor to poor performance at the secondary level. While there has been some evidence of improvement since the 1970s in the performance of primary school students on the common entrance examinations for selecting students for high school, the overall level of performance is still a cause for concern.

At the secondary level the issues surrounding performance are complicated by the introduction of the Caribbean Examinations Council (CXC) examinations. Since 1979 these have been replacing the Cambridge GCE Ordinary level examinations. While teachers and students welcome the CXC examinations, and regard the syllabi as superior to those of the GCE, perceiving their content to be more relevant to Caribbean and Jamaican realities, they are concerned that the standard of these examinations is higher than that of the GCE, thus making greater demands on the students to obtain passes (Massanari *et al*, 1984).

It should be noted that governments of the Commonwealth Caribbean established CXC to replace GCE as the external body to examine students attending secondary schools in the region. CXC began offering examinations in 1979 and hopes to offer the entire range of subjects taken by students in Caribbean high schools by 1987. It is understandable that in its initial period CXC would maintain very high standards in order to gain acceptance as being comparable to GCE, but in order to maintain the clientele gained it will need to adjust those standards downward so that they more or less equate with the level of difficulty of the GCE.

It is not clear whether student performance has actually fallen or whether social demand for examination results is much greater, but the number of students leaving secondary schools without passing any subjects in the GCE/CXC examinations is becoming a matter of public concern. This is immediately cited as one of the reasons for high youth unemployment - the lack of formal qualifications.

It was previously stated that one of the post-war trends in Jamaican education has been the shift to co-education. Hamilton (1985), in a study comparing the GCE '0' level performance of students in single-sex and co-educational high schools, found that those in single-sex institutions performed better than their peers in co-educational schools. Furthermore, she found that in rank order girls from single-sex schools performed best, followed by boys from single-sex schools, followed by boys from co-educational schools and finally girls from co-educational schools. She also found that a higher percentage of boys and girls from single-sex schools chose subjects more popular with the opposite sex than their peers in co-educational schools. These findings seem to suggest that school type may have become a factor in the performance and subject choices of high school students in Jamaica. The study seems to indicate that the impact of co-education on the Jamaican educational system needs to be evaluated, though examination performance is only one component or criterion to be considered.

Innovation:

There is no shortage of novel ideas concerning ways in which schooling and education could be reformed. Because of the fair degree of autonomy that exists within the educational system some principals and teachers have mounted modest innovations in their classes or schools. In many instances this is just done in response to some felt need in the local situation and is not even thought of as an innovaton or experiment. Areas of innovation have included work-study, school feeding, curriculum reform, school organization and school financing.

By and large most of these remain isolated efforts restricted to the particular institution in which the ideas are conceived and implemented. Usually there is no documentation of what has been done. Hence, dissemination of information concerning the innovation is very limited. In most instances these innovations do not survive the tenure of the individuals who initiate them. Some of these innovations successfully address the problems that inspired their conception and could possibly have general significance for the educational system as a whole, but are lost to the system because of the constraints of their implementation.

There have been exceptions to this general pattern. For example, the new concepts for student accommodation and boarding arrangements developed at Mico College. This college developed new designs for the physical accommodation of students based on the concept of students living in units housing twelve persons who are autonomous in making decisions concerning all the material conditions of boarding. By having students take responsibility for themselves and being as self-reliant as possible in the circumstances, living standards were raised at the same time as per capita boarding costs were reduced. Other institutions have either built or modified their buildings to accommodate this new concept and have had similar results with respect to the quality of life of students and costs.

Individual educators, particular institutions, and divisions of the Ministry of Education have been able to attract funding support for new ideas. In the main they have been able to mount pilot studies, some of which have achieved their objectives in the limited circumstances in which they were developed. The typical problems of these successful pilot projects are those related to that of going to scale. For example, Craig, in a pilot situation, developed strategies for the teaching of Standard English to Creole-speaking children. Wilson developed the appropriate primary language curriculum and supporting materials to complement Craig's strategies. In both pilot settings the teaching strategies, curriculum, and supporting materials proved that they had the potential to bring out dramatic improvements in literacy levels and reading achievement among primary school children. In 1978 the Ministry of Education introduced the pilot-tested curriculum, support materials, and teaching strategies in all primary schools in Jamaica. By June 1984, the first set of students reached primary school leaving age. There is no evidence to date that literacy levels among these students are any better than in previous years.

Massanari and Miller (1985), while noting similar outcomes across the Caribbean, observed that a possible explanation is that the success in the pilot setting is not only related to the superiority of the products developed but also to the process involved. They pointed out that in the University of the West Indies USAID Primary Education Project which was being evaluated, not only were excellent curriculum products developed for pilot testing in five schools in ten Caribbean countries but teachers were involved in the decision-making on what topics should be taught and by what methodology. They received in-service training in areas of perceived weaknesses, they were supported by periodic visits by project personnel who supplied encouragement as well as technical assistance in their attempts to master the new approaches, and they received feedback from formative evaluation. Massanari and Miller pointed out that while ten countries had adopted the curriculum products as part of national policy and had planned to disseminate these products to all primary schools in their educational system, only one country had planned to use the project process as well as the products. One of the main reasons given by Ministries of Education for not using the process employed by the project was a lack of resources. There may be some truth in the view that the problem of the allocation of economic resources is pre-eminent and that in many instances it vetoes improvements that have been proved possible through pedagogic innovation and experiment.

Evaluation:

Evaluation is a weak point in Jamaican education. Educational reforms, new policies and existing practice are seldom subject to systematic assessment involving empirical data. Notable exceptions in recent times have been the evaluations of the shift system (Leo-Rhynie, 1981) and rural education (Reid, 1981), undertaken by the Faculty of

Education of UWI at the invitation of the Ministry of Education.

Where evaluations take place, they are usually associated with externally funded projects. By and large, local efforts are not evaluated. It would seem that this dichotomy relates to different strategies employed in decision-making. Large external agencies usually require quantitative data as one of the bases for decisions. Internally, people usually think that they need only qualitative data to make decisions on matters with which they are familiar, and that quantitative data is therefore not essential.

With the growth of an indigenous research capacity there has been some shift in the educational community toward quantitative approaches, but in Jamaica the fact is that whatever the methodology of evaluation, systematic and critical assessment is not usually carried out before changes are made to existing elements within the educational system. The usual pattern is for changes to be dictated by political or economic forces supported with ad hoc statistics and questionable qualitative judgements. These changes are usually opposed by similar approaches, where opponents hurriedly gather available empirical data in support of their view and similarly questionable qualitative judgements. The end result is entirely unsatisfactory for the professional educator.

Largely through the UWI Faculty of Education at Mona, efforts have been made to analyze and evaluate different aspects of Jamaican education. Because these efforts have been constrained by what can be accomplished by one or two individuals devoting limited time to the particular exercise, the results to date have been modest. Also the issues examined have reflected more the academic interests of individual scholars than pressing national concerns. The hopeful point is that a cadre of professionals is emerging, and a body of knowledge is being developed which should more constructively inform future efforts at reform.

The Education of Boys:

At the commencement of the 1940s, school places available were more or less evenly divided between boys and girls both at the primary and secondary levels of the system. No records are available for 1940. However in 1938 the number of boys enrolled in high schools was 1,479 compared to 1,453 girls. By 1943 there were 1,609 boys compared to 1,773 girls (Blue Books of Jamaica 1938 and 1942). The expansion of educational opportunities at the secondary and tertiary levels since then has favoured girls much more than boys. Currently girls outnumber boys in secondary and tertiary institutions. In traditional high schools, where entry is determined by the Common Entrance examination, girls constitute about 60 per cent of the school population. In 1980-1981 there were 30,979 girls enrolled in high schools compared to 21,134 boys. The Annual Statistics Reports of the Ministry of Education since 1981 do not give a breakdown of high school enrolment according to gender. Girls also outnumber boys in comprehensive and technical high schools, although not to the same extent as high schools. In 1983-1984 there were 3,974 boys enrolled in technical high schools compared to 4,000 girls, while in comprehensive schools there were 3,616 boys to 4,349 girls. With the exceptions of the College of Arts, Science and Technology, the College of Agriculture and the Faculty of Engineering UWI, girls outnumber boys in tertiary institutions.

Jamaica has certainly developed a bias in favour of girls in the distribution of educational opportunities. It is certainly one of the few Third World countries in which there are more illiterate men than women (Cumper, 1976; Vincent, 1978). Usually, in the applications for jobs and for places in tertiary institutions there are more qualified females than males. The superior qualifications of females has led in the last twenty-five years to signifcant changes in the distribution of jobs as between males and females in the Jamaican labour force. In a society with a tradition of the 'working wife and mother', women have made great strides as a result of the post-war expansion of educational opportunities. This in itself is not questionable, but the issue at the present time is that post-war developments in this area have led to an imbalance which now places the male in a disadvantageous position. The preferred position ought to be one of balance in opportunities afforded to the sexes. When one considers, for example, that while lower-class girls have enjoyed most of the opportunities of upward social mobility and have left their male counterparts behind, then the long-term social implications cannot be ignored.

Several factors seem related to the phenomenon described above, and include the following:

1. A large number of families in Jamaica are single-parent and that parent is usually the mother. These mothers in their child-bearing practice exert far greater discipline over girls than boys. While the boys seem to enjoy greater freedom they may not develop the discipline necessary to make the best use of the educational opportunities provided.

2. Female teachers predominate in primary and secondary schools in Jamaica. They may not be as successful in inspiring and motivating boys to achieve as they are with girls. This may be also related to the fact that boys attend schools more irregularly and drop out in greater numbers than girls.

3. The Common Entrance examination, which is restricted to children 10+ and 11+, occurs at a time when girls are at a cognitive developmental advantage (Miller, 1969b). Appropriate adjustments are not made in the allocation of school places based on these examinations to assure balance between the sexes.

4. The trend to co-educational institutions has facilitated the growing imbalance between the sexes especially at the secondary level. A single-sex institution puts an automatic restriction on the number of places to be allocated. No such limitation is automatically imposed by co-educational schools as between the sexes. Co-educational secondary schools in Jamaica are in consequence predominately female.

The issue of the education of boys in Jamaica arises in the context in which the international concern with sexism in education focuses on female disadvantage. This presents a problem, since moves to address the issues could be interpreted as a reaction against girls and an attempt to buttress male dominance. This notwithstanding, the problems of boys in Jamaican society in general, and in education in particular, are very real. The issue will not disappear without conscious and deliberate measures designed to correct the imbalance.

CONCLUSION

From the foregoing discussion it can be seen that the contemporary issues facing Jamaican educators and policy-makers stem from Jamaica being a small, newly independent country, not in control of its own economy and not having resolved certain basic social and cultural problems. This has brought education to the crossroads of political decision-making with respect to the question of sovereignty and the means of achieving internal consensus. While education as it relates to the economic, political, social, and cultural realities of Jamaican society is in a state of crisis, there are also serious internal weaknesses that must be addressed. Jamaican education has come to the end of an era and is entering a new phase; its future course will depend on how the fundamental issues described are resolved.

BIBLIOGRAPHICAL REFERENCES

Ausubel, D.P. (1968) **Educational Psychology: A Cognitive View** (New York, Holt, Rhinehart & Winston)

Craig, D. (1969) **An Experiment in Teaching English** (London, Ginn & Company)

Craig, D. (1971) The use of language by young Jamaican children in contrasting socio-economic environments (Unpublished Ph.D thesis, London University)

Cumper, G. (1976) As reported by Martin, D. in **Jamaica National Literacy Programme: Project Findings Recommendations** (Paris, Unesco)

Gordon, S. (1963) **A Century of West Indian Education: A Source Book** (London, Longman)

Government of Jamaica (1938, 1945) **Annual General Reports** plus **Departmental Reports** (Kingston, Jamaica, Government Printer)

Hamilton, M.A.(1985) Performance levels in science and other subjects for Jamaican adolescents attending single-sex and co-educational high schools, **Science Education** 69, 4

Jamal Foundation (1984) **Lamplight: Quarterly Newsletter of the Jamal Foundation** 2, 3

Jefferson, O. (1972) **Post-war Economic Development of Jamaica** (Jamaica, Institute of Social and Economic Research, University of the West Indies)

Jennings-Wray, L. (1984) Why a reading problem in Jamaica?, **Daily Gleaner**, Monday 3 September (Kingston, Jamaica)

Kandel, I.J. (1943) **Report on Secondarv Education in Jamaica** (Kingston, Jamaica, Gleaner Company)

Kuper, A. (1976) **Changing Jamaica** (Kingston, Jamaica, Kingston Publishers)

Leo-Rhynie, E.A. (1981) **Report on the Shift System in Jamaica** (Jamaica, School of Education, University of the West Indies)

McNight, F. (1983) Education has many problems, **Daily Gleaner**, Saturday 30 July (Kingston, Jamaica)

Massanari, K., Masoner, P., Miller, E., and Klassen, F. **Report of the External Terminal Evaluation of the CXC/USAID Secondary Curriculum Project** (Washington DC, International Council on Education for Teaching)

Massanari, K. and Miller, E. (1985) **Report on the External Terminal Education of the UWI/USAID Primary Education Project** (Cave Hill, Barbados, Faculty of Education, University of the West Indies)

Miller, E. (1967) Ambitions of Jamaican school children, **Caribbean Quarterly** 13, 1

Miller, E. (1969a) Body image, physical beauty and colour among Jamaican adolescents, **Social and Economic Studies** 18, 1

Miller, E. (1969b) A study of self-concept and its relationship to certain physical, social, cognitive and adjustment variables in a selected group of Jamaican school girls (unpublished Ph.D thesis, University of the West Indies)

Miller, E. (1976) Education and society in Jamaica, in Figueroa, P. and Persaud, P. (eds) **Sociology of Education: A Caribbean Reader** (Oxford, Oxford University Press)

Ministry of Education (1978/1979, 1980/1981, 1983, 1984) **Educational Statistics: An Annual Review of the Education Sector** (Kingston, Jamaica, Ministry of Education)

Montieth, N. (1984) **Presidential Address: Jamaica Teachers Association Annual Conference** (mimeograph)

Reid, L.H.E. (1981) **Expectations of Parents, Students and Teachers in Respect of Teaching** (Jamaica, School of Education, University of the West Indies for Ministry of Education)

Vincent, F.X.(1978) Some factors associated with achievement in literacy among adults in Jamaica (unpublished M.A.[Ed.] thesis, University of the West Indies)

Whyte, M. (1977) **A Short History of Education in Jamaica** (London, Hodder & Stoughton)

Wilson, D., Craig, D., and Campbell, H. (1978) **Primary Language Arts: Book 1, 2, and 3** (Kingston, Jamaica, Heinemann Educational Books [Caribbean] Ltd)

Chapter Five

EDUCATION IN THE BRITISH VIRGIN ISLANDS: CASE STUDY OF A CARIBBEAN MICRO STATE

David Smawfield

This chapter traces the development of education in the West Indian territory of the British Virgin Islands, highlighting significant characteristics and patterns of provision. Some attempt is also made to interpret these patterns, with particular attention being paid to the significance of context. The chapter comprises three sections: background; primary education; secondary education and beyond.

BACKGROUND

The British Virgin Islands, politically a Dependent Territory of Britain, comprises a group of some forty islands lying at latitude 18° 25' north and longitude 64° 30' west. They are bounded to the north by the Atlantic Ocean and to the south by the Caribbean Sea. Approximately 60 miles west is Puerto Rico in the Greater Antilles; while neighbours to the east and south-east include Anguilla and St Kitts in the Lesser Antilles, approximately 90 and 150 miles distant respectively. Furthermore, the British Virgin Islands themselves are but one part of a politically divided archipelago; their counterparts being the Virgin Islands of the United States of America (USVI). The island of Tortola, the main island in the British Group, is separated from St John, of the USVI, by a mere three miles of water, the Sir Francis Drake Channel.

While it is proximity that is apparently suggested, and is certainly physically evident, and notwithstanding the dominating influence of the United States Virgin Islands today, the history of the British Virgin Islands has, for the most part, been one of isolation and neglect (Dookhan, 1975). Moreover, the number of islands comprising the territory, for its part, suggests intra-national isolation and fragmentation. This too is misleading. Only four islands have significant populations: Tortola, on which is located the capital, Road Town; Virgin Gorda; Jost Van Dyke and the more distant, coralline, and hence geographically exceptional, island of Anegada. Distances between the islands are small and the communications infrastructure, as of recent times, is good. Relative compactness is perhaps a suitable description. It is these four islands only with which this chapter needs be concerned, for the educational provision to be found on them comprises the entire national system.

Columbus is credited with 'discovering' the Virgin Islands in 1493. There is, however, archeological evidence indicating Carib and Arawak visitations, if not inhabitation, many years previous to this date (Harrigan and Varlack, 1975). The first European settlers were the Dutch in the early seventeenth century, though during the early years of their post-Columbian history almost every European maritime nation made a claim to the islands in one form or another (Dookhan, 1975: 1-14). Rights of sovereignty were finally settled in Britain's favour in 1735 since when they have remained British.

Piracy and subsequently smuggling were important economic activities in the period of social genesis, occupations which give some clue to the nature and character of the early settlers. Many of them were poor whites who arrived, often with their slaves, from other West Indian islands. They hoped to leave behind them poverty, war and in a not inconsiderable number of cases, debts and criminal convictions. Even when the plantation system was at its zenith the tiny elite was never really wealthy or genteel by West Indian standards (Harrigan and Varlack, 1975: 16-19). The lawless and buccaneer elements at the roots of the nascent society were not without significance for the subsequent development of educational provision. Neither was the consequent lack of a social cohesiveness, epitomized by an ethos in which every man for himself was very much the order of the day. For example, the idea of taxation, while tolerated as being necessary in most societies, was an absolute anathema to British Virgin Islanders and in the eighteenth and nineteenth centuries it was extremely difficult for legislatures to raise revenue for the provision of social services including, of course, education (Dookhan, 1975: 138).

As has been alluded to above, legitimate economic activity was founded on cotton and sugar cane and the system of slavery. To a large extent and in a broad frame, the well-documented history of the West Indies is also a history of the British Virgin Islands. The years 1735 to 1815 marked a period of economic growth and relative prosperity. This was stimulated principally by the incidence of three wars in which the territory had no direct, or only peripheral, involvement: the Seven Years War, the American War of Independence and the Napoleonic conflict. This pattern was to repeat itself in the twentieth century when the two World Wars also provided an economic fillip. Beyond 1815, the remainder of the nineteenth century was a period of disastrous economic decline (Dookhan, 1975: 61-66). This, too, may reasonably be claimed to be a part of the West Indian story, emancipation in 1834 and the collapse of the plantation system being the principal, but by no means the only, factors accounting for this demise. With the significant exception of the Depression of the 1930s, much of the twentieth century has been a period of economic upturn. From the 1960s to the present, however, what has occurred is more accurately described as a period of complete economic transformation, and this has been due almost entirely to one factor: the advent of tourism. A 1982 per capita GNP of $US 4,500 is a useful indicator of the degree of this prosperity (Dodsworth, 1985), but it provides no clue to the vulnerability of a virtual mono-economy. For the present purpose what it is perhaps most important to establish, and a consideration which will be returned to below, is that education did not play a manifest developmental role in the British Virgin Islands. Rather, economic considerations have tended to be a determinant of educational developments both directly and indirectly. An important part of this proxy influence concerns the high degree of correspondence, in the case of the Virgin Islands, between rises, falls and subsequent revivals of economic fortunes, and political developments.

In 1773, at the height of the plantation era and in line with other West Indian territories, the islands were allowed to have their own legislature. Conversely, a nadir in their political autonomy, coinciding with the period of economic decline, was marked by the institution of Crown Colony government in 1867, the 1871 Constitution of the Leeward Islands Federation, of which the British Virgin Islands became a part, and the abrogation in 1902 of the last vestiges of what by then had long been an entirely nominated legislature. Corresponding with economic upturn, though again not to overlook the arguably greater significance of a much wider influence, namely the dismantling of empire, a Legislative Council was re-established in 1950. Six years later saw the defederation of the Leeward Islands Colony and the establishment of the Colony of the Virgin Islands. In 1967 ministerial government came into effect and in 1976 responsibility for finance passed from the Governor to the Chief Minister.

While a relationship between economic and political factors exists at one level, in another sense there is a quite remarkable degree of anomaly (Augelli, 1956: 43). This is perhaps best illustrated with reference to Figure 5.1. Still British, and with all that that implies in terms of colonial legacies and political inertia, the economy of the British Virgin Islands and networks of movement, social as well as economic, are geared far less toward Britain and the Commonwealth and much more to the USA, and the USVI in particular. Even the use of pounds sterling and Jamaican and Eastern Caribbean currency as legal tender had to be abandoned in 1967 because of the *de facto* monopoly of the United States dollar. There are of course tremendous implications for educational policy and provision in attempting to accommodate these conflicting, if not irreconcilable, interests. This, too, is a factor which will be returned to below, but before undertaking a systematic examination of the development of educational provision, one further contextual consideration, itself with considerable bearing upon subsequent discussion, needs to be identified: the changing demographic make-up of the territory.

Census statistics (CARICOM, and BVI Government, 1983a) show that of the total population of the British Virgin Islands, 35.2 per cent was classified as foreign-born. Furthermore, while 28.7 per cent of the foreign-born population had lived in the territory for more than ten years, 51 per cent had immigrated in the five years and four months preceding the census, and 27.6 per cent of the foreign-born population had entered the British Virgin Islands in the sixteen months immediately prior to the census. According to the 1901 census, just two Caucasians remained on the islands (0.04 per cent of the total population). Even in 1960 the number of recorded 'white' population amounted to a mere 47 persons (0.6 per cent of the population). In 1980 the figure had risen to 778 or 7.0 per cent. But the number of Europeans and North Americans drawn to the islands in one capacity or another by the economic boom represents but a small part of the demographic transformation. Of the foreign-born population in 1980, 77 per cent emanated from other Caribbean islands, with persons born in St Kitts/Nevis being by far the most significant national group (26.7 per cent of the foreign-born population).

> The transition from small-scale agriculture to a tourist economy brought an influx of immigrants which introduced for the first time in over a century a substantial landless class whose social backgrounds differed in important respects from those of British Virgin Islanders. Insofar as the normal pattern whereby immigrants occupy the lowest paying jobs did not follow and they appeared to be getting ahead of the natives, local sentiment against the 'non-belonger' began to crystallise. (Harrigan and Varlack, 1975: 113)

Today, whether one is a 'British Virgin Islander', 'belonger' or 'non-belonger' has arguably become an even more invidious distinction with no less serious socio-political and economic implications. A number of isses facing contemporary society, including those of an educational bent, have as their basis this particular manifestation of pluralism.

PRIMARY EDUCATION

With two abortive exceptions, attempts to establish an Endowed Grammar School (1844-1846) and a Vocational School (opening in 1847 and closing - as far as can be ascertained - the same year), neither a secondary nor a government school formed part of educational provision in the British Virgin Islands until the year 1943 (Harrigan and Varlack, 1975: 81-82 and 198). Consequently the development of educational provision in the territory up to this date may, for the present purpose, be taken as being synonymous with the development of elementary or primary education. Furthermore, in view of the extremely important role played by the Church in the development of this provision it is worth noting contemporary patterns of religious affiliation for the population (see Figure 5.1). It should perhaps be mentioned, too, that in the majority of cases such affiliations are far more than merely notional. Religion forms a major part of the lives of many British Virgin Islanders; churches are very important and powerful institutions, both in the local communities and the territory as a whole. The number of politicians in the 1986 general election campaign finding it expedient to invoke God's will in concluding political speeches or statements is a telling example of this (*The Island Sun*, 6.9.86 and the *BVI Beacon* 25.9.86). However, Figure 5.1 fails to reveal some interesting inter-island variations in religious affiliation. Of the total population 45.4 per cent is Methodist, but in Anegada and Jost Van Dyke Methodist affiliation is as high as 69.4 per cent and 68.2 per cent (British Virgin Islands government, 1984). The only schools on these islands, until the government took over responsibility in the 1970s, were Methodist schools.

In the Virgin Islands as a whole, it was the Methodist missionaries, arriving in 1789, who are credited with making 'the first halting attemps at religious instruction for slaves' (Harrigan and Varlack, 1975: 76), and hence commencing the chronology of educational provision in the territory. In the early nineteenth century the Methodists were joined in their educational activities by the Anglicans, the year 1827 marking the opening of the first Anglican day school in Road Town (Harrigan and Varlack, 1975: 77). Whereas the Methodist initiative to this time was essentially one of religious instruction, Anglican activity from the outset included a significant secular dimension (Dookhan, 1975: 91). The Anglican and Methodist thrusts, and not infrequent rivalry, were to dominate educational provision into the second half of the twentieth century. As to why this should have been the case, it is difficult to over-emphasize the significance of the

Figure 5.1:

Background - Selected Demographic and Economic Data

RELIGION, 1980

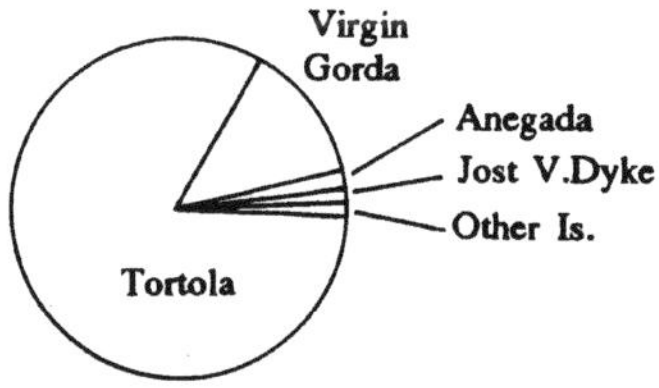

POPULATION BY ISLAND, 1980
(Tot. pop.: 10,985)

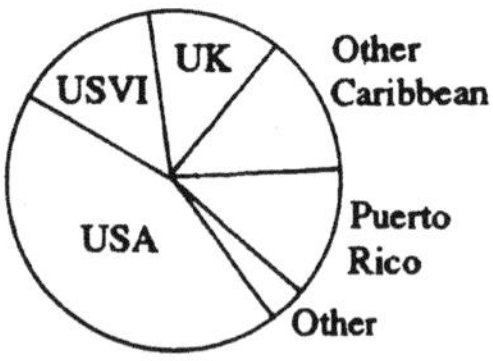

COUNTRY OF ORIGIN OF IMPORTS, 1980
($40,494,282)

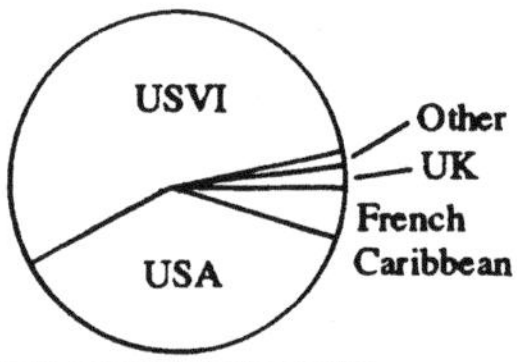

DOMESTIC EXPORTS
1980 ($507,934)

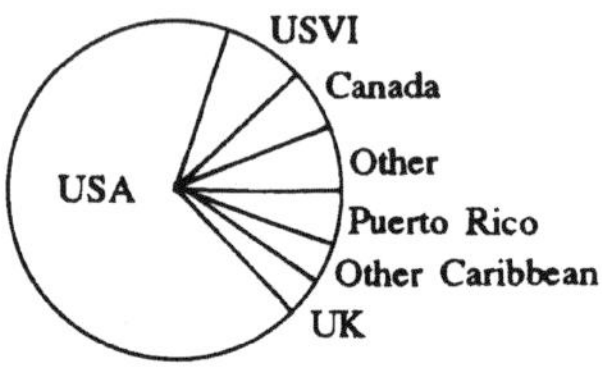

TOURISTS BY PLACE OF RESIDENCE, 1981

Data abstracted from: CARICOM, 1980-1981: 2-7, 82-83;
BVI Govenrment, 1983a: 53, 175, 179

1835 Sterling Report. On emancipation in 1834 and the decision of the imperial government to promote Negro education in the British West Indies through the means of a grant, Rev. John Sterling was given the task of recommending whether this should be made to the local legislatures or the religious bodies, that is to say, whether the responsibility for educational provision should be entrusted to the state or to the church: the latter being chosen (Gordon, 1963: 19-23). Though the Negro Education Grant was reduced progressively after five years, and withdrawn completely in 1845, an important precedent had been set and an inertia generated.

As was established at the outset, the dire state of the economy to the end of the nineteenth century had a negative effect on educational growth and with the territory's incorporation, in 1871, into the Leeward Islands Federation local educational milestones were manifestations of federal legislation modified by scale, isolation and neglect. Nevertheless, as Dookhan notes, 'It was only with the formation of the Leeward Islands Federation that some attempt was made to introduce a secular and unified curriculum throughout the Virgin Islands' (Dookhan, 1975: 182). The passing of the Leeward Islands Education Act of 1875 introduced a system of annual inspection upon which grants-in-aid were to be forthcoming should schools meet certain conditions. However, it was a further two years before even one British Virgin Islands school was able to do this. The Leeward Islands Education Act of 1890 is noteworthy in that it marked the commencement, if not enforcement, of compulsory education. Indeed, in such a brief historical resume there is a very real danger of failing to convey the inadequacies of what passed for education. Harrigan and Varlack's succinct appraisal of educational achievement to the turn of the century is all the more poignant therefore:

> Initially learning was little in the numbers it affected; subsequently, when numbers had grown, in its quality. (Harrigan and Varlack, 1975: 91)

The 1925 Elementary Education Act for the Leeward Islands, and the Code of Regulations for the British Virgin

Islands made under this act, served as the legislation upon which educational provision was based into the second half of the twentieth century even though, as early as 1938, there was official remonstrance to the effect that:

> it has become abundantly clear that the main educational legislation of the Leeward Islands needs revision... is narrow in its purview... and... unworkable in present conditions,... (Colonial Office, 1939: 12)

Despite this particular inertia, the decade of the 1940s may reasonably be regarded as a watershed in the educational history of the British Virgin Islands. In 1942 the first real Education Department was established and a full-time Supervisor of Education appointed (Leeward Islands Colony, 1953: 1-2). The following year a government secondary school was opened, using temporary accommodation until the completion of purpose-built facilities in 1947 (a development which will be discussed below when secondary education is examined). Adjoining this new site and completed at the same time, the first government primary school came into existence.

Prior to legislation in 1955, which brought about a more realistic partnership between church and state, in practice little control or guidance was effected over all the other church schools (Harrigan, 1963: 2). The period of economic transformation has, however, seen no less a metamorphosis in respect of the control of education. Table 5.1 shows this clearly in the changing enrolments in the various sectors over a period of thirty-four years. In 1954 the primary schools in the territory could be classified as follows: Methodist management - ten schools; Anglican management - one school; Seventh Day Adventist management - one school; government owned - one school; private - three schools (Leeward Islands Colony, 1954: 3). By 1973 the majority of the 'assisted' church schools had become government schools, the changes taking place as schools were moved out of churches into proper government-owned school buildings, and before the decade had ended all these schools had become government schools.

The statistics in Table 5.1 also show a marked increase in the significance of the 'private' sector, from no representation in 1950 to 20 per cent of total enrolment in 1984, but unless some further explanation is given the degree of this shift would be misleading. St George's, Anglican, Primary School is the most important institution in this sector, both in terms of its numbers and its prestige. Its clientele are the children of the more affluent of the expatriate community and the indigenous elite. Certainly its numbers have grown steadily and substantially, from about 80 pupils in 1969, the year the school was reopened, to 186 pupils in 1984 (BVI Department of Education Reports, 1969: 4 and 1984: Appendix Table III). Of even greater significance than this, however, is that more recent statistics in Table 5.1 include pre-primary enrolment and the private sector dominates this developing area of educational provision. Presently, there is only one government pre-school, on Jost Van Dyke, and this itself was not functioning in 1986 due to insufficient numbers. It would be misleading, too, not to point out that the government offers support to private pre-primary education, including training a number of the teachers who operate these schools, as well as providing some basic supplies (BVI Department of Education Reports, 1984: 6).

This would also seem an appropriate juncture at which to mention what may be termed the 'invisible private sector' in spite of the fact that it has more bearing on secondary and tertiary provision, to which more specific attention will be given below. What is meant here is those children who are sent to study abroad, often using the network of the extended family, to St Thomas, the United States mainland and other Caribbean islands. The incidence of this occurrence is difficult, if not impossible, to gauge empirically. No records are kept from which such information may be abstracted. Before the establishment of the secondary school, sending children abroad to study was the only post-primary educational option. Apart from the limited number of scholarships even this possibility was only available to those of sufficient means. There is some evidence, in the form of verbal recollection, that after the secondary school was established this behaviour pattern, whether on grounds of elitism, tradition or a genuine belief that a better education would be provided, remained for a while (Wheatley 16.9.86). The current Chief Education Officer, with his intimate knowledge of the territory, believes that today the number of children sent to study abroad for education below

Table 5.1

Primary Enrolment by Sector 1950-1984

	Non-fee paying				Fee paying		
	GOVERNMENT		ASSISTED		PRIVATE		
Year	Number of pupils	Percentage of total enrolment	Number of pupils	Percentage of total enrolment	Number of pupils	Percentage of total enrolment	Total enrolment
1950	500	32.8%	1026	67.2%	--	--	1526
1954	537	28.5%	1197	63.5%	152	8.1%	1886
1962	319	17.4%	1483	80.7%	36	2.0%	1836
1968	642	34.6%	1165	62.8%	49	2.6%	1856
1974	1278	58.6%	605	27.8%	298	13.7%	2181
1978	1430	63.5%	432	19.2%	389	17.3%	2251
1981	1724	80.3%	--	--	423	19.7%	2147
1984	1860	80.0%	--	--	465	20.0%	2325

Sources of Data: Annual Reports of the Department of Education, for the years as listed

the tertiary level is very small, perhaps even countable on one hand. If this is so, it is a cause for optimism. In the West Indian milieu the connection made between education 'worth having' and education gained abroad has been one of the most debilitating attitudinal legacies of colonialism (Brock, 1982).

Further examination of Table 5.1 permits another observation to be made: growth of total enrolment has remained remarkably small, a mere 23.3 per cent increase in the thirty-year period 1954-1984. Unlike so many countries striving toward a 'developed' status during this period, there has not been a battle of maintaining or improving the quality of educational provision against huge increases in numbers. Neither is this to overlook the fact that rapidly falling rolls can also have equally, if not more, serious ramifications. But while the validity of this comment must remain, Table 5.1 fails to reveal that within the overall enrolment pattern significant spatial variations in enrolment have in fact occurred and these have indeed caused acute problems. In the period in question the Cane Garden Bay, Meyers and Jost Van Dyke schools have experienced problems of declining enrolment 'owing to migration to the US Virgin Islands' (BVI Department of Education Report, 1974: 5). Conversely, schools in and near Road Town and also the former St Mary's School on Virgin Gorda have experienced severe problems of overcrowding and large classes 'largely due to the fact that territory's [sic] immigrant population is concentrated in these areas' (BVI Department of Education Report, 1977: 3). At the commencement of the 1986/1987 academic year overcrowding was still causing problems in the majority of schools in the south of Tortola while those in the north tended to be undersubscribed (*BVI Beacon*, 18.9.86). Mention of conditions within particular schools opens the way to a brief discussion of some of the prevailing characteristics of this level of provision.

Within the British Virgin Islands' educational system the first two years of primary schooling, commencing when a child reaches the age of five, are designated as Infant Stages I and II. With one exception, Road Town Infants School opened in 1977 (BVI Department of Education Report, 1977: 1), the infant section comprises a part of every primary school. The subsequent levels are designated as Primary Classes I to V. The implied equivalence of Class I to Grade I in the United States system (Christopher, 1974: 1), and similarly through the five levels, is an interesting example of the United States influence modifying patterns of provision. And more in common with North American than British educational practice, promotion through the different levels is not automatic but based on a criterion of attainment. The most important social event in any primary school's educational year is its annual 'graduation' and prize-giving ceremony. Above all else, this occasion pays tribute to those children who have passed the Primary School Leaving Examination and thus automatically secured entry into the 'secondary' level or 'division' of education. The social significance of this may be gauged from the fact that it is also not untypical for even Infant Stages I and II to have their own rolls of honour called during the programme.

In what may also be seen as something of a tradition, a great deal of effort is expended by primary schools annually in the organization of a major fund-raising event. In many cases this takes the form of a summer fair in which the whole community is involved - making this incomparable to, say, a British school fete. 'Prince and Princess' shows (hybrids of beauty queen/fashion shows and talent competitions in which pupils are contestants) have also proved popular with parents. In 1986 a number of schools each raised more than $US 2,000 through events such as these. As a result of this kind of effort, over the last two or three years, almost every school in the territory has been able to purchase its own photocopying machine and the possibilities for the local generation of educational materials have been revolutionized. A conjecture would be that within the next few years the majority of primary schools will posses computers purchased with funds raised in the same way. Children in the British Virgin Islands are expected to provide their own exercise books. A good proportion of textbooks, workbooks, and basic teaching apparatus and equipment are also purchased from funds schools have raised themselves. Other sources of materials include the Education Department itself and aid agencies. That far more onus is placed on schools and parents, as opposed to the educational administration, to provide what in Britain, for example, would be regarded as basic material does not make the British Virgin Islands unusual. Rather, this may reasonably be described as representing a typical Caribbean pattern.

Much of the material in use in the territory's primary schools is 'Caribbean' in origin. But what comes to mind here is De Block's concern writing of Grenada:

> How Caribbean are they really? The faces are indeed black but while they may reflect the lives of affluent urban children in Trinidad they are foreign to the majority in the region.(de Block, 1984: 82)

Particularly noteworthy among North American material, not least in that it is in fairly wide usage, is a phonics cassette kit series *The Listening Corner* published by Houghton Mifflin in 1984. From the above, it hardly needs stating that almost no material in current use is purely local in origin and it has been argued in detail elsewhere that these last-mentioned patterns of provision of educational materials are, essentially, problems of scale (Smawfield, 1985). Similarly, curriculum development initiatives also have an important bearing on the nature and character of educational materials. In the British Virgin Islands these too have been, for the most part, regional in character; the UWI/USAID Primary Education Project in the areas of language, arts, and mathematics, and in which the British Virgin Islands has participated during the 1980s, being one such example. Figure 5.2 shows a typical timetable and helps to provide further insight into the structural nature of the territory's primary school curriculum. But it should be noted that while curriculum guidelines are centrally prescribed, headteachers and teachers, in practice, have the autonomy of deciding upon the detailed organization and programming of the school day. Timetables do therefore vary from school to school.

In terms of influencing both what is taught and how, in addition to the considerations identified above, in the British Virgin Islands education system enormous downward pressure is exerted on the school by the Primary School Leaving Examination. As to the quality of teaching, and if it is reasonable to assume a correlation between teacher training and classroom performance, the problem of large numbers of untrained teachers has been an ever-present factor throughout the entire period of the territory's educational history. Even in

1984, the most recent year for which published data are available at the time of writing, 41.3 per cent of the total primary teaching force was untrained (BVI Department of Education Report, 1984). This figure may soon change substantially, however. In 1985, at the invitation of the government, the University of Hull established two, three-year, part-time, teacher education programmes operated within the territory. Twenty-eight trained and twenty-one untrained teachers are participating in these programmes. It is an extremely bold initiative and one on which many hopes are pinned, notwithstanding the fact that the present author has to declare his interest in referring to this, being the University of Hull Resident Tutor in the British Virgin Islands (1986-1988).

But even were a well-trained teaching force to be secured there are still other problems to solve (*BVI Beacon*, 18.9.86) and, in bringing the present discussion full circle, not the least of these are those related to imbalances of school enrolment. In some schools, where numbers are smaller, a common pattern is for one teacher to be responsible for two classes within one classroom; half the pupils facing the blackboard at one end of the room, the remaining half facing a blackboard on the opposite wall. At the other extreme, some school buildings and the resources within them that teachers are expected to work with are grossly inadequate for present enrolments.

Before turning attention to secondary education, it is nevertheless possible to leave the question of primary school disparity on a positive note. A distinctive characteristic of the British Virgin Islands educational system, based on the author's first-hand experience, is the well-being of outer-island schools. It is much more usual in multi-island small country systems, and Grenada/Carriacou and Grand Cayman/Cayman Brac may be cited as just two examples, to find outer-island schools substantially disadvantaged.

SECONDARY EDUCATION AND BEYOND

Moving on now to consider secondary educational provision, as with the treatment of primary education above, it is proposed to arrive at a discussion and analysis of some distinctive patterns of provision through a brief examination of the development of this level of the system. Moreover, it may

Figure 5.2

Specimen Primary Timetable: Class II, Academic Year 1985/1986

Age range of children: 7 - 10 years (Intended age range: 8 - 9 years)

	a.m.				p.m.			
Monday	General Assembly	Language	BREAK	Mathematics	LUNCH	Social Studies	Singing	BREAK	Art
Tuesday	House Assembly	Mathematics		Language		Health	Story Time		Phonics
Wednesday		Worship		Language		Mathematics	Games		Games
Thursday	Class Assembly	Mathematics		Language		Science	Art		Phonics
Friday	General Assembly	Language		Mathematics		Social Studies	Story Time		Art

be useful to establish here that this discussion itself leads ultimately to considerations beyond the present apex of the system: not just in the narrow sense of secondary/tertiary articulation, but including questions of the relationship of educational provision *per se* to such wider concerns as the territory's manpower development needs.

The history of secondary educational provision in the British Virgin Islands may be treated as comprising two distinct periods: 1943-1968, the era of the British Virgin Islands Secondary School; and 1968 to the present, the period of existence of the British Virgin Islands High School. Concerning the establishment of a 'senior' school in 1943, and in view of subsequent discussion, perhaps the first point that should be made is that both before, and for several years after, this institution was first opened there was a great deal of uncertainty and contention as to its desired form and direction. The 1938 Hammond Report had envisioned a

> junior secondary school... founded on practical work. Agriculture, housecraft, and constructional work will not be merely added to an orthodox secondary curriculum. (Colonial Office, 1939: 26)

This was completely at odds with what the majority of the population thought was appropriate: a grammar-type school and all that is implied in terms of academic standards; an institution that would not only aim to produce successes in the Junior and Senior School Certificate of the University of Cambridge but which itself would be judged on its capacity to produce such results. When, in 1947, the expressed intention of the territory's Commissioner indicated a merger of the Senior and adjoining primary school and the discontinuance of external examinations there was an enormous public outcry and demonstration (Bacchus Report, 1976: 16). This succeeded in producing a victory for majority opinion, with the school gaining official recognition as a 'secondary' school.

According to the official record, in 1950 the curriculum of the school still had 'a vocational bias' (BVI Department of Education Report, 1950: 5), but perhaps already this was little more than a preferred interpretation. In fairness, it is still possible to note an agricultural programme forming part of the curriculum in 1954, but already exempted from this was 'the School Certificate form which has had to concentrate on the prescribed work for the examination' (BVI Department of Education Report, 1954, App.A: 14). From the headmaster's report for the year 1963, however, there can be no ambiguity as to the nature of the school or its curriculum. What is even implied is a tradition already firmly established:

> The curriculum remained unchanged: - Religious Knowledge, English, History, Geography, Latin, Spanish, Mathematics, Science, Health Science, Woodwork (for boys) Cookery and Needlework (for girls). (Report of Virgin Islands Secondary School, 1963: 1)

This year also saw the school inspected by Brissett, Principal Education Officer of the Ministry of Education in Jamaica. From what has been said above it will come as no surprise that he found a school that 'was exceedingly examination-minded' (Brissett, 1963: 10). His comments concerning the teaching of English Literature are also revealing, describing

> the choice of books... running the well tramelled paths of the classics.... I cannot think of a more unsuitable choice for form II than Palgrave's 'Golden Treasury' or a book of 'Prose Selections'. There is also, generally, an undue emphasis on the plays of Shakespeare. (Brissett, 1963: 4).

But even in retrospect, whatever one's criticisms of the model or its curriculum, there can be little doubt that these early years of secondary schooling made a significant contribution toward meeting the territory's higher-level manpower needs. This may be illustrated with reference to a reunion which took place in 1986 between the school's first headmaster and some of his ex-pupils. The occasion brought together an impressive gathering of present and former holders of high office, not the least among whom was included a Chief Minister and a former Chief Minister.

Throughout the twenty-five-year history of the British Virgin Islands Secondary School it remained an extremely selective institution. Brissett refers to a figure of 8 per cent (Brissett, 1963: 18) finally emerging from a selection process which involved, at that time, internal tests set by the respective primary schools in the first instance. These sifted out those who went on to sit a Department of Education 'Assessment Test' from which, in turn, some 150 pupils emerged to sit the secondary school's own entrance examination, approximately twenty-five places being on offer (Reid, 1963: 26-27). When the British Virgin Islands Secondary School closed in 1968 it had 150 pupils on roll. By December of the same year the institution which took over its mantle had 774 pupils (BVI Department of Education Report, 1968: 2).

The British Virgin Islands High School was the outcome of the government's expressed desire to provide open access to non-selective secondary education. This remains official policy to the present day, though the deviation which has occurred in practice may be demonstrated in a changing pattern of statements extracted from five Education Annual Reports for the period 1968-1982.

> [1968] The selection of pupils for the High School was done on the basis of school recommendations and parental wishes. No examination was involved.
>
> [1970] It had not been possible through lack of accommodation to admit any new pupils in the school year beginning September 1969, so that the 1970 intake... represented a two years' backlog...
>
> [1970] Entry to the High School remains non-selective but in 1970 a fair number of children over the age of 12 who were eligible for entry were retained, at their parents' wish, for a further year in their district all-age primary schools so as better to consolidate their basic work in literacy and numeracy.

> [1971] the school cannot absorb at any one intake more than a reasonable quantity of pupils weak in reading. It was necessary therefore in September 1971 to recommend that pupils who were very weak might stay for an extra year in the primary schools.
>
> [1973] At the beginning of the new school year, in an effort to raise standards, there was insistence that all new pupils must have passed the Primary V Examination in each of the subjects offered. This directive was later modified to include another 71 pupils whose results were almost as good as of those 83 who had 'passed' and who were recommended by their Head Teacher. These pupils were put on probation for this first term.
>
> [1982] A total of 263 students... qualified for certificates and automatic transfer to secondary schools.... Of the 199 students who failed... 87 were recommended to attend a special three week summer school to upgrade.... Based on their performance during the summer school programme, 69 students were offered secondary school places.

The School Leaving Examination itself was not conceived of as an entrance examination, despite the fact that essentially this is what it has become. Rather, the intention was to provide the opportunity to work for a certificate, the only qualification that some pupils would ever be likely to attain, which had some currency with government and private employers. At least two reasons may be offered with some degree of confidence as to why such discordances should have occurred. First, the present secondary infrastructure, physical plant, number of suitably qualified secondary teachers, and so on could not adequately support open access; second, there is a problem of funding. Plans have been drawn for developing the High School campus, but an aid donor or other source of finance has still to be found. One feels that added to the above material considerations could be included an attitudinal dimension: the concern for standards and the probably justifiable fear that further expansion would compromise those standards already attained. The statements cited above would certainly appear to support such a conclusion. That there was a failure to modify the name of the school to include the word 'Comprehensive', as recommended by the Bacchus survey team, (Bacchus Report, 1976: 83) may also be symptomatic of this overriding attitudinal concern. As the Bacchus survey team pointed out, in much of the West Indies (and historically in Britain, too) the word 'High' suggests a grammar-type school (Bacchus Report, 1976: 42). But, for the sake of objectivity, the preferred influence, conscious or unconscious, of a United States role model as an equally plausible explanation should also be recognized. The term 'High School' in the United States has no similar elitist connotations.

To point to the largely academic orientation of the British Virgin Islands High School is to return to assertions more capable of substantiation. A fairly recent speech by the Minister for Health, Education and Welfare (*The Island Sun* 7.6.86) made it very clear that the credibility of the school is measured, like its predecessor, on its capacity to produce expected and desired examination results. Of such examinations, those of the Caribbean Examinations Council (CXC), for which pupils first started preparing in 1979, have, in the 1980s, overtaken in numerical importance the Cambridge Overseas GCE. Also significant, not least in the fact that it has some currency in the United States Virgin Islands as well as carrying weight in the territory itself, is the High School's own Leaving Certificate. Further reference to secondary curriculum will be made when the question of vocational education is raised in connection with manpower considerations. But before this and other selected issues are discussed it remains for two other structural developments which have substantially altered patterns of secondary education in recent years to be identified: the inauguration of the Literacy and Skills Programme and the establishment of Secondary Divisions in outer island schools.

According to the *Report of the Department of Education for the Calendar Year 1982*:

> The results of the 1982 Primary V Examinations revealed that there were a number of students in Primary V who would have attained the age of 13 years 6 months and older by December of 1982, and whose academic performance was far below average.
> A further survey of the schools' population showed that there were a similar set of students in the Primary Four grades.
> In order to help those students who were identified as old for primary school and weak in the basic skills, it was decided to separate them from the primary school population and bring them together.

The outcome was the Literacy and Skills Programme located in a specially erected building in the grounds of the old Road Town Primary School (and thus adjacent to the High School). The Programme was instigated, with sixty-nine students enrolled, in September 1982 (ibid). The following year seventeen students were able to progress to the High School. Latest published data show sixty-two students participating in the Programme in 1984, their ages ranging from 14+ to 20+.

A 'Secondary Division' was established on Anegada in September 1981 (BVI Department of Education Report, 1981: 18), that is to say, an educational facility which allows students to follow as closely as possible courses offered at the British Virgin Islands High School without leaving their own island. Students eligible for secondary entry, however, may still elect to attend the High School in Tortola should they wish. The Anegada Secondary Division forms part of the primary school building. The development coincided with the establishment of a Secondary Division on Virgin Gorda, the evolution of which is worthy of further comment. On Virgin Gorda an attempt was made, in 1978, to introduce vocational education provision (BVI Government Development Programme: 53, and Department of Education Report, 1978: 1-2). A Vocational Centre, opening that year, offered courses in the 'Visitor Industry and Electrical Engineering' to students, some of whom had already left school and some of whom were about to leave or had not taken the opportunity to attend the High School. It was conceived on a very different premise to that of paralleling what was on offer at the High School and was in fact administered by a private group called the 'Virgin Gorda Education Committee' (BVI Department of Education Report, 1981: 17). The institution became recognized as a Secondary Division when the government took over complete control in 1981. That students then began wearing High School uniform is indicative of a similar transformation in the educational colour of what had originally been a specific and much more narrowly conceived vocational education initiative. In 1982 the Secondary Division and its counterpart, the Primary Division of the former St Mary's School, were relocated in a new educational complex: the Bregado Flax Educational Centre.

In moving to some brief mention of particularly characteristic enrolment patterns, complementing earlier discussion in respect of primary provision, the establishment of Secondary Divisions on outer islands is undoubtedly of major significance when the question of spatial imbalances of secondary provision, actual or potential, is raised. That such disadvantage occurred in the past is certain. Table 5.2 clearly shows this despite the fact that its indicators are crude. However, encouragingly, the Bacchus survey team in 1976, considering the question of possible spatial disparities apropos of Virgin Gorda, noted a quite different pattern. While finding evidence of 'slight under-representation of the population of secondary school age from Virgin Gorda in the high school' (Bacchus Report, 1976: 23), they nevertheless concluded that children from Virgin Gorda 'have about an equal chance of receiving secondary education as children in Tortola'. Interestingly, particularly in view of earlier discussion of what was termed 'the invisible private sector', their reason for judging the observed disparity to be counterbalanced pertains to the fact that

> we also learnt that because of the relative economic prosperity of many parents on that island more of them were able to send their children of secondary school age to attend school overseas. (Bacchus Report, 1976)

It is too early to establish what effect the newly established Secondary Divisions have had on enrolment patterns, or will have, for example on patterns of certification. Clearly, when the time is ripe, this could be a useful area of research.

Table 5.3 shows secondary enrolment according to gender for the period 1950 to 1984. It reveals a striking pattern of disparity and one which is all the more so when it can be confirmed that at the primary level over the last twenty-five years the number of boys has always exceeded the number of girls (though nowhere near as significantly). The disparity is well recognized and there is no shortage of

Table 5.2

Spatial Disparities and British Virgin Islands Secondary School Enrolment, 1963

Percentage of total BVISS enrolment, by island*		1960 population by island, expressed as percentage of total population	
Tortola	94.4%	85.2%	Tortola
Virgin Gorda	4.0%	8.3%	Virgin Gorda
Anegada	1.6%	3.5%	Anegada
Jost Van Dyke	0.0%	2.3%	Jost Van Dyke
		0.7%	(Other Islands)

* As determined by location of primary school from which pupil recruited

Data compiled from: Brissett, 1963: 2; BVI Government, 1983a: 3 (Table 1.03)

suggested reasons as to why this pattern should have occurred or continue to occur. Some will be mentioned here, but before doing so a caveat will be entered. This concerns the danger of applying too insular or introspective an interpretation, and there has perhaps been a tendency to do this. As Table 5.4 attempts to portray, while the pattern is distinctive it should be seen as part of a wider phenomenon, as one which is perhaps more accurately described as being West Indian in character.

Among those reasons that have been voiced are included the influence of the teacher as exemplar, the teaching profession in the British Virgin Islands at primary level historically having been dominated by women (Brissett, 1963: 1). Second, and perhaps more significant, is the influence of economic pressures and the fact that traditionally boys have been expected to start earning a wage earlier than girls (Brissett, 1963). A possible third factor is the question of attitudinal ambivalence. A more considered examination of a quite different manifestation of this phenomenon leads to this chapter's ultimate objective: that of looking briefly beyond secondary education, including aspects of the possible relationship between educational provision and manpower and development needs. To conclude the immediate discussion, however, there is empirical evidence to show that in the British Virgin Islands girls display more positive attitudes to schooling than boys; but as the researchers who established this themselves comment, on its own, the factor should not be seen as particularly significant: it merely echoes similar patterns of attitudinal sex differences found in Britain and the United States, for example (Buys, Carlson, and Hourihan, 1976: 5). Table 5.3 shows a trend, in that the disparity between male and female enrolment has been a decreasing one. This perhaps gives cause for some optimism that in, say, another twenty-five years time the phenomenon may only be of historical interest.

An arguably more disquieting manifestation of attitudinal ambivalence and educational disparity concerns a societal characteristic identified at the outset: pluralism in the form of distinctions of British Virgin Islander, belonger and non-belonger status. Two, independent, empirical studies both carried out in 1976 (Buys, Carlson and Hourihan, 1976;

Table 5.3

Secondary Enrolment and Gender, 1950-1984

Year	Number of boys	Boys as % of total enrolment	Number of girls	Girls as % of total enrolment	Total enrol-ment
1950	14	24.1%	44	75.9%	58
1954	34	30.1%	79	69.9%	113
1960	35	28.2%	89	71.8%	124
1965	40	26.7%	110	73.3%	150
1968	41	27.3%	109	72.7%	150
1969	257	42.0%	355	58.0%	612
1972	332	43.6%	417	56.4%	739
1976	365	44.5%	456	55.5%	821
1980	345	43.6%	446	56.4%	791
1984* (High School only)	371	44.9%	456	55.1%	827
1984* (All secondary)	452	44.6%	561	55.4%	1013

* 1984 is included as a composite entry on account of the establishment of the Anegada and Virgin Gorda Secondary Divisions in 1981 and the Literacy and Skills Programme in 1982.

Sources of Data: Annual Reports of the Department of Education, for the years listed

Table 5.4

Average Percentage Secondary Enrolment, according to Gender, in Selected Caribbean Countries for the Period 1970-1978

Country	% Boys	% Girls	Years for which data calculated*
Barbados	46.6	53.4	1970-1977
Belize	47.2	52.8	1970-1974,1976
British Virgin Islands	43.9	56.1	1970-1978
Dominica	44.0	56.0	1970-1977
Guyana	49.5	50.5	1970-1978+
Montserrat	42.9	57.1	1970-1974,1976
St Kitts/ Nevis/Anguilla	47.6	52.4	1970-1973, 1975-1976
St Lucia	45.0	55.0	1970-1974
St Vincent	43.3	56.7	1970-1976
Trinidad & Tobago	48.2	51.8	1970-1975

* criterion being availability of data

\+ excludes private schools prior to 1976

Data compiled from: CARICOM, 1980: 117-123 (Table 41); BVI Government 1983a: 79 (Table 3.07)

Bacchus Report, 1976), the former based on 81 per cent of the BVI High School population, both confirm an aspect that BVI educators have been both aware of and uncomfortable about: namely that

> Students born off-island (non-BVI), in contrast to students born in the BVI, or to BVI parents located elsewhere at the time of birth, displayed significantly more positive attitudes toward school work. (Buys, Carlson and Hourihan, 1976: 4)

The explanations for this, although showing considerable common ground, differ in their emphasis. Buys, Carlson, and Hourihan point to the differing social and economic backgrounds of the two groups, suggesting that because there is a tendency for the immigrant community to have come from more impoverished backgrounds their motivation to improve their position through success in school is greater. They also refer to the High School Principal commenting that 'unmotivated students frequently identify with successful Tortolans who have limited formal education'. The Bacchus survey team, for its part, emphasized the doubtful value of education as perceived by some pupils. First, it made a point somewhat similar to that above: the nature of the tourist industry being as it is, individuals without much education can still quite easily obtain relatively well-paid jobs (Bacchus Report, 1976: 48). It also raised the question of belonger and non-belonger status:

> Because of the declared and commendable intention of the Government to ensure that native BVIslanders are given first preference in the selection for jobs the feeling has developed among some students that they do not have to do well educationally to be able to obtain a position. Because of the fact that they are 'belongers' by birth they have come to believe that they will be given priority in job selection irrespective of their educational qualifications.

Certainly, the attitudinal syndrome is, or was, sufficiently well known or prevalent to have engendered a colloquialism: in the form of a cynicism that an 'IBH degree' is sufficient qualification for any job (IBH being an acronym for 'I barn here'). On the other hand it is important not to lose sight of the fact that the minimal research evidence there is in connection with this particular phenomenon, actual or perceived, is now ten years old. With so much else in British Virgin Islands society changing so quickly it would perhaps be unreasonable to expect such findings to have remained static. Again, this may be an area worthy of further research.

Contemporary education, status, and manpower relationships themselves - as opposed to perceptions of them - are, however, a little more clear and in fact reveal a quite different pattern from that suggested above. From published employment statistics for 1982 (BVI Government, 1982: 4-10), it can be determined that 56.8 per cent of the workforce were 'British Virgin Islanders', the remaining 43.2 per cent being categorized as 'Other' workers. But further scrutiny also shows that within this overall picture, patterns change most markedly to the disadvantage of the 'British Virgin Islander' when the proportion of 'Other' workers occupying jobs conventionally regarded as higher status and requiring, if only for legitimization purposes, higher qualifications is compared to the proportion of 'Other' workers occupying lower-status jobs. For example, merely in comparing occupational sectors, highest 'British Virgin Islander' representation (80.3 per cent) is achieved in the sector designated 'Clerical and Related Workers', whereas lowest representation (47.7 per cent) is recorded for the arguably more prestigious sector 'Professional, Technical and Related Workers'. Within a sector, and even within a particular occupation, the common pattern is for hierarchical pyramids to further modify 'British Virgin Islander'/'Other' employee ratios to the disadvantage of the former. The composition of the Royal British Virgin Islands Police Force is illustrated in Figure 5.3 as just one example of this. A further manifestation of the phenomenon is, of course, to be found within the teaching profession itself: 68.2 per cent of primary school teachers in 1982 were 'British Virgin Islanders', but only 46.2 per cent of secondary school teachers (BVI Government, 1982a). Far from indicating that education is of doubtful value the above statistics could be interpreted as suggesting that education has an important developmental role to play.

But from this, unfortunately, far more questions are raised than are answered. Is there, for example, a *prima facie* case for extending educational provision beyond its present apex? At present the High School does not have a Sixth Form and it, like the secondary schools of many small countries, is constrained in its freedom of educational choice by the pressure it faces to turn out students with internationally marketable qualifications for further academic or professional training outside the territory (Thompson, 1977: 158). With the exception of the Hull University teacher education programmes, all that approaches anything like further or tertiary educational provision is a limited number of evening classes and a community education role played by the national library. The feasibility or desirability of establishing a community college has been a controversial issue for several years and still remains unresolved: a key question being whether on grounds of scale, it is an institution the territory can afford. Regional tertiary education initiatives have often been the recourse of small countries (Smawfield, 1986) and indeed the British Virgin Islands is, for example, a peripheral participant in the University of the West Indies. The benefits presently accruing from this relationship are however minimal. It may be that for the British Virgin Islands, contracted programmes tailored to specific needs have the potential to yield a better return for investment. This is a further reason why the outcome of the current Hull programmes is arguably of so much interest. It may of course be feasible for a community college to be an umbrella institution for such contracted educational initiatives.

Turning finally to what the implications may be for the existing educational infrastructure, much has been said about the possibilities of 'vocationalizing' the primary and secondary curricula. But such advocates would do well to examine more carefully the reasons why previous attempts to introduce vocational education have either failed or ended up serving only academic fare. This is not to decry the potential contribution of vocational education *per se*, but to share Foster's (1966) view that vocational training given in connection with real jobs-apprenticeships, in-service and on-the-job training, and such like-makes more obvious sense (especially for a small country) than providing wholesale training in skills which might never be applied.

And just as there may be lessons for vocational education, sensitivity to the different patterns that have emerged in this examination of educational provision in the Virgin Islands may also be instructive apropos of other areas of contemporary educational debate.

Figure 5.3

The Royal Virgin Islands Police Force: Nationality and Rank, 1980

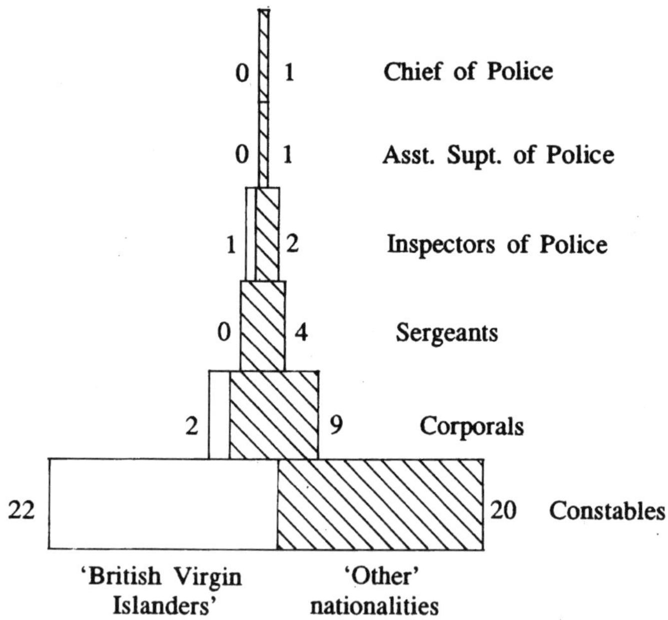

Source: BVI Government, 1983a: 127 (Table 5.07)

BIBLIOGRAPHICAL REFERENCES

Augelli, J.P.(1956) The British Virgin Islands: a West Indian anomoly, **Geographical Review** 46, 1: 43

Bacchus Report, (1976) **Report of the Survey Team on Secondary Education in the British Virgin Islands** (May 1976) (mimeograph)

Brissett, V.L.N. (1963) **British Virgin Islands: Report on Inspection Visit to the British Virgin Islands Secondary School, undertaken by Vincent L. Nathan Brissett, M.A., Principal Education Officer in the Ministry of Education, Jamaica, 28 - 31 May 1963** (mimeograph)

British Virgin Islands Government (1951) Department of Education Report

British Virgin Islands Government (1954) Department of Education Report

British Virgin Islands Government (1969) Department of Education Report

British Virgin Islands Government (1974) Department of Education Report

British Virgin Islands Government (1977) Department of Education Report

British Virgin Islands Government (1978) Department of Education Report

British Virgin Islands Government (1979) Draft: **British Virgin Islands Development Programme 1979-1982**

British Virgin Islands Government (1981) Department of Education Report

British Virgin Islands Government (1982a) **Employment in the**

British Virgin Islands, 1982, Table 4, Employment by occupation, nationality and sex, (Road Town, Statistical Division)

British Virgin Islands Government (1982b) Department of Education Report

British Virgin Islands Government (1983a) **Statistical Abstract of the British Virgin Islands 1980**, 2: 1

British Virgin Islands Government (1983b) Department of Education Report

British Virgin Islands Government (1984) Department of Education Report

British Virgin Islands Government (1984) **Census of the British Virgin Islands, 12th May, 1980, Provisional** (Road Town, Statistics Division)

Brock, C. (1982) The legacy of colonialism in West Indian education, in Watson, K. (ed.) **Education in the Third World**, (London, Croom Helm)

Buys, C., Carlson, P., and Hourihan, J. (1976) **Secondary Students Attitudes towards Education in the British Virgin Islands** (mimeograph)

The BVI Beacon, 18 September 1986

The BVI Beacon 2, 51: 7, Thursday, 25 September 1986, Advertisement: Vote for Patsy Lake of the Virgin Islands Party: candidate for the Fifth District

CARICOM **1980-1981 Population Census of the Commonwealth Caribbean: British Virgin Islands** 1: 56 (Jamaica, CARICOM)

Christopher, A. (1974) **Education in the British Virgin Islands**, (British Virgin Islands Government) p.1 (mimeograph)

Colonial Office (1939) Education in the Windward and Leeward Islands: Report of the Education Commissioners, 1938 164: 12 (Hammond Report)

De Block, L. (1984) Lessons from Grenada, in Mebrahtu, T. (ed.) **Learning from the South: what, why and how?** (Bristol, Bristol Classical Press)

Dodsworth, T. (1985) Financial Times Survey: British Virgin Islands, **Financial Times**, Monday 29 April

Dookhan, I. (1975) **A History of the British Virgin Islands: 1672-1970**, (Epping, Caribbean Universities Press in association with Bowker Publishing)

Foster, P.J. (1966) The vocational school fallacy in development planning, in Anderson, C. Arnold and Bowman, Mary Jean (eds) **Education and Economic Development** (Frank Cass)

Gordon, Shirley C. (Comp) (1963) **A Century of West Indian Education: a source book** (London, Longman)

Harrigan, N. E. A. (1963) Comments made by N.E.A. Harrigan on Mr R.S. Jordan's report (mimeograph)

Harrigan, N. and Varlack, P. (1975) **The Virgin Islands Story** (Epping, Caribbean Universities Press in association with Bowker Publishing), p.1

The Island Sun, 2014, Saturday, 7 June 1986, Minister of Education discusses appointment of new principal: speech by Minister of Education Hon. Wheatley Re: Principal BVI High School on 3 June 1986 on ZBVI

The Island Sun, 2116(A) Saturday, 6 September 1986, Radio broadcast on ZBVI, by Hon. Cyril B. Romney (1 September)

Leeward Islands Colony: Report on the Education Departments for the Year 1953, Part IV: Presidency of the Virgin Islands (Leeward Islands Colony): Report on the Education Department for the year 1953 (Antigua, Government Printer)

Leeward Islands Colony: Annual Education Report for the Year 1954, Part IV: Presidency of the Virgin Islands, British Virgin Islands Education Report 1954 (Antigua, Government Printer), p.3. In the researching of this chapter all other Education Annual Reports examined were consulted in their original typed and mimeographed format: that is to say, not as comprising of part of a Leeward Islands volume or as part of a general report on the territory. Since some of these reports were also reproduced in this alternative form page references may not always correspond. The character of the reports produced in recent years is such that they may reasonably be regarded as full publications in their own right. The reports are produced by the Department of Education and Culture, Road Town. All subsequent references to these documents will be given in abbreviated form: e.g. **Report of the Department of Education for the Calendar Year 1954**

Rhymer (23.9.86) Telephone interview with Winston Rhymer, Principal, Bregado Flax Educational Centre

Reid, L.H.E. (1963) Selection for secondary schooling: British Virgin Islands, Appendix to Brissett, V.L.N. op.cit.

Report of the Virgin Islands Secondary School for the Year Ending 31 December 1963

Smawfield, D. (1985) **An Examination of the Provision of Educational Materials in Small Developing Countries**, unpublished M.Ed. dissertation, Hull University

Smawfield, D. (1986) Form, style and extent of university provision as affecting small countries: a typology, in Smawfield, D. (ed.) **International Academic Interchange and Cooperation in Higher Education**, Proceedings of the 10th Annual Conference of the British Comparative and International Education Society, held at Ferens Hall, the University of Hull, 13-15 September 1985 (Hull, BCIES)

Thompson, A.R. (1977) How far free? International networks of constraint upon national education policy in the Third World, **Comparative Education**, 13: 158

Wheatley (16.9.86) Interview with Charles Wheatley, Chief Education Officer (Mr Wheatley became Permanent Secretary for Health, Education and Welfare in October 1987)

Chapter Six

THE POLITICS OF ADULT EDUCATION IN CENTRAL AMERICA: 1950-1980

Gonzalo Retamal

Central America is perhaps at present the most convulsive region of the Western Hemisphere. The education of adults in a society where illiterate and semi-illiterate peasants and urban dwellers constitute the majority of the population can be perceived as a tool for the battle of the minds of these majorities; for social and political awareness; or for social and political domination. Any significant analysis of adult education in a polarized society must be cognisant of its political framework, the activity being by its very nature an integral aspect of politics. Furthermore, the present situation of Central American adult education and education in general can only be understood within a framework of historical and social evolution.

ADULT EDUCATION IN CENTRAL AMERICA: THE FORMATIVE YEARS

The Central American republics share a common pattern of historical development which makes possible a common analysis. Although differences exist in the evolution of each separate country, such differentiation, according to Torres Rivas, is related to the degree of social heterogeneity observed in each country:

> The existent social heterogeneity generates a major concentration of power in proportion to

> the evident cultural-economic imbalance. This proposition, only useful for a formal analysis, helps to explain the differences among the existent forms of oligarchic power; i.e. between Guatemala (maximum heterogeneity) and Costa Rica (minimum heterogeneity), thus positioned in dissimilar situations. (Torres Rivas, 1963: 73)

The situation in Guatemala, El Salvador, Honduras and Nicaragua evolved during the present century into a variable pattern of society dominated by institutionalized terrorism, backed by US intervention. Costa Rica, however, consolidated a democratic state with a powerful but extended elite, able to bargain its own space for political national development with the fruit companies, and thus with the US policy of direct intervention. This led to a process of gradual modernization of the state apparatus and the consolidation of structures of legitimization of political power, among others, and with considerable success, a proper education system. The Liberal governments of Tomas Guardia in 1871 and Bernardo Soto in 1885 gave to Costa Rica the institutional basis of a system of education unique in Central America. A network of elementary schools was laid down with enthusiasm, and between 1870 and 1892 the illiteracy rate declined from 89 per cent to 68 per cent. By the third decade of this century, the illiteracy rate was one of the lowest in Latin America at 23.6 per cent in 1927 (Wilson, 1942: 87).

By 1937, with a population of 500,000 inhabitants, Costa Rica had a net enrolment of 73 per cent of the children between 7 and 14, that is to say 12.3 per cent of the total population was registered in the primary school system. By 1942 the Ministry of Education was at the stage of modernizing the structure of services at the rural level, where accessibility was still difficult. Peripatetic units were developed in those areas where the low density of the population and the distances made the provision of school buildings impossible:

> In such cases the teacher takes up his residence in the home of the better situated neighbours and assembles there, not only children, but also adults who may desire to attend the teaching of

> reading, writing and the elements of arithmetic. After three or four months the teacher moves to another place and in this way makes an annual rotation.(Brenes Mesen, 1942: 136-137)

Other mechanisms for tackling the problems of adult education had been developed at the time. According to a former Minister of Education, Brenes, such provision was not considered a central element in the overall system:

> As a result, perhaps, of the strictness with which the attendance of children in primary school is enforced, there has been no urgent need to organize a vast system of schools for adults. The few such schools that exist are found in the capital. The most important is the *Escuela Popular de Adultos* with a programme adapted to the demands of the adults who attend and who, as is natural, desire to fill the gaps which they discover in carrying on their trades and other occupations. (Brenes Mesen, 1942: 46)

Also a school for adults interested in learning English had opened by that time in the capital, San Jose.

Moreover, under the influence of populist leader Jose Figueres education received a new thrust, and important developments were produced between 1947 and 1950. Considerable importance was attached to the adult education provision and twenty-two schools were opened for the purpose of teaching illiterates. Also, an evening course for adults in each school of the Republic was proposed (Unesco, 1942: 125). A very important measure was the dissolution of the Army, and much of the defence budget was transferred to education. This fact gave more strength to the overall educational system and set itself as an unprecedented example to the rest of the Latin American governments, especially the dictatorships of Central America.

In the rest of Central America, political evolution had followed diverse paths. The so-called 'Liberal Republic' of the last decades of the nineteenth century was an attempt to achieve social and political stability. Especially in those countries where the coffee export entrepreneurs needed such stability, some 'enlightened' measures were taken by military or civil dictatorships. Some important achievements were observed for example under the liberal dictatorship of Barrios in Guatemala and similar developments were undertaken in El Salvador. However, Nicaragua and Honduras were very early affected by external attempts of economic and political imperialism, and thus the possibility for early internal agreement between the diverse groups of the dominant elite was not possible (Torres Rivas, 1969: 57). Furthermore, a process of political intervention, with the exception of Costa Rica, in the Central American republics began to develop. At the turn of the century, the US considered Central America as its 'backyard' and in pursuit of its 'manifest destiny' disrupted the internal political and economic affairs of Central American society:

> Colony and protectorate differed, after all, only in degree. In either case local assistance had to be made use of; in one case foreign troops would be there all the time, in the other they would be ready round the corner. Most of the time the U.S. could keep itself out of sight, there were established regimes in Central America for it to work through.... It was in the most corrupt sections of the higher social layers that America had to look for associates. The outcome was that American business interests flourished while America at large was divided between impatience at these countries not making up and making progress, and alarm whenever they showed signs of wanting to do so after their own bent. (Kiernan, 1978: 126-127)

The social cost of this association was very high. By the early twentieth century it was evident that the dominant elite had turned over control of their countries in large measure to US interests and in the case of Nicaragua even to US armed forces. From active partners they had become a dependent bourgeoisie whose role was to keep peace and stability for the foreign US investor. The shift from the coffee bourgeoisie to the ignominious role of 'Banana Republics' had been achieved.

If liberals brought forward the idea of education as a means for the social regeneration of the nation, the new *dictadores* imposed by the fruit companies and the State Department, feared that possibility as a source of subversion. The effect of this situation in the educational sphere of the Central American societies was devastating. By 1900 only 2.7 per cent of the population was enrolled in the primary sector (Hans, 1937: 535). Nicaragua devoted only 7 per cent of the national budget to public instruction at that time, while Guatemala, where attempts to acculturate the Indian majority were carried through in a forceful manner in the form of the short-lived experience of *Escuelas de Castellanizacion* which was to introduce Spanish in the Mayan-speaking community, was only marginally better at 13 per cent (Hans, 1937).

In Honduras the torch of liberal education burned dimly during this period, and by 1926 the illiterate population was a massive 73.9 per cent. Some efforts were developed by 1927 when special budgeting was considered for the purpose of undertaking adult literacy teaching at primary schools. In 1935 it was reported that the Department of Public Instruction had

> launched a valiant effort to overcome illiteracy by the use of special night schools, itinerant teachers for remote communities which are not yet possessed of schools and by organizing trade schools for adults. (Wilson, 1942: 66)

However, these important efforts were wiped out under the US-sponsored dictatorships of Tiburcio Carias (1938-1948) and the literacy rate was kept stagnant during that period. Some efforts were made under the sponsorship of the Pan American Union between 1945 and 1948 in order to promote a 'Campaign Against Illiteracy'. It was claimed that 46,000 adults had become literate. However, the overall situation did not change given the rapid rate of population growth.

Under the dictatorship of the Somoza family in Nicaragua, no special developments were produced in the educational sphere. Between 1937 and 1941, 30 per cent of the children of school age were enrolled in primary education. However, the rate of drop-outs remained very high. Also a network of 98 evening schools was devoted to a programme for adults, without following any kind of plan or even ministerial guideline.

By 1942, former Minister of Education Edelberto Torres complained:

> Public instruction is no longer marked by the trend toward reform in accordance with the movements in modern education... the Ministry of Public Instruction, in order to comply with the demands of the reactionary elements which are all power in Nicaragua, has repealed the laws, regulations, curriculum and courses of study. (Torres, 1942: 304)

To a great extent, this situation reflected the consequences of US occupation and the prolonged war against nationalist guerrilla leader Sandino. The situation of repression and arbitrary dictatorship continued after the withdrawal of the US Marines in 1933, following the assassination of Sandino. The only basis of 'modernization' left by US intervention was an effective system of repression and torture, the US-trained *Guardia Nacional*, whose chief officer, Anastasio Somoza, reigned with full powers over the country. According to Beals:

> Actually no basis had been laid. No schools had been erected, few promised roads had been built, health measures had not gone far beyond areas held by US troops; the people were illiterate, unemployed, strained. (Beals, 1974: 118)

It was only after the assassination of Anastasio Somoza in 1957 that some changes were produced in the field of rural and adult education, namely under the Pan American Union sponsorship, but only within the limits of experimental actions (Garcia, 1957: 78-84).

The situation in El Salvador was similar. Education was promoted basically at the post-primary level. Coffee planters were not at all interested in developing elementary schooling among the peasants. However, an efficient army was developed in order to keep peasants under conditions of subjugation, a mass of temporary workers needed for the coffee crop. The effects of dictatorship upon the educational structure were candidly expressed by a former professor of the San Salvador Normal School in 1940:

> The school has been carried on under conditions of hardship and restrictions imposed on it by the forces mentioned, the Church, those in power and the wealthy classes. Its influence has frequently been obliterated, diminished or changed by the interests and tendencies of these influential forces.... They need cheap labour and that becomes more scarce to the degree that workers become educated and look for higher standards of living. The well-to-do classes promote the formation of a cultured elite to serve their interests and to exercise the guardianship over the popular elements whose cultural level has to be kept low so that the cost of labour shall remain cheap. (Moran, 1942: 198-199)

Since 1929 some urban-based night schools were erratically provided, and ten years later it was still estimated that the illiterate population was more than 55 per cent. According to the Census of 1950, the situation had worsened to give an illiteracy figure of 60.5 per cent (OAS, 1963: 19).

In Guatemala, adult education was developed in the late years of the nineteenth century and some night schools were provided. However, the illusions of the so called 'liberal revolution' were unrealized. Certainly so far as indicated by the financial support given to the educational system, the claims of the *Senor Presidente* that he was a staunch friend of education were gross overstatements (Jones, 1966: 334). In 1893 the population showed an illiteracy rate of 88.63 per cent which by 1921 had only fallen to 86.82 per cent.

After a short interregnum of political factionalism which followed the end of the Estrada dictatorship, the United Fruit

Company managed to stage the accession to power of Jorge Ubic (1931-1944). This so-called 'petit Napoleon' helped to produce by 1944 a catastrophic situation where 'schools were few, teachers were not prepared and their salaries were low' (Dowbrowski *et al.*, 1970: 191).

Deprived of the unconditional backing of the US because of its pro-Nazi leanings, under the Good Neighbour policy, Ubico was swept from his dominant position in 1944. A leftist-centre revolution, led by young military and middle-sector intellectuals, put the first democratically elected President, Juan Jose Arevalo, at the head of a movement towards social, political, and educational transformation. After 1945, strenuous attempts were made to eradicate illiteracy and to institute free primary education for all children. Between 1944 and 1957 enrolment in daytime primary schools doubled (Dowbrowski, *et al.*, 1970).

The second presidency of Arbentz defined a clear programme of action where education was supposed to play a big role in the transformation of Guatemala.

> To convert Guatemala from a dependent nation with a semi-colonial economy to an economically independent country; second to transform our nation with a predominantly feudal economy to a modern capitalist country; and third to accomplish this transformation in a manner that brings the greatest possible elevation of the living standard of the great masses of the people. (Quoted by Jones, 1966: 156)

Arevalo, himself an educator, assumed his presidency as a task of 'educational redemption' in a typical populist liberal style. Educational reform was central to the revolution and aimed to provide a sense of nationalist pride and dignity. However, the acute problem of an Indian majority population and its possible integration into the political process remained untackled for a very long period. Differing from the Indian majority of the Andes, the Guatemalan Indians represent an heterogeneous variety of cultures and languages, classifiable into three 'families': Quiche, Mayas, and Araguace.

Mostly orientated to the needs of the *ladinos* ('westernized' Indians and mestizo-peasants) the First National Committee for Literacy was created in 1944, and in the next year a law was passed to promote and fund a national Literacy Campaign. The problem of illiteracy was even considered in one of the articles of the new Constitution.

Between 1945 and 1950, 98,000 adults were made literate. Cultural Missions were established and Peripatetic Units for a post-literacy programme were developed. Perhaps one of the first of this nature in Latin America, the mobile units were provided with audio-visual systems, adequate literature and highly trained personnel. The Department of Literacy at the Ministry of Education became a model of organization and educational management with the collaboration of Central American and Latin American educators. A widely distributed magazine called *El Nuevo Lector* (The New Reader) served as a means of communication with the grassroots and a support to the post- literacy work preventing a slip backward in the achievements of the Literacy Campaign. Co-ordination was developed with the Agricultural Ministry in order to integrate the newly literate *campesinos* into the project of Agrarian Reform of the government. Various rural literacy centres were transformed into rural schools (OAS, 1963: 33).

It was only late in 1949 that some serious attempts were launched to tackle the problem of Indian education. A 'pre-training' rural school was established at Santa Maria Cauque, a small village near the Guatemalan capital, with twofold purpose: to teach the children of the Indian peasant population according to their values and with a respectful sense towards their culture; also, to train the teachers who intended to remain in rural schools. Active methods were largely introduced. In cooperation with the Ministry of Agriculture, some land was provided to teach students and teachers by doing actual agricultural work and learning stock-breeding techniques. Spanish and the children's vernacular languages were studied and spoken at the school. Bilingual systems for the teaching of adult literacy were also developed at that stage (IBE, 1949: 159).

Development and nationalism were the key factors in the Guatemalan educational ideology. However, this possibility of autonomous development was to be crushed by the anti-communist lobby of the Truman and Eisenhower administrations in the USA. A CIA-organized coup d'etat, and a well-provided mercenary invasion, led by Colonel Castillo Armas, brought down the democratic government in the name of anti-communism.

The end of the Guatemalan experience marked the end of an era, where education was proposed and sought as a major element for the building of a democratic society. The liberal illusions of capitalist autonomous development, proposed by the populist government of Guatemala, were not plausible after the end of the 'Good Neighbour honeymoon'.

The educational structure laid down during this 'decade of dignity' was wiped out under the helpful assistance of the Point Four educational missions. Adult education became ostensibly under the control of the military (UNESCO, 1964: 66) and US teachers were sent in to teach Guatemalans the values of the 'American way of life'.

ADULT EDUCATION IN CENTRAL AMERICA: 1950-1980

Perhaps the central feature in the process of development observed in this area since the 1950s is the collective attempt of Costa Rica, Honduras, Nicaragua, El Salvador, and Guatemala to establish basic norms for economic, military, and cultural integration. These attempts have been initiated by the national rural entrepreneurs, such as coffee growers, and by commercial, financial, and industrial interests of a transnational character operating in the area, and mostly related to agro-business.

According to Torres-Rivas, there have been strings attached to this process of integration:

> One of the most important conditions in the social order is the maintenance, at the expense of peasant masses, of the old agrarian structure, whose modification, according to the critics of the system, is a *sine qua non* condition for actual development. In other words, if development is considered as industrialization *a outrance*, such a situation must be achieved

> with the warrant of immobility of the agrarian structure. (Torres Rivas, 1969: 175)

During the Alliance for Progress years some careful and well-planned attempts were made to reorientate and modernize agrarian production. However, repression and nearly forced labour conditions imposed upon a very unstable peasant population constituted the background to the social and political transformation in most countries concerned. The modernization of the bureaucracy, the consolidation of professional armies, plus the modernization of the educational structure, especially higher education, have been encouraged via external debt and the total control of the United States.

The impact of modernization has generated the concentration of land in Honduras, where large-scale property did not exist; and has contributed via technological input to worsen the social conditions of a rural working force of a temporary and migrant character in the other countries. The importance of industrial urban development is meaningless as it is not able to absorb rural-urban migration. In fact, perhaps with the exception of El Salvador, most of the marginal workforce, instead of concentrating in urban shanty-towns, constitutes a large itinerant workforce migrating beyond the political boundaries of the Central American countries.

This situation has produced confrontations among these governments, such as the so called 'Football War' between Honduras and El Salvador in 1969. Moreover, Central America concentrates some of the most distressing social conditions in the world. The extreme concentration of wealth together with political dependency on the USA helps to generate an explosive political and social picture, expressed at present in El Salvador and Guatemala and in the revolutionary movement of the peasant-leftist *Sandinista* coalition of Nicaragua.

Most of the decision-making in the area has been orientated and defined by the US agencies with a conspicuous and undisguised 'back-yard' style, which reaches every level of national affairs. Even in cases like Costa Rica, where democracy apparently is at work and some bargaining space still exists for the state to maintain some political independence, the situation is not really very different (Denton, 1979).

In the rest of the countries where the state apparatuses are less homogeneous and participative, such influence is 'direct' and does not need any lobby at all to impose the US outlook. Such 'aid' initiatives have been mostly related to the conformation and development of CONDECA (The Central American Defence Organization), a step towards 'integrative action' against 'subversion'. ROCAP, the USAID educational office for Central America and Panama, has been behind most of the decisions made at every level of educational reform, especially the developments in the sectors of post-primary schooling (Ramfrez, 1969).

Some criticisms have emerged from important Central American educators against this process of ideological and cultural invasion. The case of a programme for the production of standardized school texts for all Central American countries has been criticized as an attempt to reproduce an external and alienating view of the world in the minds of Central American children and adults (Aguero *et al.*, 1966). The Peace Corps and non-governmental Christian agencies have received special treatment, such as tax exemptions and special transport facilities, to develop their educational action among *campesinos*. These efforts for cultural penetration are developed within an atmosphere of political and social revolution or wherever the education structure remains stagnant and profoundly uneven, inequitable and disparate.

. . . .

A description of adult education provision in Central America needs therefore to be considered within this framework, a profoundly polarized society in search of its own political destiny as a means for national self-reliance and integration. A case where adult and popular education has been used for oppression and military control (Guatemala, El Salvador, Honduras), directed to the reproduction of liberal democracy (Costa Rica) and lately organized towards revolutionary change (Nicaragua). A wide range of experiences obtains which needs to be analysed in detail, country by country. As a further background, the table below illustrates the very low level of the workforce of Central America in 1970 in respect of its educational profile.

Table 6.1

Educational Level of the Workforce in Central America (%) 1970

Country	University	Secondary	Primary	None or incomplete primary
Costa Rica	1.4	4.9	22.4	71.3
Nicaragua	0.4	2.7	7.2	89.7
Honduras	0.5	2.2	5.6	91.7
El Salvador	0.3	2.1	11.3	86.3
Guatemala	0.6	1.4	7.2	90.8
TOTAL	0.6	2.2	9.8	

Source: ICECU, 1970

COSTA RICA

For many educators and intellectuals of other countries of the area, Costa Rica has been historically perceived as the cultural and educational *respiradero* (breath of fresh air) within the noxious environment of neo-colonial domination. Costa Rica is still in Central America the only country with a long record of democratic liberal tradition, the origins and evolution of which have been discussed above.

However, since the 1950s an elitist political and social strata has dominated the decision-making structure of the state. According to Arias, no changes in the composition of the elite are perceived in regard to social stratum, education attainment or rural and urban origin. Also there is little upward vertical mobility among office-holders. That is to say, the way to the top is to be born at or near the top. Emergent middle-class individuals are not able to work their way up through the dominant parties or through local political office into ministerial positions. In this particular democratic society, education has been a more effective force than in other Latin American democracies. It has played a legitimizing role for the elite and has helped to reproduce the image of participative democracy even among the lower strata of the population. The nearly generalized pride of Costa Ricans in their democratic institutions is to a considerable extent the outcome of a process of massive educational policy. This is, of course, relative to the region and although the retention rate after the first primary school level remains 71 per cent, at the end of the sixth grade is reduced to about 45 per cent (Arias, 1976; Waggoner *et al.*, 1971: 115).

The figures in Table 6.1 are relevant in that they show a comparative view of the sound performance of the Costa Rican system compared to the rest of the area. It is interesting to note that Costa Rica, with 8 per cent of the working population having achieved primary instruction, sets up an impressive record as compared with the average of 9.8 per cent for the Central American region as a whole. However, the inefficiency of the system (mostly because of drop-out and repetition) becomes very clear if one considers the fact that about 71.3 per cent of the adult population has in fact incomplete primary or no educational attainment whatsoever.

Changes in the pattern of land distribution and tenure, and the impact or early health improvements with the consequent population growth, have been accounted among some of the important factors working against the well-devised and rather modern educational provision of Costa Rica (Seligson, 1977: 224). With an illiteracy rate of 10.2 per cent (one of the lowest in Latin America), Costa Rica is mostly confronting the problems of quality rather than those of quantity and enrolment of human resources. According to Waggoner and others the low retention rate of the primary system should be held responsible for the reproduction of adult functional illiteracy (Waggoner *et al.*, 1971: 118).

Costa Rica has attempted to tackle the problem of training through the creation in 1965 of INA (National Apprenticeship

Institute), following the SENAI-ILO pattern. With a variable drop-out rate (26.5 to 7.75 per cent according to the kind and the time of the training tuition), the system has proved to be adequate (Rock, 1970: 29). INA provides for the training needs of a wide variety of clients from the fields of mining, industry, commerce, agriculture and cattle production, plus the state employees and officials. In this sense INA has a concentrated function, rather different from Brazil and other countries where emphasis is given to the creation of separate institutions at different levels. Moreover, this training facility covers a very small section of the total national need, in fact about 1,500 trainees yearly. By 1978 this contribution fell far from the real needs of the workforce, which grew at a rate of 3.3 per cent. In 1975 the four regional centres of INA were able to ensure the training of about 18,000 trainees; that is to say, about 20 per cent of the need (Lizano-Fait, 1981: 361-374).

Under the expertise of UNESCO official de Pienne (1974: 85-90), the Adult Education Department of the Ministry of Education was reoriented in 1970. The policy developed in Costa Rica was somehow considered as a model to be followed in the rest of Central America. As reported by de Pienne in 1972, the overall project, and especially the basic adult provision, had to consider the development of a special scheme for the training of tutors.

Similar aims to those experimented with in the Venezuelan case were attached to the Costa Rican project, that is to say, a *parasistema* of an essentially remedial character. According to the Costa Rican Minister of Education:

> We need these *para systems* to reach the students who have dropped out of the regular systems to help them on the job, to improve their economic status and train the individual to incorporate himself into the normal educational system at any time he wishes. (Quoted by Campion, 1972: 163)

Within the general provision, a salient feature is the special and unique scheme for the education of adult tutors developed in a co-ordinated effort with the Open University of Costa Rica, one of the few experimental structures of this nature produced in

Latin America. The Costa Rican *parasistema* has been developed along the pre-existent network of twenty-six night schools; two of them of a rural character. Other private organizations have collaborated in this effort, especially at the basic level. Special mention should be made of the Costa Rican Institute of Radiophonic Education (ICER) which has assumed an important role in the less-accessible regions of the country (ICER, 1976: 1-23). The influence of the Christian Protestant agency ALFALIT also seems to have been of decisive importance in the development of methodological and curricular aspects at the first levels of elementary adult education (Campion, op. cit: 104-5).

Notwithstanding these initiatives, adult education provision still faces a very important challenge. According to the Census data, the adult population without any schooling experience constitutes nearly 120,000 individuals, that is to say about 12 per cent of the total adult population of Costa Rica. It should be also noticed that there are more than 500,000 adults with incomplete elementary education. The contribution of INA and *parasistema* together cannot match up to this target. Moreover, it has been recently observed that a profound gap between aims and actual commitment exists in these Costa Rican projects (Sandi *et al.*, 1984: 233-235). In an evaluation of the ministerial provision, Campion has clearly identified and underlined this sort of problem:

> Costa Ricans are sincere and want the most but rather than build slowly upon a step-by-step successful programme, the tendency was to make it big, all inclusive, and facts were doomed to failure. The educational objectives were idealistic and not within the realm of realistic achievement. (Campion, 1972: 165)

HONDURAS

Honduras, with nearly three million inhabitants, shares the lowest record of underdevelopment in Latin America with Haiti and Bolivia, as 80 per cent of the population shares only 27 per cent of the national income, which is in any case one of the lowest in per capita figures in Latin America (*c.* US $540).

The population is mostly concentrated in the rural areas where the pattern of subsistence economy dominates the landscape, while the best land is concentrated in the hands of the US fruit companies on the Atlantic Coast, and of the big cattle-breeders of Choluteca in the south-western region of the country. This picture of poverty is compounded if one considers some of the effects. For example, more than 75 per cent of the children under five years of age suffer from different levels of malnutrition. Illiteracy in the rural areas has remained in the range of 80 to 90 per cent throughout the present century.

Attempts to produce change are normally confronted with the dominated and dependent character of the nation. In this sense, the fruit companies and their economic interests have shaped the existent political situation and established the mechanisms that prevent any transformation, such as agrarian reform, which might affect their interests. The enclave economy shades every act of government:

> The structural dependence in Honduras, leads to a situation in which the US Embassy in Tegucigalpa becomes one of the major participants in the domestic political process. (Morris and Ropp, 1977: 33)

The intervention and blocking of the mild reform attempts of the 1970s have generated a situation of increasing conservatism and economic immobility. However, the path to a civil liberal-rightist government, under controlled elections, has been explained by the US ambasssdor in Tegucigalpa as 'a victory for civic responsibility in a region plunged into the agony of revolution' (Posas, 1980: 45).

In this context the adult education work of the state has been under control. The Peace Corps actions on non- formal education at rural areas during the 1960s set down a series of patterns, for *campesino* leadership recruitment and youth formation, especially through 4-F clubs. Experience in the field in 1974 showed that this agency had left profound ideological traces of 'anti-communist' propaganda among illiterate peasants, to whom tyranny was symbolized by personalities like Fidel Castro, but hardly by their own military oppressors. However, it seems important to underline that in the urban areas a rather more nationalistic and socially orientated view towards the Honduran problems has been developed, especially in relation to governmental agencies and the US-dominated banana enclave (Retamal, 1974: 2-3). The extension work of National Institute of Agriculture should also be considered. However, its action has been mostly confined to the few *asentamientos* (co-operatives) created by the erratic agrarian reform programme of the government.

The other governmental agency for adult education is the General Directory of Literacy and Adult Education, which concentrated until recent years on basic and secondary provision at urban level, using the same methodologies and textbooks created during the 1960s under the sponsorship of the Pan American Union. Although later in the 1970s the idea of *parasistema* was introduced, it seems that provision has not radically changed its urban orientation.

During the 1970s important measures were taken in the area of literacy, with positive results. Chain's (1974: 104-117) evaluation shows a good performance. Nonetheless, this literacy programme was abandoned by the new democratic administration of Suazo Cordoba, and a literacy campaign based on materials with an impositive ideological meaning was launched after 1983. This approach utilized generative words for the literacy lessons like *soldado* (soldier), this underlining the importance of national security and other chauvinistic themes. In 1982 the Ministry of Education itself stated:

> In the last literacy campaign developed during 1980 the net enrolment was 382,710 illiterate adults of whom 86,733 were declared literate. However, given the lack of proper follow-up these have not reached an acceptable literacy standard. (Ministerio de Educacion Publica, Republica de Honduras, 1982: 35)

Probably the most important contribution to the process of literacy work in Honduras has been developed by organizations related to the Catholic Church. For example, the work developed by Church-sponsored *Accion Cultural Popular Honduna*, through its *Radio Suyapa*, has been of the utmost importance in the fight against illiteracy in that country. The goals proposed by this organization have progressed beyond an isolated and purely educational action into an explicit commitment to develop 'generative themes' in a dialogic relation between co-ordinators of radio schools at inter-personal level. Some general themes or subjects have been developed along these lines from 1968, when the experience began, up to the present day. The achievements, at the same time, have been very high; it has been demonstrated that peasants are able in many cases to read and write and use at least two arithmetic operations in a period of four to five months with twenty minutes of daily work. Although the functional structure of these particular radio schools is not different from other Latin American patterns (training centres, newspaper production and pedagogical materials), the general objectives proposed are explicitly orientated towards a larger participation and change. Specific aims for discussion each month and the peasants' cultural involvement have been outlined as follows:

Month 1 - The peasant must be considered as a person, an active element of change, a member of a family and of a community.

Month 2 - The family has a nucleus of activity; obligations of each member of the welfare of the family; family relations and contributions of the family to the community.

Month 3 - The community as a force of social integration; problems of community development; community action; the peasant as a militant member of community organizations.

Month 4 - The peasant and the Honduran reality; the peasant as a promoter of change and as a basic element of the national economy; contributions of the peasant to the cultural life of the community and of the community of Central America. (CONCORDE, 1974: 1-5)

On the basis of these open 'generative themes' the skills in the 3 R's are developed under the guidance of Freire's psycho-social method. In this sense, generative words are existentially attached to the generative themes, which peasants, by participating in the election and determination of such themes, had already defined as part of their everyday life. Though personal field experience in 1974 and 1983 suggested certain variations on the dialogic intention of coordinators of cultural circles (some were trying to impose religious subjects which are not important for the peasants; others would enforce discussions of general importance, such as problems of national politics, in the very early stages of conscientization), most of them were effectively dedicated to teaching and learning with the peasants at the same time. Thus they were turning the whole project into a decisive tool for the mobilization and conscientization of the peasant community of Honduras.

Perhaps the higher standards performed by *Radio Suyapa* (White, 1972) during the 1970s were due to the character of the wider co-ordinating agency *CONCORDE* (Council of Co-ordination for Development), which at the same time was able to co-ordinate and integrate the process of trade union organization and co-operative training with the radio schools' effort.

The most important of these links is that formed between Radio Suyapa and UNC (National Peasants Union), which defines itself as an organization whose principal goal is the construction of a workers' society along the lines of a social-Christian philosophy. It was an ex-radio school co-ordinator who led UNC to its present cell organization operating in rural highly organized co-operatives upon a self-reliant economic and social basis and along the effort of communitarian work. At the same time, *CONCORDE* operated *Centros de Capacitacion* (Training Centres) where training was given to peasants involved in educational and co-operative activities.

The effort of *CONCORDE* was difficult to separate from that of the Catholic Church of Honduras. Moreover, it might be said that this religious institution provided a sort of protective umbrella over the radical social action performed by *Radio Suyapa* and UNC, which finally was destroyed, dismantled and banned by military action in 1980. Although the first attempts of *CONCORDE* were outlined in very simple and even moderate terms around the idea of forming a coalition between urban technical and professional sectors and the lower *campesino* strata of Honduras, the whole project had evolved in its practice into a powerful organization for social change. La Belle defined *CONCORDE* of Honduras as one of the more integrated strategies of education for liberation in Latin America, while at the same time he praised its co-ordinating capacity and ideological coherence:

> Initiated in 1971, the projects of CONCORDE are normally directed to the small semi-subsistence farmer and are designed to provide a range of educational and technical services. Goals include increasing the participation of marginal populations in local, regional and eventually national decision-making processes, stimulating co-operative peasant organizations and collective decision-making, and encouraging an independent peasant destiny which provides an alternative to the consumer-orientated and U.S. dominated capitalist system. In effect, CONCORDE seeks to break the bonds of dependency and move toward a participatory social system in which liberation and collective production, consumption, and decision-making are mutually supportive and pre-dominant. (La Belle, 1976: 344)

At the time of writing, Radio Suyapa is surviving within the limits of military and political control exerted by the government of President Suazo Cordoba on all forms of nationalist or humanistic opposition to direct North American military presence in the country and any radical form of peasant organization. Nonetheless, its educational experience remains as one of the most interesting adult education schemes for illiterate peasants in Central America.

EL SALVADOR

A general descriptive framework of El Salvador can only match the economic and social underdevelopment of the Honduran case in its profound inhumanity and inequality.

Perhaps its more industrialized economy, its high population density, and a worse record on wealth concentration explains some differences. Culturally the differences are few; politically the Salvadorean civilian and military elite has proved to be more tough and inhuman. The violation of human rights has become a common and everyday pattern of life, directly attached to the machinery mounted by the US to fight against 'communism'. A hackneyed justification, which in the particular case of El Salvador is no more than an over-simplification used to denote an ample national opposition sector which:

> springs from popular organizations which date back to the last century. It unites peasants, trade unionists, priests, teachers, students, businessmen, Christian Democrats, social democrats, socialists, communists and Jesuits. It includes groups such as the Union of Slum Dwellers and the Christian Peasants' Association. (Pilger, 1981: 11)

At present the state of El Salvador is not basically interested in the development of education. The central function of the Salvadorean state is military and repressive, as denounced by the sacked US ambassador Robert White in the Senate of the USA:

> The chief killers of El Salvadoreans are the government security forces. They are the ones responsible for the deaths of thousands upon thousands of young people who have been executed merely on the suspicion that they are leftists. Are we really going to be part of all that? (Pilger, 1981: 11)

The United States has been and continues to be profoundly engaged in the process of political intervention.

USAID has played, as in the rest of the area, a central role in the process of educational reform launched in 1968. The modernization of the secondary and university subsystems was emphasized, while primary and literacy education were neglected. Still by 1978, the government was able to state that 'education is the correct means for social transformation and national development' (Fuenzalida, 1978: 775). However, CONAPLAN, the national planning agency, showed impressive deficits in the educational sphere: the general illiteracy rate was recognized as 55 per cent. Only 38.5 per cent of the children in rural areas were enrolled in the schools as against 61.5 per cent in the urban areas. Of those enrolled, only 26 per cent were able to reach sixth grade. The post-primary facility showed a growth of 75 per cent and 'no serious problems of desertion were observed in the secondary school' (Fuenzalida, 1978).

Educational decisions did not consider the problem of primary education as a central issue. Moreover, the unequal distribution of educational resources was reinforced when USAID experts pushed forward the decision to introduce high-cost technology in the post-primary level. The rationale behind the decision has been clearly defined by Davis:

> This level was chosen because secondary education was considered a key bottle-neck in manpower plans for a more diversified workforce, which planners hoped would attract foreign capital investments to the country. In addition, the small number of students enrolled at this level (only 25% of the eligible cohorts between 13-15 years of age) provided a favourable set of circumstances for successfully introducing marked educational improvements and expanding enrolments. (Davis, 1979: 156)

These measures helped to reinforce rural-urban differences in the provision of educational services, and to widen the gap between secondary and basic educational developments, making of the state-sponsored project a profoundly selective and socially regardless enterprise. As a result of this 'modernization' process, El Salvador shares with Brazil and Guatemala one of the highest rates of population without instruction (about 54 per cent). At the same time that the illiteracy rate of urbanized San Salvador, the capital, is only 17.2 per cent, the average national rate is 40.3 per cent, and in particular rural areas, like Morazan, La Union or Cabanas, the figure reaches nearly 60 per cent (OAS, 1979: 89).

As has been pointed out by McGinn and Schiefelbein (1979: 218-239) and others, educational reformers and technicians of El Salvador were aware of the negative consequences of such reforms. However, the USAID lobby had so much influence in the overall decision-making and political structure of the country, that every single attempt to re-orientate the system towards the real needs was frustrated by the AID groups at the ministerial levels. This situation was worsened when liberal-minded *tecnicos* were ousted from the managerial levels, especially after the takeover by General Romero in the mid-1970s.

The obsession with resources development as a functional tool for US investment also retarded the provision of adult education.

The Office for Fundamental Education of the Ministry has produced an erratic action of co-ordination at rural and urban levels. Between 1977 and 1987, a network of 1,246 literacy centres was established, 270 in urban and 977 in rural areas. This action developed a record coverage of 27,610 adults enrolled, of whom 15,538 were claimed to have become literate. However, some 'paper reforms' were produced after 1971 in order to create on top of the existing sections for Literacy and Basic Education, a section for *Capacitacion Laboral Urbana y Rural* (Training for Basic Skills at Urban and Rural Levels). The result of such reforms remained inconclusive by the late 1970s (Fuenzalida, 1978: 770, 774). In fact, the only conclusive aspect of adult education in relation to USAID commitment in this area was the 'Basic and Literacy Programme for the Armed Forces' (Waggoner, op. cit: 60). Moreover, those were the only illiterate individuals who, in respect of government policy, could be regarded as useful in the foreseeable future.

The emphasis on the qualification of small sectors to serve a highly modernized industry of agricultural transformation or on security personnel, coincided with the need for an unskilled and cheap labour (*campesino*) force for the production of agricultural raw materials for industry and export. According to Ungo and Valero:

> The lack of emphasis on massive literacy and the significant exclusion of the adult population are incumbent on the above reasons. This is also the reason why the reform concentrated in the higher levels of the educational pyramid.... The introduction of diversified secondary education followed the aim to produce a skilled labour force for the projects of national development, and taking into account that such action would be functional to national and international capitalism. (Ungo and Valero, 1978: 572)

The purely economic-orientated lobby of USAID in connection with adult education was pushed forward in most Latin American countries. However, such a plan had to be negotiated and accommodated in the cases of societies where a certain adult education tradition existed. The case of El Salvador and other countries of Central America, presented a weak provision, absolutely open to 'innovation' (Molina, 1978: 579-595). The creation in 1977, under the government of General Romero, of a National Council for Professional Training, has to be understood within the political context outlined above.

Against all the recommendations which emerged from a national multidisciplinary 'Seminar of Evaluation of the Educational Reforms', which pointed towards the need of re-orientating the system towards basic educational needs, 'the government sat upon the results of the Seminar and reduced publicity about it to a minimum' (Latin American Bureau, 1979a: 244). Instead, the idea prevailed of training human resources for the internal modern economic structure and even for export. This even became the basic aim of the new policy. Indeed, it was stated that the National Council for Professional Training

> will study the situation and tendency of employment for the purpose of directly satisfying the demand for skilled labour produced by the growth of national business, by the change in the production techniques of the

> different economic activities of the country and by the possible *immigration of national workers*. (Latin American Bureau, 1979a: 244)

Could it be suggested that the government was preparing a skilled and semi-skilled labour force for export?

However, at present the question still remains rhetorical, as such a possibility has ground to a halt. The only export of skilled or semi-skilled labour observed is that of thousands of refugees in UNHCR camps on the borders of El Salvador and in the other Central American countries, Belize and Mexico.

As reported by Pilger in 1981, only one enterprise flourished in war-ridden El Salvador: funeral parlours, a trade not considered in the curriculum of National Council for Professional Training.

> Concepcion Street in El Salvador is a street of funeral parlours. Every dawn the owners go scouting for bodies when the death squads have completed their shift. On the wall of one funeral parlour there is a graffiti, the words say, 'To hold down people forever, is like putting a hand up to the sun.' (Pilger, 1981: 13)

Clearly, effective adult education will have to rely on the truly informal sector until such time as a fundamental political change occurs that would favour mass literacy and broadly based skills training.

GUATEMALA

Since the abrupt end of the Guatemalan 'decade of dignity' in 1953, the country has been plunged into a situation of political violence and official terrorism. Guatemala has become a test ground for the 'counter-insurgency' policy of the US in Latin America. The reaction to military intervention, the breakdown of a process of legitimate distribution of power and wealth initiated in 1944, generated a process of social and political upheaval which set the country on a vicious circle of terror. This was carried out by the government with its 'para-military death squads', aimed at the basic population of Indians and other peasants, plus any kind of political opposition (Aguilera Peralta, 1972: 116-136).

The reversal of the Guatemalan Revolution of 1944-1953, in fact set in motion a process of rebellion which has continued for at least a quarter of a century. As defined by Whetter:

> There are many *campesinos* who received lands under the agrarian law of 1952 only to have them taken away again after the fall of the Arbenz government. They might be receptive to any revolutionary scheme that promises to restore them the land which they were the proud possessors of for such a short time. (Quoted in Melville and Melville, 1977)

However, there are also structural reasons attached to rebellion and violence. A candid description of the situation by Christian Union leader, de Lyon, in 1974 helps to explain this aspect:

> The current conditions of distribution in the agricultural sector have accentuated an unjust duality. While great plantations have mechanization, credit, corporate facilities, and above all, great extension of land, so that 82% of the agricultural land is held by a few exporters; the rest of the people, 90% of the population, live a subsistence economy, with only 6% of the agricultural capital and no necessary social and economic infrastructures.... The violence is in the system, which denies the majority of Guatemalans access to power, wealth and culture. (NACLA, 1974: 14)

It should also be said that political participation and access to communication and power were only for the *ladinos* (persons of mixed race or westernized Indians). Indeed, the Indian community of Guatemala has not been part of 'history' until recent years as nearly 45 per cent of the population constitutes a mass of Maya-Quiche and Araguace people who have remained effectively outside national politics. Their folkways and traditions have been preserved against the intervention of the white and *ladino* society, that is, until the process of 'modernization' of the countryside, based on wage relations and a money economy, affected their resistance to the white man's world. To a considerable extent the conflict has emerged from the process of 'colonization'. That is to say, the development of extensive and intensive forms of agricultural production for external markets, especially when the traditionally communal land of the Indians has been occupied by big companies and transnational interests. So, the 'integration' of the Indian population of Guatemala has been carried through at a later stage than in other Latin American cases, such as those of the Andean countries. Inevitably though, this process has followed a similar pattern of confrontation against the attempts of the state to impose a certain 'national unity'. The reaction of the state to rebellion in the case of Guatemala, was, in effect, genocide.

Some governmental actions in the area of literacy have been proposed, but mostly along the lines of enforcing *castellanizacion*, or Spanish literacy courses, with absolute contempt for the indigenous cultural values and language (Melville and Melville, 1977: 291). Adult education in peasant and Indian areas of Guatemala has not been important in quantitative terms, and it has been mostly orientated and based on strategical 'counter-insurgency actions', following social unrest and repression:

> The only real incentive for a massive aid programme to rural education seems to be in those areas of political unrest and counter insurgency which until now have been primarily Indian areas. The 'trouble spots' are the areas in which the USAID has set up its education project. The Pilot School: Chiquimula, Zacapa, El Progreso. In these areas, education is seen as an alternative to the 'politically sensitive' problem of land reforms, for raising the rural standard of living. (NACLA, 1974: 35)

For many years, the principal actions of adult education in

rural Guatemala have been under the direct supervision of the Ministry of Defence. For example, so-called 'civic-military offensives' have been launched since 1964, with a great display of propaganda, in the rebellious area of Jutiapa. In 1965 it was claimed that 57,028 people were taught to read and write in 2,465 centres of literacy under the direction of 658 literacy instructors. By 1970 proponents of 'civic-military-action' within the armed forces were able to say that 'dissident elements have gained no significant foothold within rural areas where there were meaningful "civil action" projects' (Dowbrowski *et al.*, 1970: 312)

Independent evaluation, however, has demonstrated that such military action of an 'educational' nature has had little positive impact on the population. With the exception of a very small proportion of individuals, little use of literacy skills and few changes in the customary way of life were observed. The formal education of the *campesinos* has had little or no relevance to the life and problems fashioned for them by custom and geography. Literacy has been an ornament of status rather than an instrument for improvement or a skill to be improved. Few literates read anything after leaving school or literacy courses, and many lose their literacy skills. The impact of 'civil-military action' was mostly helpful to the process of reconcentration of land, rather than to the transformation of the educational profile of the population. This process was observed in the reduction of per capita landholding and productivity of the newly made literates. For different reasons, namely increasing economic pressure and greater exposure to the other regions through forced seasonal migration, young *campesino* adults seemed to place greater importance upon literacy skills in the 1950s and 1960s (Wright, 1967).

The reproduction of this situation is based also on the poor educational efforts made by the government at the primary school level. Official sources reported in 1973 that 93 per cent of the five- and six-year-old children were not enrolled in a school of any type. 52 per cent of the children between seven and fourteen were unschooled and fewer than 10 per cent of those between the ages of fifteen and twenty were in a post-primary facility. For the population as a whole, 63 per cent of those over seven years of age were classified as illiterate. Finally, the average number of years of schooling for the

Guatemalan population over seven is only 1.2. The total adult illiteracy rate, at 52 per cent, is the highest in Latin America, but if one considers only the indigenous population, then the figure goes up to a massive 76 per cent (Chain, 1974: 78).

According to Williams this failure of the state to tackle the problems of education is rooted in two basic elements:

> The first, has been the belief that the educational system can be considered independently of the social and economic environment in which the schools are placed: the attempt to establish an academically selective system has been frustrated because of a very high wastage rate due to non academic factors... The second element in the failure to transform aspiration into achievement has been the low priority attached to empirical research.... Policy makers have acted on assumptions about what ought to happen rather than what was actually happening, and those assumptions were rarely challenged because so little information was available. (Williams, 1969: 208)

Decision-making at the educational level in Guatemala, as in El Salvador and Honduras, does not take into account non-academic problems such as property, exploitation and economic need. The dominant ideological pattern imposed at governmental level considers, in a paranoid way, that references to such problems are not acceptable in a 'society of order'.

> When someone describes the extent of the problem, he is promptly labelled a communist and an agitator and becomes open game for right-wing vigilantes or for government itself. [President] YDIGORAS refused to allow the publication of a study that attributed 50,000 infants' deaths a year to malnutrition, as a 'communist document'. Poverty is a negative concept, a lack of something, a difficult symbol upon which a power alliance can be integrated. (Melville and Melville, 1977: 283)

Such a conception of education has also pervaded the adult education provision at different state levels, in addition to the War Ministry whose civic-military action scheme has been described above.

Within the federal government of Guatemala there are two agencies dealing with the problem of adult education: The Directorate of Rural, Social and Educational Development, and the Directorate of Adult Education. This duality generates not only obvious problems of co-ordination and determination of institutional aims but also the most unintelligible bureaucratic overlapping which results in inefficiency in the field. Indeed, the structure was even more inefficient before 1971 if one considers that adult education and literacy were outside the scope of the general educational budget altogether. In rural areas these activities were financed from the proceeds of a small lottery. Thus most of the fiscal control and action became heavily dependent on the Army budget and therefore attached to 'security' attitudes and interests (Unesco, 1964: 66). However, between 1971 and 1974 a national literacy plan was launched and state and USAID money was provided. The plan's objectives were to reduce the high percentage of illiterates in the country, to co-ordinate adult basic education with programmes for social and economic development, and gradually to include in the adult education programme functional literacy and technological basic education.

In 1971 the equivalent of a *parasistema*, *Educacion Acelerada de Adultos*, similar to the one developed in Costa Rica, was proposed as a basic four-year cycle, with technical training. The primers used in the basic educational effort were developed by ROCAP (*Amanecer*) and the Army Literacy Department (*Nuevo Dia*). By 1972 there were 70 adult basic education centres in the country with a total of 15,546 students. However, the drop-out rate of the scheme was about 33 per cent. Co-ordinating efforts have been developed between the five months literacy course and the adult systematic scheme. Also some erratic efforts have been developed by the government to provide a radio school network for literacy and post-literacy programmes.

However, such action remains mostly in the hands of the Guatemalan Federation of Radiophonic Schools (FGER), following a similar methodological scheme as Radio Suyapa in

Honduras, within seven centres for the emission of educational programmes in the four principal regions of the country. This had a coverage of 7,550 students in 1976, with 830 voluntary tutors and 755 cultural centres (Radio Escuelas) (SEDECOS, 1980; Early, 1973). Despite this promising development, serious contradictions between the Church and state developed to put in jeopardy the continuity of the radiophonic school project of Guatemala.

In general the literacy efforts of the 1970s have been inconclusive and remain at present within the status and scope of experimental field actions, funded and orientated by USAID and some US university research groups. These are less conflict-based, self-defined-free-of-value researchers: different, therefore, from the FGER project.

One of these projects was the Basic Village Education Project (BVEP), a five-year experiment in communication with farmers (1973-1978). Different communication methods were compared in order to increase the effectiveness of the *campesinos'* productivity and two pilot areas have been used, one a *ladino* area, and one an indigenous-speaking location (Nesman, *et al.*, 1978: 6-7). A similar project, whose results were left inconclusive after the 1978 earthquake, was the Guatemalan Project, supported by the Pan American Health Organization and dealing with the research on radio messages and non-formal health education.

Perhaps the most consistent effort in the field is the one related to the state-sponsored *Educacion Extra-Escolar* programme (EEE). This project is based on the co-ordinated action of diverse ministerial levels in order to introduce the three basic indigenous groups (Maya, Quiche, Cakchiquel) to modern agricultural techniques. EEE has organized, under direct USAID supervision, a network of 250 *promotores* working in 125 villages. These extensionists have been trained in one indigenous language in addition to Spanish. Programme goals are aimed at improving the quality of life, increasing educational opportunities, and generating a more efficient use of material and human resources through governmental co-ordination. Such actions developed by *promotores* are supported by radio programmes, and by literacy and post-literacy materials. The pattern followed in this case seems to have been more effective, given the fact that it introduces the native language as a basic vehicle for the achievement of the 'modernization' goals. The disruptive consequences of introducing purely economic-oriented aims into traditional communities have been denounced by Guatemalan sociologists (Schartz and Eckhardt, 1971: 219-246). This action is bound to generate new social contradictions, such as the creation of sub-classes and wealth-based differences within indigenous communities.

The modernization pattern as observed in the *ladino* society in Honduras and Guatemala has generated a 'rural middle class', which tends to ameliorate the confrontation between agri-business and various strata layers of *campesinos* who were expelled from community property, deprived of all rights, submitted to wage relations, and forced to become itinerant workers.

The EEE project appeared, after the different 'militarized' approaches to the problems of rural adult education in Guatemela, to be a sound and 'efficient' scheme for the manipulation of the Indian community of that country and its integration to transnational investment. This assumption can be substantiated by an analysis that shows that minority groups which are able to acquire literacy skills among Guatemalan *campesinos*, are more exposed to accept the introduction of agricultural technical innovation proposed by governmental agencies. Such an effect seems to have greater importance, not among literate small land-holders, but basically among those with a middle-sized property. According to Silva-Freire (1980), this situation would be demonstrative of 'advancement through literacy'.

Nevertheless, if one considers that the majority of Guatemalans are landless and illiterate one should identify the contrary view that governmental literacy action of the EEE type reproduces social segregation, economic selectivity and class differentiation, rather than 'advancement' or 'integration'. This situation is even more clear if one considers that the programme is of a purely pedagogical nature and is not related to any form of land redistribution, or any other policy of wage and job stability in favour of the great majority of peasants living in subsistence conditions.

More conclusive in this respect seems to be Chain's evaluation of the state-sponsored literacy action of Guatemala, according to which fewer than one-third of the adults who have acquired literacy skills feel that such knowledge has helped to improve their lives in respect to income, health, job satisfaction, housing, or their social life in general (Chain, 1974: 130).

On the other hand, it is important to underline the fact that since 1979, the government has weakened its educational arm and instead has concentrated its efforts on military-based initiatives. The massacre of Indians, peasants and middle-class intellectuals by para-military and police forces, on the basis that '50,000 subversives' will have to be eliminated in order to produce 'social peace', illustrates this bias well (NACLA, 1981: 30-35). It shows that in Guatemala there is very little space left for any sort of genuine adult education.

NICARAGUA

Nicaragua exhibited until recently a typical 'enclave economy', characterized by an anachronistic state structure, mostly under the domination of the personal power of the Somoza family. Although in the rest of the area the US-imposed authoritarian regimes had moved towards a rather 'modernized' and less personal dictatorship of the military type, the characteristics of the 1930s and 1940s had been able to survive in Nicaragua. With the open backing of the USA, this family dictatorship proved to be a long-lasting agency of exploitation and suppression. As defined by Millet before the revolution:

> In 1976 Nicaragua was clearly a nation occupied by its own army. Far from producing a professional, non-political force, United States influence had helped create one of the most totally corrupt military establishments in the world: a force that functions more as the guardians of the SOMOZA dynasty than as the protectors of Nicaraguan sovereignity and freedon. Part of this responsibility for this situation falls upon the American military, which created the *Guardia* and which in subsequent decades has helped train, equip and

> support this force: while rarely, if ever, questioning the uses to which this training and equipment were put. The impact of this aid has been crucial. (Millett, 1977: 251)

The concentration of wealth in the hands of the Somoza family was impressive. Virtually every single business from agro-export to shipping, from industry to recording companies, computers, boutiques, newspapers, and even exports of 'cheap' human blood plasma, were under the control of Tachito Somoza and his family (Latin American Bureau, 1979b: 107).

Such personal concentration of wealth was based on the shadow-partnership of the regime with transnational capital investment in the Central America region. While the Gross National Product had grown during the 1960s and 1970s at an annual average of 7.1 per cent, the process of social deprivation and exploitation related to such investments generated one of the most appalling social conditions in the entire world.

According to Census data, in 1971, 47 per cent of Nicaraguan homes had no sanitation, 80 per cent of the houses of Managua, the capital, had no running water, and 55 per cent had no electricity. In 1975 the calorie intake had been reduced in relation to previous decades at the same time that peasants had been expelled from the land in a process of concentration towards export agriculture, that is to say, cotton and coffee production. As a result of this situation, more than 83 per cent of Nicaraguan children suffer from some degree of malnutrition. Infant mortality was in 1975 as high as that in Haiti or neighbouring Honduras, almost the highest of the world.

Needless to say, the maldistribution of wealth and power in Nicaragua was paralleled by the extreme disparities of educational opportunity. In 1963 it was estimated that the average years of formal schooling of the total population were 2.5 in urban areas, and only 1.5 in rural areas. Such figures were as low as those of Guatemala even though the population of Nicaragua contained a great majority of Spanish-speaking *ladinos* (Waggoner *et al.*, 1971: 89).

The adult illiteracy rate had been 63 per cent in 1952 and 65 per cent in 1962 (Pan American Union, 1964). By 1970 this had been reduced to 42 per cent but it went up again to 47 per cent in 1976 and to 50 per cent by 1980. However, the illiteracy rate of the capital, Managua, was only 28 per cent, while the average for the rest of the country remained still similar to the 1962 figures, with the extreme cases, such as Rio San Juan, Jinotega, and Matagalpa, showing much higher rates of more than 70 per cent illiteracy. All this despite the fact that between 1950 and 1979 Nicaraguan educational efforts were governed by the general US policy for the area in which priority was given to post-primary provision, there being a retention rate of only 5 per cent beyond the primary sector (Black and Bevan, 1980: 75).

Following this pattern of education, experimental developments were proposed within the narrow problem-solving scheme of USAID experts and without any consideration of social and political problems. The Nicaragua Radio Mathematics Project, should be considered as a typical example of this strategy. Only developed at experimental level, its results proved inconclusive and were not widely extended. At a time when not even the basic facilities of schooling were provided, educational hardware technologies were considered as *the* panacea! (Searle, 1975; McAnany, 1977: 130-134)

Given this approach, it is not surprising that basic/adult education, which could have confronted not only adult illiteracy but also the resulting problems of inadequate home support for primary school children, exhibited (perhaps with Honduras) the worst and most erratic profile in the region. A succession of misconceived projects occurred. For example, in 1951 an ill-fated campaign against illiteracy followed a Pan American proposition of 1949. The only result was the creation of bureaucratic structures under the supervision of the National Directorate of the National Literacy Campaign. Schemes such as the *Escuela de Cultura Obrera* with a special basic skill training for urban workers, and the reorganization of the *Escuela Nocturna* with a full programme of six years similar in all aspects to the daily children's curriculum, were organized at ministerial level. By 1953 there were 61 centres of this kind in the Republic. A supplementary course of handicrafts and secretarial skills were set up by 1960 with an enrolment of about 2,000 students. Some early but unfortunately short-lived radio school experiments were produced in 120 literacy centres.

About 1,600 adults were made literate by 1962; however the drop-out rate of the provision was 41.4 per cent. The overall exercise of 1962 however, given its discontinuous action proved to be fruitless, especially if one considers that the target illiterate population of the country was about one million adults (Pan American Union, 1964).

As in Guatemala, the central educational action for adults was part of the 'anti-subversive' operations of the *Guardia Nacional*. Special civic-military actions were planned, of which the *Plan Waslala* was the best known and most publicized, because of its final political outcome. Within the aims of these actions, security agents were trained as literacy teachers so as to help in counter-insurgency operations as *soplones* or 'grasses'.

> These semi-literate 'teachers' were employed to help the soldiers and local para-militaries root out the peasants who sympathised or co-operated with *Sandinista* guerillas; as a cover they taught elementary literacy to a few of the peasants. This operation was financed by the Ministry of Education itself, but the training of those agents was so poor that they managed to achieve very little. For the peasants of Northern Nicaragua, literacy was only taught when conceived of as an instrument of counter-insurgency. (Black and Bevan, 1980: 26)

However, one must recognize that such actions considering adult basic education as a 'geopolitical' instrument or a structure attached to the doctrine of 'national security', were not totally alien to Nicaragua's history. They had been tested by the US marines during their occupation in the 1930s and also in the 1950s. An example of this approach was the Rio Coco Pilot Project, launched in 1955 under the advisership of the Pan American Union and the US Point Four Programme, which was defined as a 'frontier experiment' following the results of a mini-war over the territories of the Atlantic coast of Nicaragua and Honduras. As proposed by the general director of the project:

> The basic aim of the Rio Coco Pilot Project is to link up this region politically and spiritually with the rest of the country the point of departure being the objectives pursued by fundamental education. (Garcia, 1957: 80)

The process of *castellanizacion* of the local Miskito and Sumo indigenous population, its integration to the money market, the introduction of modern agricultural techniques and health measures were central to this project of 'national integration'. It was followed with high regard by the conspicuous US timber companies, with which the Somoza family was associated in the Rio Coco Basin. The real purpose and impact of this pilot project, as with most of the 1950s experiments of fundamental education in Latin America, has not been accurately assessed.

However, the fact that the target region in question still holds one of the highest illiteracy rates in Nicaragua helps to provide some indication of the real purpose of the exercise. Also, the US and *Somocista* counter-revolutionary actions have been using this area to launch 'anti-communist' propaganda and even separatist propositions against the *Sandinista* government which replaced Somoza. They have found a malleable and pro-US leadership among the Miskito Indians, a leadership generated under the educational actions of the previous years of intervention and cultural invasion in the area. Such examples constitute only a small sample, an isolated case, if compared to the overall process of political struggle which had occurred in the country since the beginning of the 1970s.

The boundless greed and the savage political control exerted by Somoza over the country had reached unbearable proportions even for some sectors of the elite, which were not part of the official clique around the *Jefe Supremo*. The abuses and diversion of international relief sent into Nicaragua after the 1972 earthquake, which killed about 12,000 people, by the officials of the *Guardia Nacional* and by the Somoza family itself, and the assassination of the Christian Democrat leader of the opposition and newspaper man, P.J. Chamorrow, are some of the causes of the fall of *Somocismo* and the emergence of *Sandinismo*. The desperate war against the *Sandinistas* and the genocide perpetrated upon the peasant population of collaborators helped to isolate the regime from every sector of Nicaraguan society. When the Carter administration took over in the USA and Somoza openly rejected the calls of the US government to bring his political strategy into line with the new American human rights policy, the most effective and long-lasting power basis of the dynasty began to crack and in mid-July 1979 Somoza fled into exile. Thus ended 42 years of domination by the Somoza family (Van Eeuwen, 1980: 507-538).

Despite the extraordinary display of courage and popular faith exhibited by the population, the war left profound scars. Some 40,000 people were killed, 100,000 wounded and 40,000 children orphaned. Somoza escaped with all the reserves of the Central Bank except US $3.5 million leaving an international debt of US $1.6 billion dollars.

The outcome of the Nicaraguan Revolution is a gradual approach towards socialism, orientated by the *Moviemiento Sandinista de Liberacion* (MSLN), the mass organization of workers, peasants and students. A profound agrarian reform has been launched, and the over-exploited *campesinos* working under nearly forced-labour conditions in the cotton and coffee lands of the Somoza family (over 50 per cent of the best cultivable land of the nation) have been assured full employment and acceptable wage conditions. Cooperatives have been created in other sectors. Diversification of agriculture in order to satisfy the national market of foodstuffs is being considered, while the distribution and control of export agricultural products is under state control.

The reactivation of agricultural production has proceeded satisfactorily: unemployment immediately declined from 32 per cent in 1979 to 20 per cent in 1980, in which year exports, in value terms, exceeded pre-war proportions in sugar, meat, shellfish, bananas, gold, and chemical products. 'Given the level of destruction and shocks of war, the level of recovery has been amazing and the reactivation programme in economic terms has to be termed a success' (Petras, 1981: 81).

However, the external debt, a heritage of Somoza, makes the Nicaraguan Revolution vulnerable to US pressures. In consequence, internal agreement must be reached in order to avoid a weak flank and avoid direct US intervention on the principle of 'anti-communism'. Such intervention is, however, already there in the form of support for the counter-revolutionary 'contra' movement, arms for which form the preoccupation of the foreign policy of the ageing Reagan presidency. The *Sandinistas* have to be sure to maintain a broad support in the country. As Petras has observed, the task is one of pragmatic reconstruction:

> The problem is in the first instance political and ideological.... The latter includes the totality of social reality - the historic role of capital in destroying productive forces in pre-revolutionary society and the paramount need to reconstruct the working class through the reconstruction of productive forces. (Petras, 1981: 81)

This process of reconstruction of the productive forces of the new society has as a central element the consideration of dialogue between the FSLN direction and cadres on the one hand and the peasants and workers on the other. As pointed out by Gutierrez, a high official of the Agrarian Reform Institute (INRA), 'An erroneous dynamic could lead to a separation from the masses, and thus bureaucratization' (NACLA, 1980: 20). The ideological dimension is clearly crucial. However, the possibility of dialogue requires the development of certain skills for communication between the FSLN and the majority of the illiterate *campesinos*. Such is the basic aim behind the massive educational mobilization which has been generated in Nicaragua; a revolutionary transformation of the educational sphere where profound changes can be observed, if compared to other Latin American countries. According to Bevan and Black:

> (a) in Nicaragua today the distinction between the school as an institution and society as a whole has been removed;
> (b) the relationship between teachers and students has been revolutionised, and teachers are having to overcome the legacy of decades of rote learning and authoritarian teaching methods;

> (c) the school curriculum has been thoroughly revised to be relevant to the needs of the children of Nicaragua (and not to those of the ROCAP experts);
> (d) the state has taken responsibility for pre-primary education of children and the formal and non-formal requirements of the young;
> (e) the University has been placed at the service of the community and socio-economic barriers removed. Also special programmes for adults have been developed, aiming at the workers' educational and training needs;
> (f) the rigid division between ministries has been removed, and educational provision now depends on the advice of social welfare planners, agrarian reform experts, artists and popular grassroots organizations like the Sandinista Defence committees. (Black and Bevan, 1980: 30)

Attempts to democratize the overall structure of the educational sphere are expressed not only in quantitative terms by increasing, in two years, the primary provision by up to 19 per cent and the secondary enrolment by 30 per cent, but also by considering as a first priority task the upgrading of the non-formal and workers' education provision. According to a high official of the Ministry of Education:

> The main thrust of education in Nicaragua today is not towards the formal sector. This is the hour of non-formal education in Nicaragua. Educational concepts here, unlike Europe, are not fixed and sterile, because our society is in a period of dynamic change. The possibilities are endless, and it is up to us to define the state apparatus. The educational system is a gigantic upsurge, like a tidal wave, which shows itself in the mass media, the newspapers, in a CDS meeting, in every facet of the class struggle. The participation of the masses in the

> whole range of economic and other activities, through non-formal education outside the classroom, is building up revolutionary ideology in all sections of the population. The school system as such is only one element of this. The school itself, the role which the school will play as an institution, is to back up the wider concept of non-formal education. We see the two as totally linked, two sub-systems, formal education on one hand and non-formal on the other, combining dialectically. There is an unbreakable link between the formal school system, and what we might call the 'agencies' of non-formal education like the Sandinista mass media. In the schools, children are studying themes related to our national life, the revolutionary process with all its aims, tasks and problems. (Black and Bevan, 1980)

While the other countries analyzed above are still searching for an adult education solution of a selective character, an approach obsessed by human resources productivity, the *Sandinista* Revolution emphasizes the resolution of illiteracy and popular basic education as a first priority. Why popular education instead of *parasistemas* or training systems for a small sector of the working force? As pointed out by the Ministry of Education of Nicaragua in connection with the massive National Literacy Crusade:

> To carry out a literacy project and consolidate it with a level of education equivalent to the first grades of primary school, is to democratize society. It gives the popular masses the first instruments needed to develop awareness of their exploitation and to fight for liberation. Therefore, literacy training was something that the dictatorship could not accept without contradicting itself. (Arnove, 1981: 245)

This is, of course, anathema to the USA and its interests in the region, which include non-formal literacy schemes linked with the military, but to date the Nicaraguan revolutionary regime has stood firm. Facing the threat of a US invasion, the Nicaraguan ideological meaning and value attached to education becomes increasingly appealing to the masses of *campesinos* and workers.

As pointed out by Father F. Cardenal S.J., senior organizer of the Literacy Crusade:

> We believe that in order to create a new nation we must begin with an education that liberates people. Only through knowing their past and their present, only through understanding and analyzing their reality can people choose their future. Education, therefore, must encourage people to take charge of their lives, to learn to become informed and effective decision makers, and to understand their roles as responsible citizens possessing rights and obligations. A liberating education nurtures empathy, a commitment to community, and a sense of well-worth and dignity. It involves people acquiring the knowledge, skills, and attitudes necessary for their new community responsibilities. Education for liberation means people working together to gain an understanding of and control over society's economic, political, and social forces in order to guarantee their full participation in the creation of the new nation. Literacy and permanent programmes of adult learning are fundamental to these goals. We believe they are essential to the building of a democratic society in which people can participate consciously and critically in national decision-making. The struggle to achieve these aims is long, and we are just beginning. (Cardenal and Miller, 1981: 6)

This ideological proposition not only emerges from the experience of the liberation, but is also nurtured by a profoundly humanist and progressive view of adult education. It is informed by a wide ensemble of ideas and experiences, such as President Nyerere's view on national self-reliance, and Paulo Freire's direct collaboration in the organization of the project. The contribution of Peruvian, Mexican, Cuban, and Panamanian teachers and UNESCO experts have all been significant in the design of this massive and successful educational breakthrough. The instruments of this campaign are the literate youth of the country. As early as 1980, secondary and university students were organized with military symbolism to engage in the battle for literacy, reminiscent of the Cuban effort in 1960:

> Just as six guerrilla armies victoriously converged on Managua on July 19, in the wake of Somoza's flight from the country, so on March 23, 1980, six 'armies' left Managua to wage war on illiteracy. (Arnove, 1981: 248)

This 'People's Literacy Army' comprised a massive 65,000 *brigadistas*. Six national fronts were divided into 'brigades' on a geographical basis. Before the campaign, *brigadistas* received a basic instruction by 7,000 volunteer teachers through workshop activities developed during the six months prior to the field action. At the same time, and along the lines of the existing and war-ravaged network of state schools, a People's Literacy Teachers Organization of some 35,000 members mounted a parallel effort. In all, more than 225,000 literate adults volunteered to participate in the Crusade. The total population of Nicaragua is only about 2.5 million and the target is a staggering three quarters of a million illiterate persons over 10 years of age. So as to give continuity to the field action, university students and lecturers were organized in peripatetic units which helped to reinforce aspects of communication, health and in-service training for teachers and *brigadistas*.

There was, of course, US-generated opposition. The opposition newspaper, *La Prensa*, linked to right-wing national sectors, reacted by accusing the government of attempting the 'Cubanization of the youth minds' and other similar anti-communist cliches. There was even massive support by the US for the pro-Somoza 'contra' movement which has been enabled to sustain itself and provide a significant military thorn in the side of the Sandinista government. This problem is still rampant in the late 1980s.

The definition of 'militant educational action' has been clearly expressed by Father Cardenal:

> The choice of military metaphors was designed to help young volunteers integrate the memories of the past, transforming terms related to the war into positive associations with teaching and sharing. Military terminology also helped the brigadistas see the Crusade as a vital part of the nation's continuing liberation struggle and to understand that, as such, it demanded the seriousness, dedication and discipline of a military offensive. In essence, we wanted to make clear that peace-time battles demanded the same selfless, disciplined commitment as did the war effort; in fact, they demanded more.
>
> The use of military terms and the naming of fallen heroes had a deeply spiritual significance. The Crusade owed its very existence to the Revolution and to the sacrifice of thousands of men and women who fought and died for liberation. By calling forth their names and memories, the young volunteers kept alive the courage and example of their fallen compatriots. A spiritual bond joined the living with the dead. It inspired greater levels of commitment and compassion and it spurred people on in moments of difficulty. Over 40,000 Nicaraguans died in the struggle's violence. The Crusade and its symbols were a living testimony to their sacrifice, dedication, and faith in the future. (Cardenal and Miller, 1981: 8)

Each *brigadista* became not only a literacy teacher but also a person learning about the social conditions of the peasants by sharing their everyday life for five or six months. In itself the *Cruzada* became a most important process of dialogic education. The young generation of Nicaragua by being confronted with reality, by discussing in cultural circles the different generative themes in the literacy primers, designed along the lines of Freire's method, and most of all by sharing with the poor their work and style of life, became educated to a new sort of political and social awareness. As put by a peasant to the mother of his young literacy teacher, 'your son ma'am, has learned to read from our book' (Cardenal and Miller, 1981).

However, even in the late 1980s to define the final impact of the process seems still to be rather premature. Assessment of the continuity or decline of popular support for the Sandinista Revolution may come in the future as the popular evaluation of the Literacy Crusade makes itself clear. Nonetheless, even mere quantitative results can help to prove the fact that a small and underdeveloped country like Nicaragua, with few resources, is able to cover and give drastic solutions to the central and most pressing problem faced by adult education in Latin America and the Third World, the problem of illiteracy. Within nine months the Crusade had reduced the illiteracy rate of the population over 10 years of age, to 15 per cent, from a starting point of over 50 per cent. This means that 406,056 Nicaraguans learned basic reading and writing skills during that time, but 21 per cent of the people remain ignorant of reading and writing. Special programmes of a bilingual character were developed to cope with indigenous minorities and English-speaking West Indian immigrants from the Atlantic Coast.

A permanent network of adult education, based on community learning groups, trained by peripatetic teams and radiophonic networks, was developed. Additional learning materials and an impressive boom of book production and newspapers is being encouraged by the Nicaraguan government. All these efforts are being developed in Nicaragua within the framework of a war which still disrupts family and social life in a most radical and violent way. The open decision of the US government to back the terrorist actions of ex-*Somocista* guardsmen and poor *campesino* mercenaries in a war of intervention and erosion, has disrupted efforts towards education and improvement of the social conditions of the illiterate masses of the country. Nonetheless, the experience of an adult education for national self-reliance and social justice still remains alive in Nicaragua, as in other countries of Central America, as part of a long-lasting and increasingly valuable tradition of Latin American adult education.

BIBLIOGRAPHICAL REFERENCES

A National Apprenticeship in Costa Rica (1966) **International Labour Review** 93

Aguero, A. **et al.** (1966) Numero Especial sobre textos ODECA/ROCAP, **Boletin de la Academia Costarricense de la Lengua**

Aguilera Peralta, G. (1972) El proceso de terror en Guatemala, **Aportes** 24

ALFALIT (1969) **Cartilla para Centro America y Panama** (Alajuela, ALFALIT)

Arias, S.O. (1976) **Quien gobierna en Costa Rica?** (San Jose, Ed. UCR)

Arnove, R.F. (1981) The Nicaraguan Literacy Crusade of 1980, **Comparative Education Review** 25, 2

Beals, C. (1974) **Latin America** (Westport, Greenwood Press)

Black, G. and Bevan, J. (1980) **The Loss of Fear: Education in Nicaragua** (London, WUS)

Brenes Mesen, R. (1942) **'Nicaragua', Educational Year Book of the International Institute** 133-150

Campion, M.M. (1972) An analysis of the goals of the Department of Adult Education in Costa Rica (Ph.D dissertation, Arizona State University)

Cardenal, F. and Miller, V. (1981) Nicaragua 1980: the battle of the ABC's, **Harvard Educational Review** 51, 1

Castilla, V.M. (1972) **Educacion para la modernizacion en Nicaragua** (Buenos Aires, Paidos)

Chain, B.J. (1974) An analytical description of three adult literacy programs in Bolivia, Honduras and Guatemala (Ph.D dissertation, Columbia University)

CONCORDE (1974) **Consejo de Coordinacion para el Desarrollo: Que Es?** (Tegucigalpa, CONCORDE)

Crawley, E. (1979) **Dictators Never Die: a Portrait of Nicaragua and the Somoza Dynasty** (London, C.Hurst & Co.)

Davis, L.R. (1979) Educational reform with television: the El Salvador experience, **Comparative Education Review** 23, 2

Denton, C.F. (1979) Costa Rica: a democratic revolution, in Wiarda, H.J., and Kline, H. (eds) **Latin American Politics and Development** (Boston, Houghton-Mifflin)

de Pienne, A. (1974) Realisations et tendances de l'education des adultes en Amerique Centrale, **Convergence** 7, 4

Dobrowski, J. **et al.** (1970) **Area Handbook for Guatemala** (Washington, The American University)

Early, J.D. (1973) Education via radio among Guatemalan Highland Maya, **Human Organization** 32, 3

Fuenzalida, R. (1978) Caminos de la educacion de adultos en El Salvador, **Revista Inter-americana de Educacion de Adultos** 1, 56

Garcia M.M. (1957) The Rio Coco Pilot Project in Fundamental Education, **Fundamental and Adult Education** 8

Guzman-Bokler, C. and Herbert, J.L. (1971) **Guatemala: una Interpretacion Historico-social** (Mexico, SXXI)

Hans, N. (1937) Comparative study of education in countries of Latin America, **The Year Book of Education** (London)

Honduras, Ministerio de Educacion (1973) **Primer Seminario sobre Planificacion de la Educacion de Adultos en Honduras** (Tegucigalpa, MINED)

Honduras, Ministerio de Educacion Publica (1982) **Politicas y Estrategias para el Desarrollo Educativo Nacional 1982-1986** (Comayaguela, D.C., MINED)

IBE (1949) **'Guatemala' Bulletin of the International Bureau of Education** 23, 93

ICER (1976) **Experiencias y Perspectivas** (San Jose, ICER)

Jones, C.L. (1966) **Guatemala: Past and Present** (New York, Russel & Russel)

Kiernan, V.G. (1978) **America: the new Imperialism** (London, Zed Press)

La Belle, T.J. (1976) Goals and Strategies of Non-Formal Education in Latin America, **Comparative Education Review** 20

Latin America Bureau (1979a) **El Salvador under General Romero** (London, LAB)

Latin America Bureau (1979b) **Nicaragua: Dictatorship and Revolution** (London, LAB)

Lizano-Fait, E. (1981) Toward a national employment policy: the case of Costa Rica, **International Labour Review** 120, 3

McAnany, E.S. (1977) Why educational technology? **Educational Broadcasting International** 10, 3

McGinn, N.F. and Schiefelbein, E. (1979) Educational planning as political process: two case studies from America Latina, **Comparative Education Review** 23, 2

Melville, T. and Melville, M.B. (1977) Oppression by any other name: power in search of legitimacy in Guatemala in Nash, J. **et al.** (eds), **Ideology and Social Change in Latin America** (New York, Gordon & Breach)

Millet, T. (1977) **Guardians of the Dynasty** (Maryknoll, NY, Orbis Books)

Ministerio de Educacion, Nicaragua, and Departamento Ecumenico de Investigaciones (1981) **Nicaragua Triunfa en la Alfabetizacion** (San Jose, Costa Rica, DEI)

Molina, H. (1978) Sistema Educativo y estructura socio-economica, **Estudios Centroamericanos** 33

Moran, F. (1942) **'El Salvador', Educational Year Book of the International Institute**: 195-206

Morris, J.A. and Ropp, S.C. (1977) Corporatism and dependent development: a Honduran case study, **Latin American Research Review** 12, 2

NACLA (1974) **Guatemala** (Berkeley, NACLA)

NACLA (1981) **Report on the Americas** 15, 3

Nash, J. **et al.** (1977) **Ideology and Social Change in Latin America** (New York, Gordon & Breach)

Nesman, E.G., Rich, T.A. **et al.** (1978) The Basic Village Education Project, **Development Communication Report** 6-7

OAS (1963) **Campanas de Alfabetizacion y Educacion de Adultos en America Latina** (Washington, OAS)

OAS (1979) **Los Deficits Educativos en America Latina** (Washington, OAS)

Pan American Union (1964) **Yearbook of Education, Scientific and Cultural Development in Latin America** (Washington, PAU)

Petras, J. (1981) Nicaragua: The transition to a new society, **Latin American Perspectives** 8, 2

Pilger, J. (1981) The slaughter of El Salvador, New Statesman 18 September

Posas, M. (1980) Honduras at the crossroads, **Latin American Perspectives** 7, 2-3

Ramfrez, S. (1969) Balcanes y volcanes, in Torres Rivas, E. **Procesos y Estructuras en una Sociedad Dependiente Centroamerica** (Santiago, PLA)

Ramirez, R.A. (1975) **La Educacion de Adultos en Guatemala** (Guatemala, n.d.)

Retamal, G. (1974) Como visualiza el hondureno la existencia del enclave? **Boletin de Ciencias Sociales y Economicas** - UNAH 13

Rock, J. (1970) Selection and guidance for vocational training in Latin America: The case of Costa Rica, **International Labour Review** 102, 2

Sandi, M. **et al.** (1984) Analisis del curriculum de la educacion Nocturna Formal de Adultos, **Revista Educacion** 8

Schartz, N. and Eckhardt, K. (1971) Values, ethnicity and acculturation in Peten, Guatemala, **Cultures et Developpement** 11, 2

Searle, B. (1975) The Nicaragua Radio Mathematic Project (Paper presented at Educational Testing Service, Princeton, NJ, 10 September 1975)

SEDECOS (1980) **Informe sobre la Federacion Guatemalteca de Escuelas Radiofonicas** (FGER) mimeographed document (Santiago, SEDECOS)

Seligson, M.A. (1977) Agrarian policies in dependent societies: Costa Rica, **Journal of Interamerican Studies** 19, 2

Silva-Freire, M.E. (1980) **Assessing the Role of Education in Rural Guatemala** (Ph.D dissertation, University of California, Berkeley)

Torres, E. (1942) **'Nicaragua', Educational Year Book of the International Institute**

Torres Rivas, E. (1969) **Procesos y Estructuras en una Sociedad Dependiente Centroamerica** (Santiago, PLA)

UNESCO (1942) **International Year Book of Education** (Paris, UNESCO)

UNESCO (1964) **Literacy and Education for Adults** (Geneve, UNESCO)

UNESCO (1972) **Education in Costa Rica: A Reconnaissance in Depth** (Paris, UNESCO) Annex 18

UNESCO - Ministerio de Educacion (1974) **Informe Final de la Segunda Etapa del Proyecto Experimental de Educacion Funcional de Adultos Realizado en el Dpto. de Solala, Guatemala** (Guatemala, Ministerio de Educacion)

Ungo, G. and Valero, L.F. (1978) Fundamentos socio politicos y fines de la Reforma Educativa, **Estudios Centroamericanos** 33

Van Eeuwen, D. (1980) Du Somozisme au Sandinisme, **Cultures et Developpement** 12, 3-4

Waggoner, G.R. **et al.** (1971) **Education in Central America** (Lawrence, Kansas University Press)

White, R. (1972) **The Adult Education Program of Accion Cultural Hondurena** 2 vols (St Lois, St Lois University)

Wiarda, H.J. and Kline, H. (eds) (1979) **Latin American Politics and Development** (Boston, Houghton- Mifflin)

Williams, T.D. (1969) Discrepancy Between Goal and Function in Educational Planning: The Guatemalan Experience, **Comparative Education Review** 13, 2

Wilson, C.M. (1942) **Central America, Challenge and Opportunity** (Oxford, Oxford University Press)

Wright, P.C. (1967) **Literacy and Custom in a Ladino Peasant Community** (Ph.D dissertation, Columbia University, New York)

Chapter Seven

EDUCATION IN THE LARGEST CITY IN THE WORLD: MEXICO

Guadalupe Gonzalez-Paredes and David Turner

MEXICO: THE CITY

There are difficulties in making precise statements about the size of a large city especially a city which is growing rapidly; it may have outgrown its administrative boundaries and may be so closely linked economically to other towns and cities that they form part of a single urban unit. These considerations apply with some force to Mexico City, which is the fastest growing city in the world. According to Hall, United Nations statisticians have estimated that by the year 2000 Mexico City will have a population of 31 million, and will be the 'greatest mass of urban humanity the world will ever have seen' (Hall, 1985: 214).

Until the 1960s, the term Mexico City was more or less synonymous with Mexico DF, the Federal District, which was the administrative area of the city. The Federal District is bordered by the State of Mexico on all sides except the south. The built-up area of Mexico City and the relevant administrative boundaries are shown in Figure 7.1. The rapid growth of the urban area now means that roughly half the city lies outside the Federal District in the State of Mexico. The government is now planning on the basis of a Central Metropolitan Zone of Mexico, a new administrative unit which includes all the Federal District, a large part of the State of Mexico, and a small part of the State of Hidalgo. However, the

Figure 7.1

Map of the Central Region of Mexico

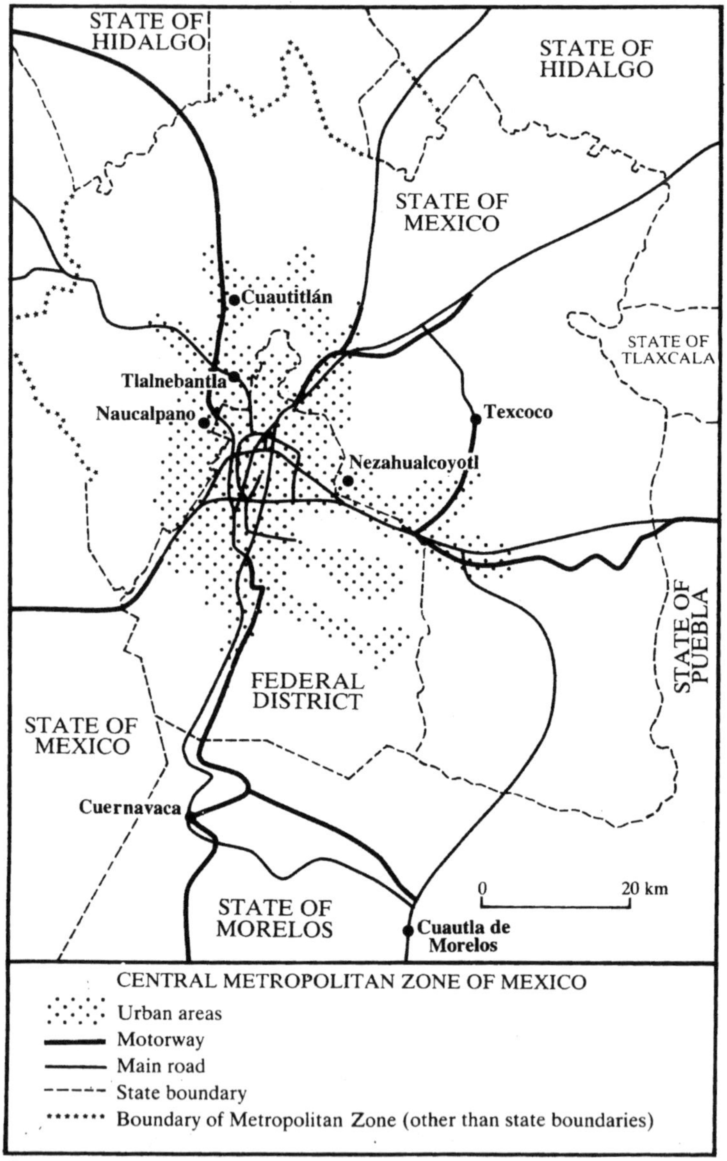

Source: After Gobierno Constitucional de los Estados Unidos Mexicanos, 1983: 13

Table 7.1

Population of Mexico City over the Decades 1940-1980
(in thousands)

Year	Population of Mexico	Urban Population	Population of Mexico City
1940	19,649	3,928	1,559
1950	25,779	7,210	2,970
1960	34,923	12,747	4,907
1970	49,050	22,004	8,362
1980	-	-	15,032*

Sources: Silvers and Crosson (1980)
* Hall (1985)

Central Metropolitan Zone has not yet replaced the Federal District for all administrative purposes.

Estimates of the 1980 population of this urban complex vary according to the unit in question: from 9.3 million for the Federal District, 15 million for 'Mexico City' to 18.4 million for the whole conurbation (Hall, 1985). Whatever the total, there is no doubt that the growth of the city, in both physical and demographic terms, has been rapid. At the turn of the twentieth century less than one and a half million people, or 10 per cent of the total population, were living in urban centres. Even as recently as 1940 the population of Mexico City was less than two million. Its meteoric growth over the years 1940 to 1980, roughly doubling in population every ten years, is set out in Table 7.1.

This rapid growth does not mean that Mexico is a new city. In 1519, when Mexico City was first seen by Europeans, it was quite possibly even then the largest city in the world.

Estimates of Davies (1982) and Cockcroft (1983) are of 200,000 to 1.5 million respectively. Conquest by Spain reduced the size of the city, and it did not grow again to this size until the twentieth century. However, throughout the colonial period it remained the largest city in the Americas, and that position was only later challenged by the emerging industrial conurbations in the United States of America.

There are two common patterns of urban problems in major world cities. The first, which is generally associated with European and North American industrial centres, comprises: a declining core, built in the last century, where the sewers, roads, and building stock have fallen into decay. As central areas become derelict, there are competing groups which attempt to take advantage of the opportunity which this offers. Migrant groups occupy the inner city zones, commercial enterprises take some areas for redevelopment, and the middle classes attempt to 'gentrify' specific neighbourhoods. The migrant groups, poorly equipped to compete with the other groups, find themselves squeezed into slum districts. Such development is characterized by successive patterns of changing land use.

The second pattern of urban development, usually associated with cities in the developing countries, is characterized by the rapid growth of hastily built, poor-quality districts at the edges of modern or modernized city centres. One example of this rapid growth at the edges of the city is the urban development of Netzahuacoyotl. Although physically part of the urban development of Mexico City, it lies outside the Federal District and is therefore technically a separate city. The growth of this city, which hardly existed in 1960, has been so rapid that it has now overtaken Guadalajara and Monterrey, and is the second largest city in Mexico (Hall, 1985). These outer regions of the city are often of doubtful legality, and inadequately supplied with services.

Mexico City, with its ancient centre and mushrooming suburbs, does not fall neatly into one pattern or the other. It exhibits problems of an old city and a new city at the same time. Its central zone, Zocalo, is built in classical colonial style on the ruins of the Aztec city. The sewerage and water systems, greatly overloaded by the expansion of the city, are suffering from age. The need for improving the infrastructure of the city is recognized by the government, although action has been inhibited by Mexico's financial position. In the competition for scarce land in the central area, poorer communities have lost out to commercial interests as land use has changed. For example, the Zona Rosa, once a 'bohemian' residential area, has become, in fairly rapid succession, first a tourist attraction and then a business centre (Gonzalez-Casanova and Flores, 1980).

The peculiar geological conditions beneath Mexico City only serve to exacerbate the decay of the city centre. The city is built on the site of a, now, largely dried-up lake. Originally chosen in fulfilment of a religious vision, Mexico City was founded where the wandering Aztecs came across an eagle, perched on a cactus, eating a snake, in the middle of a lake. (This myth is celebrated in the central emblem on the Mexican flag.) The Aztecs used their engineering skills to divide the lake into fresh water and waste water regions, and the city flourished. They used their military might to subjugate neighbouring tribes and to establish an empire in central Mexico. Some of this heritage remains in a capital which is the political centre of an administrative structure which is federal in little more than name. Perhaps it also remains in the fact that Mexico City has a safe water supply. But the geological conditions present considerable difficulties for construction engineers, any large building being in danger of settling into the mud and cutting itself off from its own water supply and waste disposal. A new, deep sewerage system and improved water supply from distant reservoirs have long been projected (Gobierno Constitucional de los Estados Unidos Mexicanos, 1983). The tragic earthquake of 19 September 1985 serves to underline the vulnerability of any 'permanent' underground structures in Mexico City. The result is that Mexico City has inner city deterioration on a scale which would be well beyond the experience of the administrators of New York or London.

Alongside the problems which arise from Mexico being an old city, is its rampant juvenility, with over half its growth coming from the rapid influx of people not only from rural areas, but also from other parts of Latin America. These new migrants have settled areas in the central plain of Mexico at the edges of the city. The aforementioned rapid growth of Netzahuacoyotl offers an example of the way in which urban growth, once generated, tends to feed on its own dynamic. In Netzahuacoyotl one of the major industries of the formative period was the sorting and disposal of rubbish collected from Mexico City, and the salvage of anything worth preserving. As the congestion and pollution of the centre increased, so Mexico City spawned this symbiotic satellite which provided an invaluable service, as well as providing a livelihood for many of its poorest inhabitants.

Land reform was one of the major causes around which the Mexican Revolution was fought, at least notionally, to redistribute the massive land holdings of a small land-owning class. As in many countries, such land reform was only partly successful, with redistribution happening first among the families of landowners, and complex arrangements to hide real ownership. Even where distribution was successful, the land-ownership may be complicated by a system of corporate ownership unique to Mexico. Corporately owned, or *ejido*, lands are not easily divided into manageable property rights when the land is urbanized (Varley, 1985). Many of the new settlements are therefore in areas where the ownership of the land is not clear, and where, even when it is clear, the political will may not exist to enforce the rights of the original owners, or to transfer ownership to the large numbers of people now who occupy the land, including those comprising part of the expansion of Mexico City.

In addition to this, with the development of Mexico City beyond the administrative limits of the Federal District, there is as yet no single administrative bureaucracy which is responsible for the provision of services in the city. Even a service as basic as water is not supplied to every house. Indeed, as recently as 1977 the government estimated that one and a half million people did not have a water supply connected to their house (Gonzalez-Casanova and Flores, 1980). Development is haphazard, with the spreading slums now competing with heavy industry for space on the margin of the city, and frequently encircling heavy industrial plants with poor-quality housing. This fact is also unfortunately and graphically underlined by the explosion of a liquefied petroleum gas plant at San Juan Ixhuatepec, Tlanepantla, which devastated an area of poor housing late in 1984 (Proceso, 1985).

The general description of the city illustrates the extreme

difficulty which providing any service to the inhabitants of Mexico City presents. In the case of education this applies even more than to other services, as Mexico shares with much of Latin America a demography which means that more than 50 per cent of the population are below fourteen years of age (Wilkie and Perkal, 1984: 149). In looking at the demographic patterns in Latin American countries, and comparing them with those in Europe and the United States, one of the most striking features is how large a percentage of the population is very young. The typical pattern for Europe is that the populations have stabilized so that roughly the same proportion of the population is under twenty as is between forty and sixty. In Latin America, this is very far from being the case. One may look for explanations of this in the strength of the Catholic Church, or in the uncertain economic conditions which promote large families for mutual economic support. The latter analysis is supported by the reducing size of families of the middle classes. However, whatever produces the demographic pattern, it is clear that the large number of young people needing education places a disproportionate burden on the resources of the country.

In such circumstances it is perhaps more remarkable that there is any education system at all in Mexico City than that it has shortcomings. And yet Mexico boasts a prestigious and beautiful university, which, with 800,000 students, is among the largest in the world, in addition to a wide range of specialist institutions of higher education, and primary and secondary education enough to prepare students for entry.

MEXICO: THE COUNTRY

During the nineteenth century, there were many and diverse influences on the young country. Quite apart from the direct influence of Spain, and the Aztec and Mayan heritage, Mexico was on the receiving end of a number of military adventures. In the post-independence period, the United States annexed half the territory of the country, after first occupying Mexico City itself (Riding, 1985: 50). The French imposed a government of their choice by force of arms (Riding, 1985: 52). There were also strong trading links with the United Kingdom, when any enemy of the United States was a friend of Mexico. Booth (1969) illustrates the control of foreigners over Mexico's economic resources which show that the average foreigner owned more than one hundred times as much as the average Mexican, while the English were on average ten times as wealthy as other foreigners. But intellectually and economically the strongest links with Europe have always been with France.

Mexico is a secular republic. The Constitution owes much to the French, both through the direct intervention of France in the post-independence period, and, more positively, through the Constitution adopted by Benito Juarez in 1857. Juarez, a pure-blooded Zapotec Indian gained his early education in a seminary, but preferred the study of law. Later, as a practising lawyer, he frequently defended peasants against the powerful landowners and tenants in cases which involved the Church. The combination of his liberal and legal studies, and of his practical experience, brought him to the conclusion that the Church should be separated from the power of the state.

The exact wording of the Constitutions has changed from time to time, but the secular aim of education is succinctly expressed in Article 3 of the 1917 Constitution:

> Instruction is free; that given in public institutions of learning should be secular. Primary instruction, whether higher or lower, given in private institutions, shall likewise be secular. Private primary schools may be established only subject to official supervision. (Booth, 1969: 1)

Thus, religious education is prohibited in all schools, and the state is the main provider of higher education. All educational qualifications have to be recognized by a government committee before they can be accepted for government employment, and the system of registration of qualifications and professional status is rigid and unavoidable. In a country which is predominantly Catholic, this secularism is curiously extended to prohibit expression of religious belief in public, and to exclude priests from the full rights of citizenship.

One of the major historical events shaping the present

political development of Mexico was the Revolution of 1910-1922. Originally a Revolution to oust the Dictator, Porfirio Diaz, it was successful in its main objective within six months (Riding, op cit: 55-56). The ensuing twelve bloody years brought land reform, and established in power the Partido Revolucionario Institucional or PRI. The land reforms, which introduced a land-ceiling for individual ownership and collectivization for certain tracts of land, continue to have a significant impact on the development of Mexico City. The PRI has been in power ever since. It is not a monolithic party, having factions within it. It does, however, have extensive control over the machinery of state, the police, and the army, with which it has become inextricably linked. A party which is ostensibly committed to socialist principles, to free speech, and to the development of the country, it has been determined, and occasionally ruthless, in its suppression of opposition, particularly when this opposition took revolutionary form. An example of this was the suppression of the student movement in 1968 (Mabry, 1982: 262-266). The memory of the Revolution also has its influence on the many opposition parties, which have generally sought to avoid open confrontation with the PRI.

Mexico is not a developing country in any stereotypical sense of the term. It is an industrial country, with a well-developed oil industry, an associated chemical industry, a thriving steel industry, aluminium smelting, a motor industry, and so on. Industrial activity extends into modern technology, with a number of corporate giants from the United States using Mexico as a centre for manufacture.

These close links with the United States are not unproblematic for Mexico, which is particularly susceptible to pressure from the United States over the pricing of her products, especially oil. Close trading links with the United States have also promoted the import of consumer goods from the north, and aspirations to a lifestyle beyond the economic reach of Mexico. Indeed, with heavy investment from the United States in Mexican industry, with Mexico supplying cheap labour to the United States, both qualified and unqualified, legally employed in Mexico and illegally employed in the United States, and with many families in Mexico depending on money sent by relatives working in the United

States, the economy of Mexico cannot be seen as separate from that of the United States. Economically, Mexico is an exploited region of the United States, and is dependent on the United States in much more concrete and direct ways than any other country. Mexican politicians point to the massive national debt as a symptom of United States economic policies, and an element of United States foreign policy, and Mexican dependence is presented in a simplistic and sloganized way. This should not be allowed to detract from the fact that the analysis is substantially correct.

Agriculturally, Mexico is one of the few countries in the Western Hemisphere where the 'Green Revolution' has made a major impact. The introduction of tractors and machinery, of fertilizers and irrigation, have led to a rapid increase in agricultural production, particularly of cash crops. This has led to some anomalies in development, with rice growing being more common in the north, where irrigation can be implemented and regulated, rather than in the south, where the climate is more appropriate. Also, very large areas of fertile land in the north are devoted to the production of cash crops, particularly fresh fruit and vegetables, for the United States' market.

These changes of farming methods have radically changed the social organization of rural areas, providing more stable jobs for those associated with large-scale industrial farming, but making peasant farming and casual farm labouring impossible modes of life. This has contributed substantially to the flow of people from the countryside to the cities, especially Mexico City.

Developments which pushed people from the land were supplemented by the considerable attractions of the city. The majority of people who work for government and government-related agencies in Mexico work in Mexico City; this amounts to more than one million relatively secure and well-paid jobs (Hall, 1985: 218). The urban population benefit from an above-average per capita expenditure on health, housing, and education. And the urban wage for those in work is well above rural wages (Silvers and Crosson, 1980: 70).

Migration to the cities has been rapid. More than half of Mexico City's expansion in the 1950s and 1960s was due to migration, although this has now dropped back to around 45 per cent (Silvers and Crosson, 1980: 22). Since these figures refer only to primary migration, and do not include children of recent migrants, the overall effect of migration on the population of Mexico City is therefore probably much higher.

A general description of the economic and administrative conditions in Mexico would be incomplete without some mention of corruption. Corruption is identified by Mexicans as the primary fact of economic life, and often forms the basis of jokes which refer to contemporary political figures. But even the word corruption carries many of the wrong overtones (Riding, 1985: 140-164). Payments to officials secure the rapid consideration of documents from driving licence applications to government contracts, and while providing additional income for officials ensure that they push essential business forward promptly. What is called 'corruption' is, in effect, little more than a tax paid to cover the costs of administration. The alternative of higher levels of official taxation and payment of the necessary salaries would be politically unacceptable.

Like any other form of taxation, general statements as to the morality of the practice are misplaced. On the other hand, like any other tax it involves the redistribution of wealth, and it makes sense to ask, 'Who pays?' and, 'Who benefits?' The unofficial nature of corruption makes it difficult to answer these questions. In general, it would appear most importantly to be a corporation tax on those businesses which need official sanction or government contracts, which transfers wealth from the business community to the politicians and officials of the bureaucracy. But there are more general benefits, which include a functioning administrative system, and more general social costs, which include substandard work being accepted on government contracts. The latter may well be the most important consequence for education, a disproportionate number of schools having been severely damaged in the recent earthquake.

Mexico, therefore, presents a number of different facets which are difficult to integrate into a coherent picture. A country with agricultural and industrial wealth, she has one of the largest national debts in the world. She is a strongly Catholic country, at the same time as being rigidly secular. And although she has a free press and theatre, there is little organized and effective opposition to the PRI.

EDUCATION: THE NATIONAL SETTING

The education system of Mexico has been very strongly influenced by that of France. This is linked to the more general Constitutional influence of France and the influence of the ideas of the French philosophers associated with the French Revolution. The secular nature of education has already been mentioned. The educational system has also been open to other influences, particularly from the United States.

In 1933, Article 3 of the Constitution was amended and expanded to make the secular, even anti-Church, orientation of education more explicit. At the same time the aim of providing a socialist education was made clear.

> The education imparted by the State shall be a socialistic one and, in addition to excluding all religious doctrine, shall combat fanaticism and prejudices by organizing its instruction and activities in a way that shall permit the creation in youth of an exact and rational concept of the Universe and of social life.... In view of this, religious corporations, the ministers of cults, the organizations which preferably carry on educational activities, and the associations or societies bound directly or indirectly to the propaganda of a religious creed shall in no way intervene in primary, secondary or normal schools, nor shall they be permitted to assist financially. (Booth, 1985: 2-3).

The stress on the socialist nature of education drew upon the revolutionary history of the country. But in the precise interpretation of socialist education Mexico turned to the progressive educationists of the United States. Dewey had shown interest in the educational development of Mexico, as he had with the Soviet Union and other post-revolutionary societies, and Mexican educators reciprocated by according Dewey a special place in the exposition of socialist education (Dewey, 1964). At a meeting of the Progressive Education Association in Mexico in 1935, educators from Mexico and the United States were able to agree on practically all principles, but differed as to whether they were discussing progressive education or socialist education (El Excelsior, 1935). Progressive ideas found more concrete expression in the details of other government documents which set out the rights and duties of the child, which reflect the goals of a child-centred education programme.

More recently, and perhaps more easily reconciled with the administration of education in Mexico, the ideas of Bloom, that the curriculum should be directed towards specific objectives, have found considerable influence. The Secretariat of Public Education (SEP) issues detailed aims and objectives for each subject taught. These specify objectives in terms of Bloom's taxonomy of educational activities, requiring recall, analysis, comprehension and interpretation (Consejo Nacional Tecnico de la Educacion, 1973). The goals are not always appropriately linked to the activities which are supposed to promote them, but the influence in official documents is quite clear. In saying that the goals of progressive, or socialist, education have not been achieved in practice, it would be difficult to be more critical than some of the documents produced by SEP itself (Consejo Nacional Tecnico de la Educacion, 1981: 47-51). There is a recognition that the implementation of such ideas requires the training and retraining of large numbers of staff, while the expansion of the system has made it necessary to run very fast even to stand still.

Detailed curricula and syllabuses for all subjects are prepared by SEP, and a minimum list of textbooks is prescribed. Primary school textbooks are published and provided free for all pupils, and, although it is possible for private schools to supplement these with other textbooks, the Ministry-prepared textbooks represent the normal course for children in schools. The system of testing children on the prescribed syllabus, using an examination set by the SEP, and of scrutiny by inspectors appointed by the Ministry, ensures that the Ministry guidelines are the minimum which is covered in all schools, while the general level of material support and the relatively poor training and conditions of work of teachers also ensures that it is the maximum. In addition to the compulsory system of examining students on content, many schools set their own exams at monthly or termly intervals.

All education provided by the state is free. This includes state kindergarten where provision was more than tripled over the period 1970 to 1980. The eventual goal was to provide pre-school education for 70 per cent of five-year-olds by the academic year 1982/1983, but by 1980/1981 only half of this number were in kindergartens (Consejo Nacional de la Educacion, 1981: 36). Although the law requires that education be free, where there is a shortage of supply, cases of corruption are not unknown, with the directors of schools demanding money to secure entry to their institutions (Proceso, 1982).

Primary education is compulsory for all children. It usually lasts from the age of six to twelve, but children may remain in primary education up to the age of fourteen if they have not completed the sixth grade of primary school. The curriculum of the primary school is broadly based, having been revised in 1961 to ensure that a wide range of studies which are relevant to the experience of the pupils is presented. The four major divisions in the curriculum are: (a) language (Spanish), (b) mathematics, (c) social science, and (d) natural science. In addition there is physical education, art education, technological education, and health education. There are also experimental programmes which include regional studies related to the specific locality of the school. A fine example of a project based on a specific locality within Mexico is the work of the Centro Michoacano Para La Ensenanza de la Ciencia y la Tecnologia. The centre produces two journals, *El Barco de Papel*, which relates the material of the curriculum to local concerns and interests, and is intended for students, and *Redes*, which gives additional information and advice on introducing new material to teachers. This project therefore addresses a number of important aims, including adult education, relevant curricula, improved science education, and in-service support for teachers who lack the confidence to innovate. However, over the country as a whole major problems remain with pupils repeating grades, or dropping out, although both problems have been reduced in recent years (Consejo Nacional Tecnico de la Educacion, 1981: 59).

Progress from grade to grade within the primary school is decided on the basis of examinations set by SEP and marked by the teachers in the school. Most importance is attached to performance in Spanish and mathematics, and unsatisfactory results in the examination make it necessary to repeat the grade. A considerable amount of grade repeating, and dropping out, mean that 20 per cent of pupils reach the end of compulsory schooling without completing primary education. In addition, a large number of schools in rural areas do not offer courses for the full six years (ibid: 58). While there has been an effort to improve primary education, and performance is now better than in earlier years, the absolute numbers of students not completing primary school is large, and means that this continues to be a matter of concern.

Lower secondary education is provided through the *media basica* in common schools. There are also a number of specialist schools providing technical and agricultural education at the lower secondary level. The majority of these schools are in urban areas.

The curriculum of the general secondary schools is broad based, including study of Spanish (language and literature), mathematics, chemistry, physics, biology, geography, history, civics, technological education, a foreign language (usually English), art, and physical education. Since 1973 there have been some attempts to introduce integrated science and social science, but these have been largely unsuccessful.

Transfer to the next grade of secondary education at the end of each year is dependent on the successful completion of end-of-year examinations. If the student does not achieve satisfactory marks in up to three subjects, he or she is required to retake the examinations before the start of the following year. These examinations are called *extraordinarios*, and failure in these means that the academic year has to be repeated. Failure in four or more subjects automatically means that the year has to be repeated.

Upper secondary education is divided into separate institutions. The *bachilleratos* provide a two- or three-year course leading to the *bachillerato* examination. These institutions, which are directly responsible to the universities for their curriculum and organization, are primarily concerned with the preparation of students for university. The *bachillerato* confers the right to sit entrance examinations for the university. Recent reforms have given students who pass the *bachillerato* with sufficiently good marks the right to enter federal and state universities without sitting an additional examination. Private universities still require applicants to sit for formal entrance examinations. Technical and vocational education at the upper secondary level is provided in separate technical schools.

Since 1966 the SEP has been experimenting with closed-circuit television for the teaching of secondary school courses, introducing the *telesecundaria* to supplement traditional schools. Following the initial launch of programmes, special facilities were introduced in many areas, including the Federal District and State of Mexico, so that people unable to attend regular schools would be able to follow the courses. This was part of a general move to make secondary education 'open' and available to all who wanted it. Despite promising completion rates achieved in the early years, the *telesecundaria* must still be regarded as an interesting experiment, accounting for only 3 per cent of all lower secondary places in 1980/1981 (Consejo Nacional Tecnico de la Educacion, 1981: 116).

The high levels of illiteracy in the country have meant that adult education, especially literacy programmes, have been a major priority for SEP for a long time. Since the 1920s the government has from time to time introduced legislation to make adult education more widely available, although until recently the practical impact of this legislation was very little. In 1981, the government established an independent agency, INEA (The National Institute for the Education of Adults). The Institute was to coordinate and integrate the programmes offered to adults, especially evening primary classes, and secondary programmes for workmen. These programmes were promoted by the National Law on Adult Education of 1975, but the complexity of the problems led the government to believe that a single co-ordinating authority would be able to bring greater effectiveness to adult education.

Like all branches of the administration in Mexico, SEP suffers from sexennial dislocations. Although the PRI has been the party of government since the Revolution, each six years the new President appoints his own men and women to key positions. The hierarchy of SEP is deeply affected by these political appointments, which can extend a considerable way down the hierarchy. While each six-year period may be marked by striking and frequently imaginative initiatives in adult

Figure 7.2

The Organization of Institutions of Education in Mexico

Age	3 4 5	6 7 8 9 10 11	12 13 14	15 16 17	18 19 20 21 22 23
Stage	Pre-School	Primary	Lower Secondary	Upper Secondary	Higher
	Pre-Compulsory	Compulsory	Post-Compulsory		
		Primaria	Media Basica	Bachille-rato	University
			Technical Vocational Schools	Scientific Technical Agricult.& Commerc/l Schools	Degree Level Techn-nical Educ.
					Teacher Training

Source: Gonzalez-Paredes (1982: 42)

education or programmes for the indigenous peoples of Mexico, the planning process lacks the continuity which one would expect from such a long period of single-party rule.

Mexico City has been the main centre for higher education for the whole country since the university was first founded there in 1551, on a European model. It was closed on and off during the forty-year period following independence. Its name was changed three times, finally becoming the National Autonomous University of Mexico (UNAM) in 1929. The university has 151 faculties and schools in the Federal District. In 1982 the university had more than 370,000 students, and was growing rapidly, having increased by over 300 per cent in the previous three years (ANUIES, 1984).

The university offers courses in a very wide range of subjects, but specializes in the more academic subjects, and adheres proudly to its traditions. The negative side of this is that the university has been rather conservative in responding to technological change and providing courses in some branches of engineering. In the mid-1970s the *Universidad Metropolitana* was opened on three campuses in the Federal District, to introduce courses which were much more similar to current practice in the United States. Courses are followed for credits, and seminars, tutorials and programmed learning were substituted for the traditional formal lecture. In addition to these two universities, Mexico City has more than a hundred other institutions of higher education. But UNAM remains, in terms of its sheer size and prestige, the most important institution of higher education in the country, attracting students from all parts.

On the supply of teachers, the government is under pressure to introduce reforms which would effectively reduce the supply of teachers for primary schools. As in many other countries there has been a move towards training teachers in universities and institutions of higher education rather than in normal schools. In 1979 the Pedagogical University was founded, to prepare students for first and higher degrees, and to improve the academic quality of teacher preparation. The old normal schools retain both their name, and their function of preparing the majority of teachers, but since the academic year 1983/1984 entry requirements and course requirements have been raised to bring them into line with tertiary education establishments. This moving of primary teacher training from the secondary to the tertiary level of education is undoubtedly desirable in terms of teacher efficiency and proficiency, but works directly counter to the more pressing imperative of supplying enough teachers.

EDUCATION IN MEXICO CITY

The main objective of teachers and educational administrators in Mexico City is to provide an education which is relevant to the everyday circumstances of the pupils. They have this in common with educators throughout the country, and, for that matter, in many countries of the world. However, in the environment of Mexico City, this objective takes on an urgency which is outstanding. Take a walk down any main thoroughfare in the city, or spend a minute or two in a traffic jam, and you will find children cleaning shoes, washing cars, selling chewing gum or newspapers, or engaging in one hundred and one economic activities. If education cannot provide an immediate economic return, there are other occupations which an intelligent and hopeful youngster can turn his or her attention to (Garmendia, 1981). If educators fail in providing a relevant education, then they will be left with empty schools. The immediacy of this challenge means that when teachers in Mexico City talk of providing a 'relevant' education, one feels that it is much more than rhetoric. The diversity of economic activity which one sees children involved in suggests that they are not entirely successful, particularly for the poorest groups in the city, but that should not be allowed to detract from the fact that there are some extremely hopeful developments, particularly in lower secondary education.

Besides the shortage of private resources, which means that the poorest families simply cannot afford to let their children go to school, there is also a shortage of public resources. Quite simply, there are not enough schools in Mexico City. Nor are there enough teachers. It is difficult to get an accurate picture, as SEP does not provide separate figures for Mexico City. Normally one has to draw general conclusions from figures which are available for the Federal District and the State of Mexico. In general, the capital is better provided with educational institutions at all, and particularly at pre-compulsory and post-compulsory, levels than the country as a whole. However, it is difficult to gain a clear picture of the problems in those recently developed areas of Mexico City which come within the State of Mexico. Some indication can be gained from the shortage of teachers in the State of Mexico. But in both the Federal District and the State of Mexico, the terminal efficiency of primary schools, the number completing as a percentage of those initially enrolling, is above the average for the nation as a whole (Consejo Nacional Tecnico de la Educacion, 1981: 95).

Probably the most pressing problem is the shortage of school buildings. The distribution of primary schools over Mexico City is not even, and some areas are badly undersupplied. In recognition of this fact, in the late 1970s the government introduced a system of double shift schools. In effect this meant a more economic use of buildings, by operating two independent schools in the same building, with completely separate staffs, one school working in the morning and the other in the afternoon. While this results in an immediate saving in capital investment, it is not at all clear what the long-term effect on efficiency will be, not only in terms of wear and tear on the building and plant, but also in terms of wear and tear on the staff.

The government of Mexico is by no means alone in preferring to talk about problems after they have been solved. Jose Lopez Portillo was President of Mexico from 1976 to 1982. During his six-year period of office, he set himself an ambitious programme of building enough schools for every child in compulsory education in the Federal District. In 1981 he claimed to have achieved that goal, and an article in *Proceso* gave some indication of the difficulties which had been overcome.

> The ambitious aim of the programme of classroom construction in the Federal District, to eliminate completely the shortage of classrooms at the primary and secondary levels, has been achieved in this six year period. Around 10,000 classrooms have been built by the present administration give children the schools that they deserve; and one feature of the programme deserves to be stressed, that the

> schools have not been built just where there happened to be space for them, but where the children needed them....
>
> Previous governments, to save money, built schools where they could find land, even if this meant that they were a long way from the areas and estates where children live. It was an ill considered saving, as it ended up costing the families much more in transport, time, and above all safety.... There is now no shortage of classrooms, but, naturally, given the continuous demographic growth of the city, the regular increase in the number of schools is necessary in order to keep pressing forward....
>
> As one can imagine, the majority (of the schools) are devoted to the *Delegaciones* (boroughs) where one finds the greatest concentrations of people with modest economic resources. (From an article entitled, 'Ni una sola aula falta ya in el D.F.' [Not even one classroom short in the Federal District now] in: Proceso [1981], translated by the authors)

There are, unfortunately, three good reasons for supposing that the difficulties which the education of Mexico City faced in 1976 have not been solved once and for all. The first reason is mentioned in the article: that is, that Mexico City continues to grow apace, more or less doubling its population every ten years. Even if every President set himself the same task as Lopez Portillo, an even more daunting target would await his successor. Second, the article mentions only the Federal District, and as has already been made clear, by 1980 the bulk of the growth of Mexico City was in fact taking place outside the Federal District in the State of Mexico. Well over one-quarter of the schools built were in Ixtapalapa, the *Delegacion* bordering on Netzahuacoyotl. Moreover, the plight of those 'people of modest economic resources' outside the Federal District was likely to be complicated by other problems, including poor housing, poor water, and poor sanitation. Third, the earthquake of September 1985 has had a devastating effect particularly in the area of school buildings. Ironically, the buildings worst affected were large buildings which had been constructed since 1956, the last major earthquake before 1985. Government buildings and schools were proportionately over-represented among the numbers of buildings damaged. In one way, this is a rather sad tribute to the Herculean efforts the government has made to provide new school buildings, hospitals and housing since 1956.

Similar problems have faced secondary schools as have faced primary schools in the city. The majority of secondary schools now operate two shifts, one in the morning and one in the afternoon, while a number operate a third shift in the evening.

But if Mexico City is short of resources, it is short of neither hopes for the future nor opportunities. The United States of America is never far away, literally and metaphorically, and the television, radio, cinema, shops full of industrial products, industrial complexes, and cars are an ever-present reminder of a lifestyle that the majority of Mexicans aspire to, and an increasing number already enjoy.

This juxtaposition of extreme poverty and considerable luxury provides the major opportunity for the educational system to provide experiences which are worthwhile, and lucrative, for the pupils. While many forms of manual labour are cheap, skills which are related to the modern industrialized way of life are well rewarded. In this context, two developments in lower secondary education have been crucial in increasing the relevance of education over the past fifteen years. The first is the vocationalization of general secondary schools, and the second is a rapid increase in the number of technical secondary schools.

Both these developments are part of national programmes for education, but they take on special significance in Mexico City. The vocationalization of general secondary schools was designed to make the schools move away from their purely academic traditions, and include courses in practical skills similar to those offered in the technical secondary schools. The old schools were not well equipped with laboratories and workshops to cope with such a development, but in Mexico City it has been possible to build special centres, servicing three or four local schools, which provide these extra facilities and the staff to teach the courses. In this way it has been ensured that the introduction of these new courses has been taken beyond the stage of rhetoric and into the realm of action.

The increasing number of technical secondary schools has also been part of a national movement, but the technical and vocational skills taught at each school are intended to be closely matched to the immediate neighbourhood. Figure 7.3 shows the distribution of these schools in the Federal District, which can be compared to the distribution of general secondary schools in Table 7.2. The majority of the technical secondary schools are in the industrial and commercial areas of the city, with a large number of the newer schools being situated in Ixtapalapa, near Netzahuacoyotl. (The number of the school indicates the age of the school, School No.1 being the oldest.)

The technical secondary schools usually offer seven or eight different 'workshops', which teach specific vocational skills, and occupy one-fifth of the pupil's time in school throughout the three years of lower secondary school. While, nationally, these workshop programmes can be chosen from a range of over 100, including aspects of fisheries, forestry and agriculture, all the schools in Mexico City come under the general heading of 'schools of industry, commerce and service industries'. Most offer workshops for electricians, electronic technicians, carpenters, welders, typists and dressmakers, along with one or two more specially selected to fit in with their immediate locality (Turner, 1986). After the induction semester, in which a pupil may try two or three different workshops, the pupil selects a programme of practical skills with the help of teachers and the results of aptitude tests. Each individual pupil then follows one specialized workshop course for the remaining two and a half years of lower secondary education.

The schools are well equipped in terms of buildings and capital equipment, but receive no money for expendable materials, which the pupils have to provide for themselves. Once again, this means that the need for relevance is immediate; if the pupils do not see the benefit of a particular exercise, they will not bring the materials to work with. As a consequence, the courses are intensively orientated towards specific skills which are saleable in the city. The electricians concentrate on domestic wiring and the repair of domestic electrical equipment, the dressmakers make garments they would want to wear or can sell, and so on.

Figure 7.3

The Distribution of Technical Secondary Schools in the Federal District

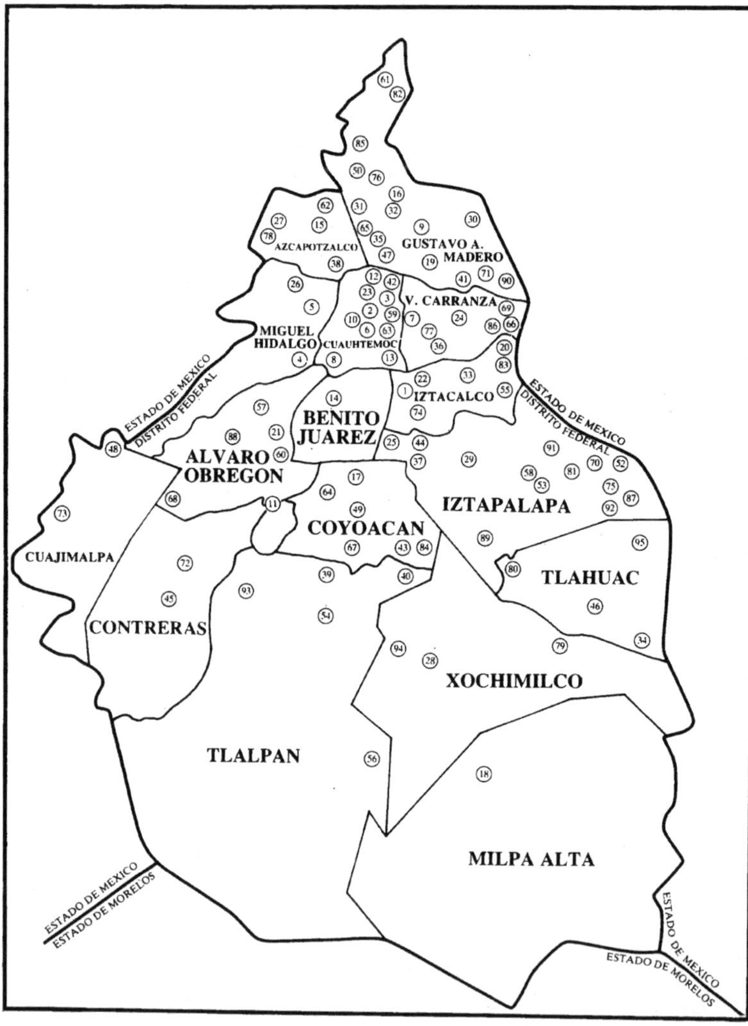

Source: Secretariat for Public Education, Directory of Secondary Technical Schools in the Federal District

Table 7.2

The Distribution of General and Technical Secondary Schools in the Federal District

Delegacion	Number of technical secondary schools	Number of general secondary schools
Alvaro Abregon	6	16
Azcapotzalco	5	22
BenitoJuarez	2	14
Contreras	2	5
Coyoacan	6	22
Cuajimalpa	2	3
Cuauhtemoc	11	28
Gustavo A.Madero	17	47
Iztacalco	7	20
Iztapalapa	14	41
MiguelHidalgo	3	18
Milpa Alta	1	2
Tlahuac	4	5
Tlalpan	5	9
Venustiano Carranza	7	22
Xochimilco	3	8
Total	97	282

Source: Direccion General de Educacion Secundaria, Directorio de Escuelas 1981-1982
Figures for 1982. By 1985 the number of general secondary schools had risen to 303.

Apart from the courses followed in the workshops, the curriculum in the technical secondary schools is the same as that followed in the general secondary schools, and leads to a final qualification of equal status. This, combined with the vocationalization of the general secondary schools, ensures that the technical secondary schools are not seen as an inferior form of secondary education. In a country where aspirations are high, and education is seen as a doorway to social mobility, it is crucial to ensure such parity of status between the technical and general secondary schools if the technical secondary schools are to be successful.

The unique combination of circumstances in Mexico City, of schools offering vocational skills which operate either in the morning or the afternoon, and an economic structure which rewards certain industrial skills highly, has opened up a new range of possibilities. Many pupils in lower secondary school are now able to work their way through school, using the skills acquired in school to pay for their education, while many working adults are able to complete their secondary education or acquire new vocational skills by attending evening schools. This does not yet mean that all young people are able to afford to go to school, but it does mean that education is economically achievable for a broader spectrum of the urban population.

These are hopeful indications for education in Mexico City, but it seems unlikely that the government will be able to produce lasting solutions to the problem of inadequacy of provision. The economic situation of Mexico generally has clear implications for a school building programme on the scale that would be required, which would, as a minimum estimate, be one new school for each school standing, every six years.

If the government is facing severe difficulties in providing sufficient places to meet the demand for education, the scale of the problem is so vast that it seems unlikely that any non-governmental action can solve it either. Less than one in twelve primary schools is privately run, and less than one in four lower secondary schools. Only at the upper secondary and higher levels of education are private schools making as large a contribution as the government institutions. During the late 1970s an attempt was made by groups of students of the national university in Mexico City (UNAM) to establish 'free' schools with literacy training for children who would not or could not attend state schools. Whether the setting up of these schools was politically motivated or not, they did represent a major threat to the Ministry of Education's monopoly of curriculum design. The students found that the Ministry put what obstacles it could in the way of these 'free' schools, and the movement rapidly became politicized and a major bone of contention between the students and the university.

It is unfortunately easy to be over-critical and to form negative conclusions about the provision of education in Mexico City. This is, however, really to turn things round the wrong way. Mexico City has a problem of rapid urbanization unparalleled in the world. In the face of this problem the efforts to supply educational facilities have in many ways been heroic. It was almost quixotic for Lopez Portillo to set himself the target of providing schools for every child in Mexico City, yet he not only attempted it, but had some success.

Lopez Portillo also put forward plans for extending compulsory education, so that it would include, not only primary education, but also lower secondary and one year of kindergarten. These various stages of education would be incorporated within a single programme of basic education. These plans have been retained, and the present government is encouraging discussion as to how such programmes could be achieved in practice (Secretaria de Educacion Publica, 1985).

In the face of these difficulties and shortages of resources, the government continues to adopt ambitious targets, and some imaginative solutions have been put forward. The *telesecundaria*, the programmes of adult education set up by INEA for the bilingual, Indian communities, and the expansion of technical secondary schools are examples.

But the problems of education in Mexico City are not soluble in the sense that the city continues to grow. Up to the present time, the problem of providing complete primary education for every child has been so pressing that plans to extend compulsory provision have not been implemented. In 1980, 187 schools were built for 140,000 pupils. It was not enough, but 140,000 children were in school, who would not have been if attempts were not being made to provide more and better education for the largest city in the world.

BIBLIOGRAPHICAL REFERENCES

Asociacion Nacional de Universidades e Institutos Ensenanza Superior (ANUIES) (1984) **Anuario Estadistico 1983** (Mexico, ANUIES)

Booth, G.C. (1969) **Mexico's School-made Society** (New York, Greenwood)

Cockcroft, J.D. (1983) **Mexico: Class Formation, Capital Accumulation and the State** (New York, Monthly Review Press)

Consejo Nacional Tecnico de la Educacion (1973) **Programa de Quimica para Secundaria Basica** (Mexico, SEP)

Consejo Nacional Tecnico de la Educacion (1981) **Educacion** 7, 4a, 37

Consejo Nacional Tecnico de la Educacion (1984) **Consulta Nacional sobre la Integracion de la Educacion Basica de Diez Grados** (National Consultative Document on the Integration of Ten-year Basic Education) (Mexico, Secretaria de Educacion Publica)

Davies, N. (1982) **The Ancient Kingdoms of Mexico** (London, Allen Lane)

Dewey, J., (1964) **John Dewey's Impressions of Soviet Russia and the Revolutionary World, Mexico - China - Turkey, 1929** (New York, Teachers College, Columbia)

Diario Official (1981) 31 August (Mexico, Government of Mexico)

El Excelsior, 1 September 1935

Garmendia, A., (1981) **Los Mil y Un Oficios de Los Desocupados de La Ciudad** (Mexico, Editores Mexicanos Unidos)

Gobierno Constitucional de los Estados Unidos Mexicanos (1983) **Programa de Desarrollo de la Zona Metropolitan de la Ciudad de Mexico y de la Region Centro** (Development Programme for Mexico City and the Central Region) (Mexico, Gobierno Constitucional de los Estados Unidos Mexicanos)

Gonzalez-Casanova, P. and Flores, E. (eds) (1980) **Mexico Hoy**, 4th Edn (Mexico, Siglo Veintiuno Editores)

Gonzalez-Paredes, M.G. (1982) **School Chemistry Courses, Analysis of Mathematical Requirements through Case Studies of British and Mexican Practice** (unpublished M.Ed. thesis, King's College, London)

Gonzalez de Turner, G. (1987) Disparities, contrasts and developments in contemporary Mexican education, **International Journal of Educational Development** 7, 3: 183-189

Hall, P. (1985) **The World Cities**, 3rd Edn (London, Weidenfeld & Nicolson)

Mabry, D.J. (1982) **The Mexican University and the State: Student Conflicts, 1910-1971** (College Station, Texas A & M University Press)

Proceso (1981), 258

Proceso (1982), 301: 28-29

Proceso (1985), 428: 28-29

Riding, A. (1985) **Vecinos Distantes** (Mexico, Joaquin Mortiz), originally published in English in 1984 under the title, **Distant Neighbours: a Portrait of the Mexicans**

Secretaria de Educacion Publica (1985) **Foro Nacional Sobre La Educacion Basica in Mexico** (Mexico, Secretaria de Educacion Publica)

Silvers, A. and Crosson, P. (1980) **Rural Development and Urban-bound Migration in Mexico** (Washington, DC, Resources for the Future Inc.)

Turner, D.A. (1986) **Secondary Technical Education in Mexico** (London, University of London Institute of Education, Department of International and Comparative Education, papers of the Vocationalizing Education Conference)

Varley, A. (1985) Urbanisation and agrarian law, the case of Mexico City, in, **Bulletin of Latin American Studies** 4, 1

Wilkie, J.W. and Perkal, A. (eds) (1984) **Statistical Abstracts of Latin America** 23 (Los Angeles, UCLA Latin American Center Publications)

Chapter Eight

THE EVOLUTION OF THE COSTA RICAN EDUCATION PROFILE

Pilar Aguilar

INTRODUCTION

Costa Rica is the second smallest of the Central American Republics, with a population estimated at about 2.2 million and an area of 51,000 square kilometres. Most of the population is concentrated in the central part of the country, with the capital city, San Jose, having over a million inhabitants. Writers generally underline the special character of Costa Rica as compared with the rest of Central America. It is seen as a politically stable country in the middle of a sea of conflict and social polarization: a long-standing democracy amidst authoritarianism and revolution. However, the characteristic that gains the attention of most authors, and makes Costa Rica a peculiar country, is the lack of an army. Indeed, barracks have been transformed into schools, and budgets for the purchase of arms have been used instead to serve the purpose of education.

Why is the importance given to education so high? What have been the results of this policy? The answers to such questions can only be ascertained by investigating the evolution of the Costa Rican system, and within this analysis describing the profile of a unique and highly developed educational system for an underdeveloped nation.

THE DEVELOPMENT OF THE SYSTEM

Since its colonial origins Costa Rica has been defined as a very particular society and the relative development of Costa Rican education should be understood within the special characteristics of its socio-economic framework.

While in the remainder of the Central American area rather important poles of colonial development were generated, Costa Rica remained marginal to the economy and trade of the Spanish Empire. This was systematically reinforced by the restrictive measures taken by the Captaincy General and the Royal Audience of Guatemala, whose ruling elite of an absolutist and centralized mentality did not wish to entertain a competitor in the distant southern border. In consequence they enforced regulations to prevent Costa Rican *colonos* allocating their agricultural surpluses to available markets in the region or elsewhere (Vega Carballo, 1983).

The consequence of this situation in social terms was the development of a structure of relatively homogeneous character composed of a majority of white *mestizos* living on subsistence agricultural production and exploiting the land as small property owners. Thus, the weak urban colonial population of Cartago never became a centre for the development of a powerful *criollo* class of merchants and large-scale landowners as happened elsewhere in most areas of Latin America during the colonial period.

The *Escuela de Primeras Letras* constituted the only existing educational provision in the country which survived permanently in Cartago, the colonial capital of Costa Rica. However, many times during the colonial period the people of Cartago, because of their state of poverty, were not able to pay the schoolmaster (Gonzalez Flores, 1978). The curriculum of colonial schooling, as of 1735, was confined to the teaching of Christian doctrine, reading, writing and counting. Also, the teacher was supposed to go out with the children to meet religious obligations such as *viacrucis*, and at the same time to lecture pupils on Christian ethics (Gonzalez Flores, 1978). The *cartilla* was the fundamental text used in the teaching of reading and doctrine.

By the end of the eighteenth century there were very few schools and they were in a precarious condition. The colonial school had an impositive system, discipline through fear prevailed, and physical and psychological punishment was common.

As defined by Monge and Rivas (1984), the transition between the colonial regime and the Republic in terms of educational development was not abrupt; indeed, the social and economic situation of Costa Rica remained stagnant as compared with other countries of Central America during the first four decades of the nineteenth century. During the colonial period, the few Costa Ricans who had gained access to secondary and higher education enrolled at the School of San Ramon in Nicaragua, and subsequently at the University of San Carlos in Guatemala. However, the municipality of San Jose did found the *Casa de Ensenanza de Santo Tomas* in 1814, the Chancellor elected being Rafael Francisco Osejo, Professor of Philosophy in the School of Leon in Nicaragua. The aim of the *Colegio* was to serve as a basic education provision and as a centre for higher education.

After Independence in 1824, Professor Osejo became the main character in the educational sphere of Costa Rica. He wrote the first law for compulsory primary education. The following year a teacher, Juan Mora Fernandez was elected as first Chief of State. His administration founded elementary schools in most of the urban areas of the country. The liberal motto: 'education is the base of a free government' was central to the development of a more formalized provision for education in a Republican context. However, until mid-century the actual development of schooling scarcely covered the urban population, let alone reaching out to the countryside (Table 8.1).

By mid-century Costa Rica was a country of about 120,500 inhabitants, mostly concentrated in the rural areas where, according to the 1864 census: 'illiteracy in the countryside was probably beyond 90 per cent' (Gonzalez Flores, 1978).

Costa Rican liberal educators were instrumental in the definition of a structure of state-sponsored education and centralized educational decision-making. This was the principal aim of Dr Castro Madriz as the first Chancellor of the University of Santo Tomas, created in 1844. Apart from developing traditional academic careers the university had a

Table 8.1

Distribution of the Primary School Population: Costa Rica 1827

Town	No. of Schools	No. of Students
San Jose	20	722
Cartago	7	414
Heredia	7	385
Alajuela	7	499
Barba	2	99
Ujarras	1	73
Union	1	50
Curridabat	1	25
Pacaca	1	24
Cot	1	30
Quircot and Tobosi	1	8
Total	50	2,429

Source: National Archives (1857) Expediente 11150, 36: 154.

supervisory role in the overall organization and promotion of secondary education, and in 1849 the Council of Public Instruction was established by the highest authorities of the university, having as a central aim the promotion of primary schooling.

By 1856 the country faced serious turmoil when it was entirely mobilized in a military campaign against the North American William Walker, a mercenary who tried to conquer Central America on behalf of expansionist economic interests based on the Southern States of the USA. These wars profoundly affected the social and educational structure of Costa Rica, but helped to consolidate a sense of nationality which had not been apparent hitherto.

In 1857, a report of the Ministry of Education gave information about the situation in the province of San Jose:

> It is most discouraging to assess the number of children attending school in this province, if compared with the number who were actually registered a few years ago. Primary school figures which showed a registration of more than 1,000 students have been reduced at present to barely 300 or so (National Archives, 1857).

However, just over a decade later, in 1869, primary education was declared compulsory and free: financed by the state as per the national Constitution. The administrative responsibility was placed at the local county level, with supervision centralized at the Ministry of Education (Gonzalez Flores, 1961). Within these guidelines, new laws were passed regulating primary, and for the first time, secondary education. Nevertheless, the democratic educational principles were far from being fulfilled. Though the authoritarian system softened somewhat, punishment still existed. The monitorial system of Lancaster appeared to be a useful tool, because it helped in the instruction of a great number of children with few teachers, although it relied mainly on rote learning, regimental discipline and a basic '3Rs' curriculum. Religion had a central place in the curriculum.

The first steps for regulating and defining a legal framework for the development of education emerged as a consequence of profound changes occurring in Costa Rican society during the last three decades of the nineteenth century and which helped to stimulate a most important breakthrough in provision.

The concept of education as a means of social mobility, and as an instrument for development, was conceived very early and became a most important feature in the ideology of the Costa Rican state. So the development and modernization of state-sponsored education as early as the 1860s was part of an overall process of consolidation of a social structure and a political system which would in due course inform the particular character of contemporary Costa Rica.

On the one hand, the impact of foreign capital and the control and development of external production, based principally on coffee and other export commodities, was not concentrated in a small powerful elite as happened elsewhere in Central America. The distribution of land as a result of the export enterprise came under the control of the government. A system developed of the state operating as administrator and legal referee as between the interests of rural entrepreneurs and the urban and more cosmopolitan elite in relation to the export enterprises. As pointed out by Vega Caballo (1983):

> The new urban centred demands, the need to control the new emerging social groups, and also the legal regulation of contracts over concessions to foreign capital investment gave way to the consolidation of a strong liberal State of rather small bureaucratic proportions. This State was not easily manipulated by the commercial-financial elite and was prepared to mediate upon the needs of the new urban groups, thus helping to develop a series of public regulations on their behalf.

Comparatively, this process does not seem to be different from similar developments observed in other countries of Latin America during the same period.

Moreover, it is interesting to underline the specific impact which this process had in the development of education. As well as in Argentina, Chile or Uruguay at the end of the nineteenth century, Costa Rican liberal educators and politicians, such as Mauro Fernandez, were successful in the development of schemes for primary and secondary education. From an economic point of view the dominant elite was able to meet adequately the integration of their interests to an external market which required better standards of production and distribution. Thus, via state-sponsored education, the skills of the working population were upgraded and provided a contribution in the achievement of higher productive standards. Probably, the most important components of educational provision in this respect were the educational structures which began to develop by the turn of the century in the areas of teacher training and higher education.

Before 1886 there was no '*education normale*' in the country: teachers had no specific training. It was presumed that any person who had knowledge of a subject was able to teach it. In 1887 the *Liceo de Costa Rica*, a secondary school, was founded. As a special part of the *Liceo*, a teacher training department was created under the guidance of Swiss teachers hired especially for the purpose. By the end of the century, two further teachers colleges, one for men and one for women, had been created. These *Ecoles Normales* were mostly inspired by the educational ideas of Herbart and Froebel, and in 1915 were merged into The Normal School of Costa Rica, in the city of Heredia.

Most influential in the development of this new teacher training college were the ideas of Dewey on democratic education. Also significant was the experience and knowledge acquired by educators, such as Roberto Brenes Mesen, who were trained between 1894 and 1902 in the Superior Normal School of Chile, and in the Pedagogic Institute of the university of that country. This group of educators was most important, basically because they were in a position to push forward the educational reforms of 1917, which set up for the first time in the country curricular guidelines at the primary level. Moreover, they realized that their implementation could not be effective without a clear educational philosophy and a systematic scheme for the education of teachers. Brenes Mesen and Garcia Monge (1908) criticized the prevailing intellectualist education. They wanted to promote the contact of the student with nature through observation and research: 'in school we have to learn to face life and to acquire abilities not only to fulfill programmes and to sit for exams'.

Notwithstanding the crisis of the international coffee market due to World War I and its aftermath, precise guidelines for the training of teachers and for development of a primary school curriculum were issued by the Ministry of Public Instruction in order to face the economic crisis in the countryside. These were aimed at reinforcing skills in the area of production (Ministerio de Educacion Publica, 1921). The Normal School of Costa Rica had developed a national catchment by means of scholarships offered by the government, and offered a higher secondary programme of six years' duration. This was divided into two levels: a lower general secondary, and a higher level dedicated to professional training. Attached to this scheme was a primary experimental facility for the practical training of the future *maestros* (Gonzalez Flores, 1978).

By 1935 the results of state-sponsored primary education in quantitative terms were very high. According to an evaluation of a Chilean Mission of that year:

> Primary education in Costa Rica has deserved the permanent attention of all governments during the last half century. Because of this the Republic heads all other neighbour nations with the figure of 88% of schooling population in elementary classrooms. (Galdames, 1935)

However, a central problem observed by the Chilean Mission was a trend of dislocation, which proved to be recurrent in the following decades of Costa Rican education, between centralized curricular guidelines set up during those years on the basis of the Centres of Interest of Decroly, and the actual implementation and supervision of those guidelines at the classroom level (Monge and Rivas, 1984). In effect there had been an oversimplification of the four centres proposed by Decroly. The social aspect was completely omitted from the plan, and at the classroom level the programmes had no clear philosophical or psychological approach.

One cannot overlook the importance of the Chilean Mission of 1935 in the history of Costa Rican education. The Chilean educators spent nearly a year trying to modernize the system, its basic tenets and structures. Unfortunately, Costa Rica was not prepared for such a big upheaval as the integral reform of teaching. Nonetheless, two projects of the Chilean Mission were taken into account:

1. the creation of the National University of Costa Rica based on the project of the Chilean educator Luis Galdames;

2. the application of the global method of reading and writing, first as a project method in a few schools and then to the whole country.

In fact, Costa Rica had founded her first university in 1842, the University of Santo Tomas with two Faculties: Letters and Law. However, in 1886 the Minister of Public Instruction had abolished the university by law as the only means of removing the conservative opposition that from within criticized the reforms instigated by the government of the day. Although the institution stopped being a university, the School of Law remained in being, and gradually the Schools of Pharmacy and Agriculture were created. Eventually the National University of Costa Rica was established in 1940 with the new Schools of Letters, Philosophy and Sciences.

During the 1940s Costa Rica faced deep social and political transformations. Nicaragua under the dictatorial regime of Anastasio Somoza invaded Costa Rica in 1948-1949 in order to stop the Social Democrat leader of the opposition, Jose Figueres. This invasion was due to the fear that Costa Rica would become a socialist state, especially during the Cold War years. The potential advance of communism was feared by Washington. In the event, Figueres succeeded and was able to overcome the Nicaraguan invaders. After his victory, apart from repressing the communist leadership, he nationalized banking, and strengthened the Welfare State through Social Security, Health and Education. He also created *Partido de Liberacion Nacional*. This political party was instrumental to his nationalistic and social-democratic ideas (Vega Carballo, 1983). The *Junta* headed by Figueres organized the new Constitution of 1949 in which four major educational changes were introduced:

1. education to be perceived as an 'integral process' complemented in its different levels from pre-school to university;

2. free secondary education was to be instituted to complement free primary education which had been available for a hundred years;

3. the Superior Education Council (*Consejo Superior de Educacion*) was created to be in charge of the general direction of public education and to guarantee continuity in educational programmes;

4. secondary education was incorporated to the newly restructured Ministry of Education. Hitherto, the Ministry had been mainly a 'Primary Education Ministry'.

In addition, for the in-service training of teachers a special unit was created. The National University of Costa Rica (UCR) was strengthened to promote the training of professionals in all areas. Autonomy and adequate financing were guaranteed.

Until 1950, the expansion and universalization of primary schooling had been the main educational goal of the state. That same year, the enrolment of primary education was 66.5 per cent for the population between 6 and 13 years old, with 1,046 elementary schools serving mainly the urban areas (Rojas, 1984).

The old liberal motto of universal and compulsory education was bound to be modernized with a more technocratic language. Not only was Costa Rica in need of dynamizing the traditional bureaucratic structures, but the new character of foreign investment began to press upon the Ministries of Education of nearly all Latin American countries. The need to meet foreign investments, mostly directed to the modern industrial and more dynamic sector of the Costa Rican economy, with qualified human resources able to manage this emerging sector, was central to the new educational approach.

Along these lines and during the 1960s, a profound change took place in the ideological approach towards education and its value. Costa Rica was not an exception to this external influence, for the United States - and especially the Agency for International Development - was instrumental in the implementation of such an approach throughout Latin America. According to Denton (1979)

> The United States Agency for International Development (AID) can also be termed a Costa Rican political interest group. In return for its assistance, perceived by the government as necessary for achieving certain kinds of developmental goals, AID demands certain rules and regulations be adopted by the Costa Rican government. AID lobbies both directly and indirectly for its programs through press contacts and by talking to political decision-makers.

As a result of the above-mentioned influence during the decade of the 1970s higher education expanded tremendously. Up to this point, only one university existed, and one normal school. In addition to the National University of Costa Rica, a Technological Institute, The National Autonomous University, and the Distance Learning State University were created. Also, the first private university was allowed to operate: Central American Autonomous University. There was a proliferation of new institutes and colleges offering short-term career training in various fields.

At this stage, more education meant better occupations and increased social mobility. According to census data for the period 1963-1973:

> structural mobility in Costa Rica was one of the highest in Latin America... education

> played a central role in the stability of the system by becoming the most expedite channel for social mobility and also because of the social integrative function which generated expectations for future mobility in the groups which were left behind. (Garcia, 1977)

However, the long-standing liberal Costa Rican tradition, with its historical concern over universal primary education, continued to give importance to that level of education. This two-fold effort generated a most important leap forward and during the 1970s the highest levels of educational enrolment in Latin America were reached at all levels of the system. The expansion of primary and especially secondary education during these years obviously had a quantitative consequence. The number of elementary schools increased from 1,175 in 1951 to 2,856 in 1971 and 3,482 in 1981. The number of secondary schools increased from 37 in 1951 to 142 in 1971 and to 261 in 1981. The net enrolment rate at the elementary school level increased from 66.55 per cent in 1950 to 80.30 per cent in 1963, to 95.00 per cent in 1973 and eventually reached 98 per cent in 1980. At the secondary school level, the net enrolment rate proceeded from 5.89 per cent in 1950 to 20.96 per cent in 1963, to 36 per cent in 1973 and exceeded 50 per cent for the first time in 1980 (Rojas, 1984).

CONTEMPORARY PROVISION AND OPERATION

The aim of this section is to describe the present structure of the Costa Rican system and attempt some general conclusions about its performance. Figure 8.1 provides a graphical overview of the system as currently operating.

Pre-school and Primary Provision

Pre-school education is free and state-sponsored, but is not compulsory. Those attending normally do so for the period of one year. The enrolment rate for this sector is estimated at about 50 per cent in the mid-1980s in respect of the population between 5.6 and 6.6 years of age. It is developed primarily in the urban areas.

Primary education is also free, compulsory, and state-sponsored, with a basic duration of six years. At the end of this period the student receives a diploma that serves as a qualification for employment in low-paid occupations. However, primary education, when articulated to secondary education, forms the basis of a General Education of nine years' duration. The total population eligible for Basic General Education between 6 and 15 years (first and second cycles) is now approximately 500,000. Of the total the system absorbs about 70 per cent, including repeaters.

Secondary Provision

Secondary education is free but not compulsory, and is state financed. Its structure helps to assist the vocational and educational needs of adolescents with a five-year programme. First, there is a general curriculum of three levels which aims to be a formative period, including general and supplementary subjects. During this period the main goal is to ascertain the abilities and interests of the student.

The second cycle includes general studies and special programmes for diversified and vocational education. It is a two-year period. At this level students have optional areas of study such as:

1. Sciences and Humanities (two years), where at the end of the period students will get the title of Bachelor of Sciences and Humanities at the secondary level;

2. Industrial and Commercial education (two years) in order to gain the title of Industrial Professional Bachelor, and Bachelor of Commerce; or Farming Education (two years) for the title of Bachelor of Farming;

3. Arts Education (three years) leading to the title of Bachelor of Arts (Dance-Ballet-Theatre-Music and Arts);

4. Technical Education, in which apart from having

Figure 8.1

The Costa Rican Education System in the 1980s

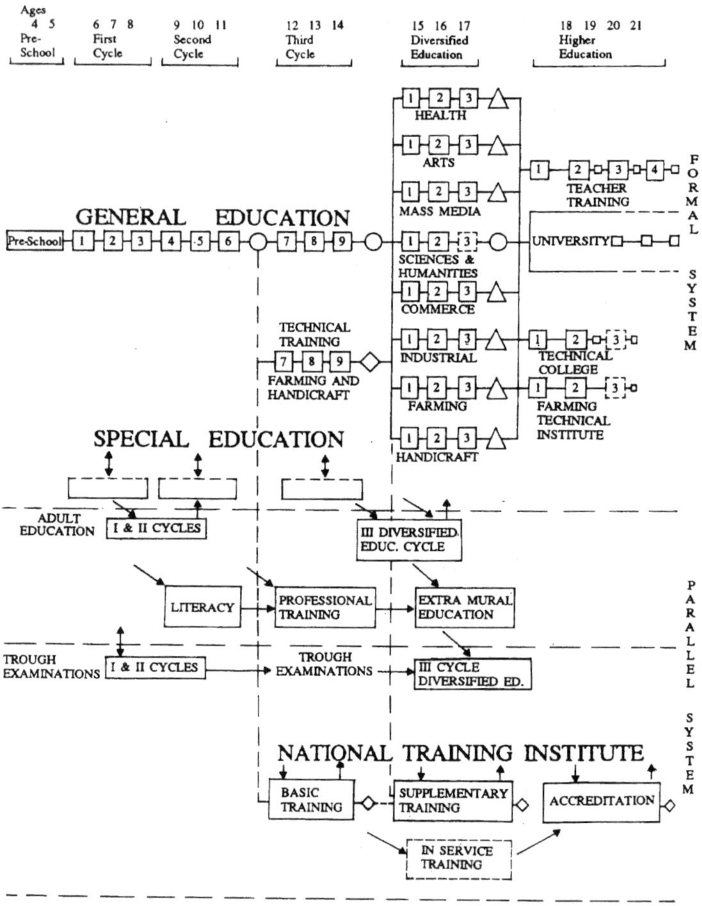

Symbology

○ Academic Certificates (All levels)
◇ Technical Proficiency Certificates
△ Secondary Level Professional Diplomas
□ Technical/Professional Degrees

Source: Ministry of Education Statistics

completed the first six grades the student must continue for another three years, with such specializations as Mechanics and Electricity.

All official secondary institutions are state-sponsored and under the direct control of the Ministry of Public Education.

The Tertiary Sector

Higher Education comprises three state universities:

1. The University of Costa Rica (*Universidad de Costa Rica*);

2. The National Autonomous University (*Universidad Nacional Autonoma*);

3. The Distance Learning State University (*Universidad Nacional Estatal a Distancia*);

and one private university:

The Central American Autonomous University (*Universidad Autonoma Centroamericana*).

As a counterpart to the university at a higher vocational level is the Technological Institute of Costa Rica, located in the city of Cartago and mostly concerned with the training of engineers.

From a population of about 290,000 young people between the ages of 19 and 24 years, the state system of higher education contains an estimated proportion of 18 per cent (Gonzalez Orellama, 1985).

A recently published report on higher education in Central America underlines the situation of Costa Rican university provision in a comparative perspective with the rest of Central America:

> The only Central American universities doing substantial research are the public universities in Costa Rica. The University of C.R. in San Jose has 17 M.A. programs and a graduate

> program in medicine, which trains 90 per cent of the physicians in the country. The development of a strong graduate program has given special impetus to research, including the social sciences, psychology (educational testing), economics, health, law, the natural sciences such as nutrition, agricultural economics, and animal foods. Some of these research programs are carried out with the collaboration of the U.S. universities, such as the University of Kansas. The M.A. program in sociology is carried out with CSUCA, and has a regional focus designed for students from all Central American countries. Although there is a lively and well-qualified faculty in the social sciences (mostly with advanced degrees) some complained that Conacit, the national funding agency for research, has given very low priority to the social sciences and in 1985 excluded them entirely. (Safa, 1985)

This is clearly an accolade for Costa Rican higher education and lends strong support to the conventional wisdom in respect of the place of Costa Rica in the Latin American educational spectrum.

Non-formal Education

Among other programmes of education at the tertiary level is the National Training Institute (INA), created in 1965. This institute trains apprentices and workers in nearly all areas and levels of the economic sector. It is administered autonomously and is probably the most efficient component of the entire system, having a very high trainee turnover.

General Trends

Since 1948 there have been major changes in Costa Rican education. These changes are interrelated with economic and political trends. For example, throughout the economic expansion of Costa Rica, education has developed in parallel with the growth of other services, such as health and social security, sponsored by the Welfare State. Now that the economic recession has become ingrained, although - indeed partly because - Costa Rica has a highly expanded and developed provision, severe problems are being experienced. In the mid 1980s the state has relatively fewer financial resources and so the educational apparatus is becoming harder to maintain and support, let alone develop. Therefore, it must be appreciated that the quality of education is lower at present than in previous years. The growth in drop-out rates is one of the manifestations of the problems that the state must come to terms with. Table 8.2 illustrates the magnitude of this issue.

Table 8.2

Dropout Figures for the First, Second and Third Cycles: Costa Rica 1981-83 (Public and Private Institutions)

	Absolute figures			Relative figures[a]		
Level of teaching	1981	1982	1983[b]	1981	1982	1983
Pre-school	n/d	n/d	993	n/d	n/d	3.0
I & II Cycles[c]	13,247	14,293	10,452	3.8	4.2	3.0
III Cycle & Diversified ed. (day-time)	13,526	16,803	13,526	10.0	12.9	11.2
III Cycle & Diversified ed. (evening)	8,548	9,943	7,799	23.4	28.4	29.3

n/d no data available
a percentage calculated over the initial enrolment
b evening schools not included
c preliminary figures

Source: Memoria 1984, Ministry of Education, San Jose, C.R.

According to Table 8.2 the system has a high level of retention for the first six years of schooling. However, at the following levels the drop-out rate increases to nearly 13 per cent, with the worst situation being that observed in evening and diversified education where a growth of the drop-out rate to nearly 30 per cent obtains. It is perhaps a paradox that despite the great expansions of the past, including that of social mobility through education, it is still a rather traditional structure of state-sponsored education that has to cope with the quantitative wave generated by previous years of reformism and economic growth. Thus, instead of putting more emphasis on the qualitative aspect of education the system is forced to an exhausting expansionist effort of a quantitative nature. We can assume that there are large discrepancies between educational ideals and reality with regard to access to and quality of education. Simple access to school is not enough, the quantity and quality of inputs to the educational system need to be analysed, but in Costa Rica there has been a failure to generate in a systematic manner, the multiple choices of information which are needed for longitudinal research of educational performance. Moreover, the information currently available does not analyse the outputs of the system which is a most relevant factor in the understanding of performance (World Bank, 1980).

Sanchez *et al.* (1977) have shown that 31.1 per cent of the drop-outs from the primary and secondary levels recognize that the principal reasons for desertion are:

> bad relations between teachers and students, between students themselves and students and the educational institutions. Moreover, what was mostly underlined was the inadequate methodologies and the lack of interest shown by teachers.

It is also important to stress that in this research it was found that economic reasons for drop-out were only slightly more relevant (34.6 per cent) than those which referred to the qualitative side of education. Also, a fairly recent evaluation by Wahab (1983), apart from underlining the existence of a rote, narrow, superficial and unpractical education, points to other problems such as the lack of textbooks, supportive services and well-trained teachers. It also mentions the heavy American influence on curriculum planning, and in general the declining cost-effectiveness of the system.

At present, more education does not mean necessarily upward social mobility:

> in fact, it will be very difficult for occupations in the service and commercial sectors a) to ensure constantly expanding labour market and b) to remunerate with income according to the educational development reached. (World Bank, 1980)

In brief, nearly all recent administrations have been concerned with educational expansion, and they have made a real effort to try to contribute to it, thus the educational budget has been increasing. In 1951, education represented 15.61 per cent of public expenditure. This went up to 21.29 per cent in 1963, to 22.6 per cent in 1971, and to 29.13 per cent, or 5.9 per cent of the GNP, in 1981. When it is realized that the unusually high figure of 97 per cent of the Ministry of Education's budget goes for the payment of salaries, leaving only 3 per cent for operation expenses, one begins to identify a potentially difficult problem in a period of economic stagnation.

Indeed, one of the most pressing reasons, apart from the profoundly rooted liberal tradition towards access to education, for the continued growth of the system and the consequent drain on public funds is the pressure exerted by the Costa Rican 'army' of 22,883 teachers. This corporative group is highly organized and constitutes the most important social pressure group in Costa Rican society. Thus, apart from purely technical or ideological considerations, the growth of the system is also based on the politcal influence of the organized teacher unions on the system. Even as recently as 1983, the growth in recruitment to the teaching force was 4.5 per cent for that one year alone (Ministerio de Educacion Publica, 1985). With this sort of commitment to the profession, little scope is now available to improve other aspects of educational provision, such as the quality of the curriculum, supporting materials and physical plant.

The maintenance of *Partido de Liberacion Nacional* as the most important political force in the country since 1948 is to a very large extent based on its popularization of the notion of education as the door towards social upward mobility, economic distribution and democracy. On the other hand, faced with the present economic crisis, the Costa Rican state is forced to cut on public expenditure, including education. Thus, the belief of Jose Figueres that 'education is the indispensable key in order to open the most valuable resources of the nation - its human resources' (Mauck, n/d), though valid in essence, needs to be reassessed within the scope of the economic and social crisis of Central America in general and Costa Rica in particular.

BIBLIOGRAPHICAL REFERENCES

Brenes Mesen, R. and Garcia Monge (1908) **Proyecto de Programa de Instruccion Publica** (San Jose, Tipografia Nacional)

Denton, C.F.(1979) Costa Rica: a democratic revolution, in Wiarda, H.J. and Kline, H. (eds) **Latin American Politics and Development** (Boston, Houghton Mifflin)

Galdames, L. (1935) Informes, Informes y Trabajos in **Mision Educacional Chilena en Costa Rica**, Vol.1 (San Jose, Juan Arias Impresor)

Garcia, J. (1977) **Educacion y Desarrollo en Costa Rica: sobre la Base de los Censos de 1963 y 1973** (San Jose, Confederacion Superior Universitaria de Centro America - CSUCA)

Gonzalez Flores, L. (1961) **Historia de Desarrollo de la Instruccion Publica en Costa Rica** (San Jose, Ministerio de Educacion Publica)

Gonzalez Flores, L. (1978) **Evolucion de la Instruccion Publica en Costa Rica** (San Jose, Costa Rica)

Gonzalez Orellana, C. (1985) **Los Educadores y la Escuela Paralela en Guatemala y Costa Rica** (Guatemala, Universitaria de Guatemala)

Mauck, W.(n/d) **The Role of Education in Technical Assistance Programs: Building a Better Hemisphere** (Washington DC, The Institute of Inter-American Affairs)

Ministerio de Educacion Publica (1921) **Programmas de Educacion Primaria Escuelas Rurales** (San Jose, Imprenta Nacional)

Ministerio de Educacion Publica (1985) **Indicadores de Matricula Inicial, Personel Docente, Instituciones, Educativas y Fuerza de Trabajo** (San Jose, Imprenta Nacional)

Monge, C. and Rivas, F. (1984) **La Educacion Tragica de Nuestra Democracia** (San Jose, Porvenir)

National Archives (1857) **Expediente 11150, 36** (San Jose)

Rojas, Y. (1984) The politics of an educational reform process in Costa Rica: a case study (Vol.1 of unpublished doctoral dissertation, University of Wisconsin)

Safa Helen, I. (1985) The Central American crisis and its impact on the university, **Latin American Studies Association Forum** 16, 3

Sanchez, Z. et al. (1977) El impacto de la crisis socio-economica en la desercion del sistema educativo Costarricense, **Educacion** 1

Vega Carballo, J. (1983) **Hacia una Interpretacion del Desarrollo Costarricense: Ensayo Sociologico** (San Jose, Porvenir)

Wahab, Z. (1983) Education in Costa Rica: an overview (Paper presented to the Annual Conference of the Western Region of the Comparative and International Education Society)

World Bank (1980) **Costa Rica: Education Sector Memorandum** (Washington DC)

Chapter Nine

EDUCATIONAL REFORM IN VENEZUELA: THE 1980 LAW

Lilia Borrero and Eyra Jimenez

INTRODUCTION

This chapter is mainly concerned with the Venezuelan educational reforms proposed in the 1980 Education Law.

The main efforts made by the Venezuelan government in the 1980s have been in the implementation of basic education throughout the country. From 1980 to 1983 experiments in basic education were carried out in 1,500 schools throughout the country. Resulting from these trials, curriculum schedules and study programmes throughout the country were readjusted and have been implemented from 1985. In that year the first cycle of basic education (years 1, 2, 3) were put into operation; the second cycle (years 4, 5, 6) and the third (years 7, 8, 9) followed.

The methodology used in this chapter involved a survey of official documents coming from the Ministry of Education related to basic education. It is relevant to add that the authors' direct experience contributes to an explanation of many of the issues in this chapter. Both authors worked in the Venezuelan Ministry of Education and have been involved within the whole process of implementing basic education in Venezuela.

HISTORICAL REVIEW

Many reforms have taken place in the Venezuelan educational system with the aim of improving educational standards and raising teaching quality in Venezuelan society. These changes have been aimed at democratizing education, improving the level of compulsory education, and providing free public education.

In 1870 President Antonio Guzman Blanco established universal free and compulsory primary education. The result of this was a massive enrolment in schools which created the need for specialized teacher education and training in 1876. Immediately the need for an educational administration arose and the Ministry of Education was founded in 1881. In 1914 Felipe Guevara Rojas, then Minister of Education, divided primary education into two levels: an elementary level from the first to the fourth grade, and a higher level from the fifth to the sixth grade (Ministerio de Educacion, 1982a: 6). On that occasion the reform extended schooling by two years, making six years in all.

In 1936 the government brought a group of educational experts from different countries to assist and cooperate in the development of new educational projects such as teacher training and school administration. In the same year the Pedagogic Institute of Caracas was created as a teacher training college for the secondary sector. An Education Law in 1940 recommended different primary school provision in rural and urban areas. It took into account as main objectives the pupils' moral development and relevance of the curriculum to the environment. This particular law also reformed secondary education, increasing it from four academic years to six, and divided it into two levels. The first level was dedicated to the study of humanities and sciences, while the second was a pre-university course in which students specialized in particular subjects which they aimed to study at university.

The 1945 Education Law reduced the secondary school to five academic years and kept the first level as general basic education, linked with primary schooling in order to offer a complete cultural and scientific progression. This implied that a pupil with the first level of secondary education was ready for the world of work without proceeding to the second level or a pre-university course (Marrero, 1960: 5). In 1947 a Ministry resolution resulted in the opening of an experimental school which extended primary schooling to seven grades in order to provide integral education. The General Assembly of The United Nations in 1948 proclaimed that primary education should be the basic education for every person. It suggested that each country should make basic schooling a priority in their educational policy.

As in 1945, so the 1958 Education Law attempted to relate general education to work. In addition, evening classes were offered to adult students with the same curriculum as in day schools (Marrero, 1964: 38). As Armas Chitty (1976: 15) points out, by this time a large illiteracy campaign was operating within the country. An important outcome of the implementation of the 1958 legislation was the creation of an Integral Planning Office whose functions were:

1. to centralize all education projects;

2. to coordinate and run the necessary research to develop any project;

3. to stimulate inter-institutional cooperation and public consultation in educational planning;

4. to supervise, advise and provide specific assistance while any project is being developed;

5. to evaluate the implementation process and the results of any particular plan. (UNESCO, 1965: 73)

By 1958, primary education lasted six academic years. Primary school leavers could either take a general secondary education in order to go on to higher education, or undertake a specialized secondary education as teacher education and technical, commercial or agricultural education, thus providing the opportunity to be trained in a particular occupation.

From 1965 an experimental design in basic education was tried in a few institutions which extended primary education from six to nine academic years. Nevertheless in 1969 a Presidential Decree established the first level of secondary education as being divided into two cycles: a basic common cycle for all primary school leavers lasting three academic years; a second diversified cycle of two or three academic years. Primary school leavers who did not proceed to secondary education at all could take short part-time courses in private institutions, adult education centres, or in the National Institute for Education Cooperation (INCE) in order to gain pre-vocational or craft experience. In the 1970s adult education developed new strategies to provide the primary and secondary programmes in a shorter period than involved in day schooling. This was achieved by using flexible methods more suited to adult learning needs (Urriola, 1973: 7-18).

Democratization, innovation and autonomous development were the main principles of Venezuelan educational policy by 1974. Such a policy motivated a general reorganization of the education system, so as to relate to the new goals of the nation. Thus in 1975 a pilot project was tried in a sample of primary schools with the object of extending primary education from six to seven grades throughout the whole country. In 1976 the Ministerial Planning Office undertook a major survey of the primary and basic secondary cycles. This study identified many problems in relation to school attendance, teacher training, general educational quality, and level of resources. It was decided that a new curriculum design was required and so the 1976 Basic Education Project was established (Zambrano, 1983). As early as 1977, the Ministerial Planning Office, in co-ordination with Primary Education Directorate and other Ministerial offices, sought official approval to extend the pilot project to other schools, and this was given. Even by the following year, great efforts were being devoted to developing a theoretical basis for the extension of the pilot project throughout the country. This involved the design of a new educational policy and strategies for basic education, which in Venezuela is understood as lifelong education for the whole population. Therefore, in order to design the new curriculum, many different variables were taken into account, such as: learning resources, educative communities, school buildings, assessment and evaluation, school administration study programmes, guidance and counselling, and teacher training.

It is relevant here to mention the Mexico Declaration of 1979, which was signed in the Unesco Regional Conference of Ministers of Education from Latin America and the Caribbean. Some of its agreements were:

1. all member states must offer a general basic education with no less than eight to ten academic years;

2. to enrol into the school system all children within school age, before 1999 according to its educational policy;

3. to adopt an energetic policy for the eradication of illiteracy by 1999;

4. to make a special effort to relate the curricula to the needs of less favoured and minority groups;

5. to establish new teacher training systems (UNESCO, 1983).

By 1980 the new Venezuelan educational law established basic education as including the second level within the formal system, and in 1980-1981 a project began with 71 schools throughout the country, though only first, fourth and seventh grades were taken as samples: 18,952 pupils and 525 teachers were involved. By 1981-1982, the project was extended to 178 schools with an enrolment of 80,000 pupils and the involvement of 4,000 teachers. The project had been extended to cover first, second, fourth, fifth, seventh and eighth grades. Finally by 1982-1983, 1,312 schools throughout the country were included, with an enrolment of 757,215 pupils and with 29,431 teachers involved. This phase, that of implementation, covered all nine grades.

In 1984 a national evaluation was instituted to assess the progress, benefits and failures of the project in order to determine the reforms necessary to curriculum redesign, and to the extension of basic education to all schools in Venezuela (Ministerio de Educacion, 1985a).

THE VENEZUELAN EDUCATION SYSTEM: AN OVERVIEW

The state, through the Ministry of Education, is responsible for all aspects of the national system. Legislation controls almost every aspect of provision and operation. To carry out these obligations the Ministry is divided into several directorates and departments (Figure 9.1). The legal bases upon which the education system rests is determined by the 1961 Constitution (Articles 78 to 82) plus the Education Law of 1980. This legal structure can be further complemented by presidential decrees.

In Venezuela the education system is highly centralized, and because education is the monopoly of the state, its planning is almost entirely the responsibility of the Ministry of Education. Political power, however, lies with the National Executive with the President as head.

The aims of the Venezuelan education system are established in the national Constitution:

> Education will have, as its aim, the development of personality, the training of citizens for life, and for the exercising of democracy, the encouragement of culture and the development of the spirit of human solidarity. The state will orientate and organize the education system to realise the accomplishment of these aims. (Constitucion de la Republica de Venezuela, 1961: Article 80)

According to this article, the principal responsibility in providing universal free education seems to rest in the hands of the state. However, there are a large number of private schools which in effect help the state in the task of providing schooling. Without the private sector the state would be unable to provide sufficient places for the compulsory school age-group, which is of course always rising in numbers. Even given the clearly expressed national goals and the private provision, the state has not reached the entire age-group because, *inter alia*, educational planning has lacked an integral model which allows flexibility and adaptation to regional and local circumstances and takes note of the variety of student characteristics, needs, and expectations.

In order to examine the Venezuelan education system it is important to note the new structure of the system that has been developed since 1980 (Figure 9.2), since the educational law of that year brought profound changes which may be summarized as follows: new *sectors* established:

Figure 9.1:

Ministry of Education: Structural Diagram

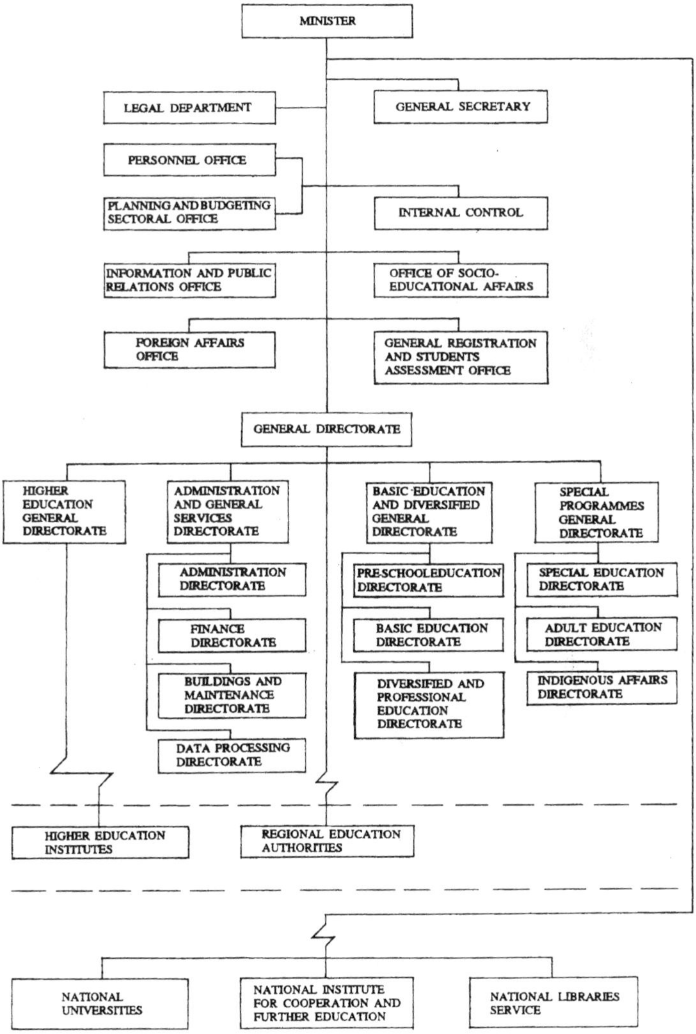

Source: Ministerio de Educacion (1984) Memoria y Cuenta, Caracas, Venezuela

1. pre-school education (4 - 6);
2. basic education (7 - 15);
3. diversified and professional education (16 -18);
4. higher education (18 +).

Additional *modalities* recognized:

1. special education;
2. adult eductaion;
3. arts;
4. military;
5. extra-school education.

In the following sections general information as to quantitative and qualitative aspects of the levels structure are described in order to complete the organizational context within which our main analysis of basic, including adult, education must be seen.

Pre-school Education

According to the current law, so-called 'pre-school education' is the first level within the system and it is compulsory. Nonetheless it is not available for the whole population under the age of six because the state is not able to provide such capacity. Until 1968 pre-school was mainly provided by the private sector, and the Ministry of Education could offer places for only 20,000 children throughout the country. Furthermore, standards varied considerably from school to school. It was in order to try to overcome such disparities that the state began to assume direct responsibility for this sector and give some priority to improving the quantity and quality of provision.

From 1969 to 1974 official enrolment increased to more than 45,000 places; and in the 1979 to 1982 period to 400,000 places (Ministerio de Educacion, 1982b: 6-7). By 1984, statistics show that 34 per cent of Venezuela's pre-school children received formal education which still leaves two in every three without a place (Ministerio de Educacion, 1984a: 13). In analysing the 1982 statistics the Ministry of Education pointed out: 'even though the provision does not reach the desirable goal the rate of growth is positive and continuous' (Ministerio de Educacion, 1982b: 7), a statement that is clearly positive of intent.

In qualitative terms it might be said that the new pre-school programmes particularly seek to develop sensory-motor and thinking basic skills, to correct and improve speech, and provide a sense of discipline. Normally the child will not be taught to read, because that is considered a primary school task. The programme is often reliant on participation of voluntary staff from the community, who provide vital assistance to the teachers (Ministerio de Educacion, 1984b: 11).

Basic Education

This embraces the former primary schooling and the first cycle of secondary school. This sector now has nine grades and is compulsory, thus significantly extending the universal dimension of Venezuelan education. Even by the 1983-1984 school year, the enrolled population in basic education was 3,368,223 which represented 88 per cent of children in that age range; the remaining 12 per cent were either out of school, or never attended school, or had attended and dropped out (Ministerio de Educacion, 1984c). It is clear that the main Venezuelan reform post-1980 has in fact been brought about at the basic education level, and an analysis of this sector forms the major part of this chapter.

Diversified and Professional Education

The main aim of this level in Venezuela is to continue the general cultural preparation of basic education while introducing further specialization in either humanities, sciences or other professional branches. The diversified cycle of secondary education is the traditional route to the university. This level has a duration of not less than two years, and in some cases three, and its satisfactory completion confers the certificate of 'Bachiller' (Bachelor). In Venezuela the diversified level still needs urgent attention in order to establish the necessary integration with basic education and also to prepare the student for employment as well as the possibility of further or higher education. By 1984 the enrolment in this level was 236,520 pupils, or 20 per cent of the age range in question (Ministerio de Educacion, 1984a: 13). Furthermore, of this minority who manage to proceed beyond compulsory schooling, only 22 per cent are involved in technical education, leaving nearly four in five studying the traditional specializations within the sciences and humanities. This has to be evaluated in the light of Venezuela's manpower needs as an industrializing society. Indeed, there appears to be an increasingly negative attitude towards technical education as an alternative to university. Technical training is always tied up with work experience and some form of apprenticeship, much of it is administered jointly by the state and the representative trades and industries concerned. It does not have status but the paradox is that the pupils emerging from this kind of education seem to be better oriented towards local employment and also cope better with the demands of higher education if and when they do proceed to it. A vital constraint is that the state does not provide enough places at this level because this kind of education is deemed too expensive; there is obviously the problem of providing technical equipment, maintaining it and keeping up to date with the latest machines.

In fact, the diversified level has not been reformed according to the requirements of the 1980 law. It is supposed to provide scientific, humanistic and technical capacities to students in order to develop qualified and skilled manpower. However, the Ministry of Education has provisions for the necessary developments at this level to be implemented by the 1987-1988 session.

Higher Education

The fourth level of the pyramid is higher education. The definition and main goals of this level are set out in Articles 25 to 28 of the 1980 Education Law, according to which any 'Bachiller', or graduate from technical education, may be admitted to universities, universitarian colleges, pedagogic institutes and polytechnics, providing the student fulfills the particular requirements of the given institution and/or specialization within it. Official statistics from 1984 show an enormous imbalance as between the numbers matriculating in universities and those leaving. They revealed that from the 376,109 students matriculating, 351,276 dropped out of the system; which means a 93.4 per cent failure rate, which is by any standards of comparison an incredible and undesirable state of affairs (Ministerio de Educacion, 1984c: 412). It would seem to indicate that reform of Venezuelan higher education is urgently needed, but the government has probably been correct in identifying the priority of the basic compulsory education in terms of attention, and it is to this central core of provision that we now return.

A DESCRIPTIVE ANALYSIS OF VENEZUELAN BASIC EDUCATION

Following the 1980 Law basic education provision involved the re-orientation of the philosophical, psychological, legal, administrative, organizational bases of the curriculum, including such fundamental variables as pupils' profiles and teachers' profiles. Greater parent-school integration has been fundamental to the reform. The policy behind the reform is clearly stated within the VII Plan of the Nation (1984-1989) which, for basic education, laid down:

1. adjustment of different schools' curricula to a unitary curriculum for each level of education. This means that schools which are following the six-grade model or three years basic cycle or other models now have to adjust to the nine-grade basic education;

2. working out new methods of administration and organization for basic schools;

3. evaluation and reorganization of the experimental basic schools and the development of curricular reforms.

In respect of these demands, the Ministry of Education began by assessing the experimental project in two ways: that is to say, documental revision and field work applied to a sample (25 per cent of schools from among the 1,312

Figure 9.2:

Venezuelan Education System Since 1980

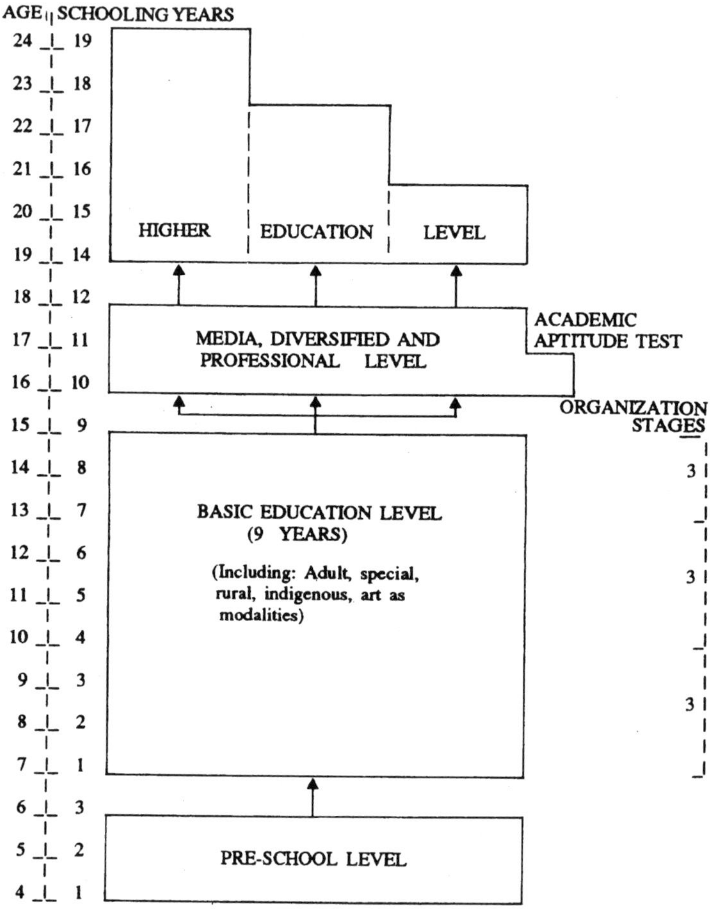

Source: Ministerio de Educacion (1985) Plan de Revision Curricular de los Diferentes Niveles y Modalidades Caracas, Venezuela

institutions within the project). Some of the main conclusions from this research were as follows:

1. the need to re-define basic education provision, the school's plan and new syllabuses to be approved;

2. to expand and disseminate the new basic education to most schools;

3. to leave a small sample of schools as experimental schools in order to obtain new experiences while still including them in the regular system;

4. to include adult education, special education, rural and indigenous education within the parameters of basic education, but using different teaching and learning strategies as appropriate to each curriculum component when being offered to special groups such as these.

As a result of this new dynamic policy, working within the legal bases of Venezuelan basic education, as provided in 1980, the second level may be characterized now as follows:

1. *efficient*: because the government is responsible for the inspection and management, the co-ordination of the teaching process in the nation's schools, as well as for providing and controlling teachers' integrity and training;

2. *integrated*: because the system now guarantees a curricular sequence throughout the nine grades, as well as co-ordination with other modalities and levels within the education system;

3. *democratic*: because all have the right to be educated up to this level;

4. *formative*: since the system must develop moral values, looking for the whole development of the personality. It prepares children as good citizens within a democratic system, providing for the development of skills in order to enable them to participate in the social change process;

5. *active*: in that basic education's main innovation is to relate it with work training for the demands of the labour market. Pupils are trained in some basic skills and to develop their artistic or technical aptitudes;

6. *humanistic*: because pupils in basic education are acquiring information and gaining knowledge of their cultural heritage and the social values of their community and country;

7. *scientific*: because research bases are taken into account to develop research skills and logical capabilities for analysis and reflexion;

8. *creative*: in being concerned with development of the imagination, with initiative and originality in order to maintain and develop a capacity for innovation in the Venezuelan population.

So the new basic education takes the necessary steps to establish a balance between individual needs and the social and cultural values of the wider community in which the individual can participate; being a democratic society. Venezuelan basic education is based on scientific eclecticism on both philosophical and psychological grounds.

Philosophical Principles of Basic Education from 1980

(a) Self-determination:

Education is a public service which provides equal opportunities for all. Consequently it is compulsory, universal, and free. It demands moral fitness from teachers and pupils alike; an individual respect for the freedom of all. National defence of Venezuelan democracy and community participation in it are also basic aims towards which those experiencing basic education are led. In order to achieve self-determination within these broad parameters, the physical, emotional, social, intellectual, and environmental context of pupils provide the reality within which basic education must concentrate its curricular design in order to succeed. Basic education provision is looking for a close relationship between teacher, pupil, and school community, within which self-determination can be promoted while group, local, and national considerations are properly understood.

(b) Self-realization:

This is another principle within which the idea of providing pupils with learning skills for decision-taking can rest. It has to do with responsibility and initiative. Teachers are required to be competent professionals, and their professional freedom is respected. This allows them to develop their own lessons within the guidelines of the school syllabuses. They have to satisfy their pupils' needs, and in so doing are free to choose whatever teacher methodology meets the demand. At the same time, a democratic teaching system helps to develop community activities and tolerant attitudes towards the ideas, beliefs, and actions of others, individually and collectively.

Psychological Principles of Basic Education from 1980

The psychological bases are also founded on scientific eclecticism. Thus Nacarid Rodriguez points out that psychology contributes to the curriculum in two ways:

1. by providing a learning theory which gives guidance to the planning of teaching;

2. by providing a conception of child development whereby it is necessary to select and organize the content and method of teaching-learning according to the age of the child and the stage of development reached (Rodriguez, 1983).

There are in fact four main psychological elements behind Venezuelan basic education as reformed in 1980.

(a) The Influence of Behaviourist Theory:

First, the school syllabuses are designed in terms of behavioural objectives. These objectives identify pupils' needs in order to facilitate their assessment according to the achieved objectives. Second, the teaching process must consider pupils' motivation as a way of stimulating their responses from the acquired knowledge. Finally, the need for practising and reinforcing the abilities and skills which have not been totally achieved must be recognized.

(b) The Influence of Cognitive Theory:

On the one hand, human development study is included in order to obtain a better comprehension of the individual, but on the other, basic education includes the study of thinking skills such as problem-solving and reasoning.

(c) The Influence of Humanist Theory:

From this theory the conception of lifelong education was taken to be applied to Venezüelan basic education: self-realization and socialization, which are specially linked to social and environmental change, are by nature dynamic and long-term concepts.

(d) The Influence of Social Psychology Theory:

The importance of environmental context to the communication process is fundamental to work, individually or within a group, since a variety of human types and groups comprise the grist of the education process. They include pupils, parents, teachers, and community agencies. With this in mind the 1980 basic education reform was also founded on accommodation of the following social-psychological dimensions: individual differences; motivation; feelings and values; participation. Sensitivity to these dimensions of human psychology is fundamental to the spirit and content of the reform.

Pupils may learn by themselves against the traditional system in which learning used to be memoristic. According to this conception, Humberto Anzola points out that such an approach promotes new attitudes in which a double process is achieved. On one side the teacher's role is to operate as a guide in the learning process; on the other side the pupils learn by doing, creating, and working (Anzola, 1985: 6-7).

The formative influence of the various philosophical and psychological theories is quite evident in the article of the 1980 Education Law that refers to basic education:

> Basic Education has as its aim, the contribution to the integral education of pupils through the development of their skills and their scientific, technical, humanistic and artistic capabilities; it has the task of running pupils' exploration, educative and vocational guidance and to initiate them with the learning of some disciplines and techniques which allow them to perform a socially useful function; it stimulates the wish of knowing and develops individual capabilities according to their aptitudes.
>
> Basic Education will last no less than nine years. The Ministry of Education will run craft courses in this level which allows pupils to acquire training in an occupation. (Ministerio de Educacion, 1985b)

Main Elements of the Post-1980 Basic Education Curriculum

(a) Content:

In Venezuela the curriculum plan for basic education is a part of the educational policy of the country, and it constitutes a scientific and technical tool. It includes study areas and subjects which have been set out on a legal basis, designed for this level and with a specific number of hours per week by grade.

The nine-year programme is divided into three stages with three grades within each, and a set of goals for each. The *first* stage stresses development of reading, writing, and elementary numeracy skills as well as the creation of certain habits based on accepted moral and spiritual values. The *second* stage concentrates on providing linguistic competence and strengthening those values related to national identity. The *third* stage emphasizes technical, scientific, and humanistic training. During this period the pupil is supposed to acquire the competence for making decisions in relation to proceeding to further education or seeking employment (Ministerio de Educacion, 1985c).

Arising from these stated objectives, the composition of the formal basic education curriculum that has emerged, comprises the following subjects: Spanish language, mathematics, Venezuelan and world history and geography, citizenship, aesthetics, sciences, physical education, health education, biology, physics, chemistry, English, and 'education for work'. Virtually the whole programme is compulsory, only workshop training becoming an optional subject in the three final years. This curriculum plan postpones as late as possible the final choice as between vocation and further studies. Table 9.1 sets out the exact composition and the duration of each component.

There is some flexibility in this programme according to the location of particular schools and communities. For example, in relation to rural education, the programme schedules vary the number of hours per week in some subjects, in order to attend to the population's main characteristics. The subject 'cooperativismo' in social studies is included within the plan. This subject looks for the training of citizens who can promote their own work. The inclusion of this subject within the programme is an attempt to reduce migration which normally results in unemployment in marginal urban areas. Nonetheless, Venezuelan rural education still faces the problem of teaching factual and relevant knowledge, and reference materials continue to be very theoretical and unrelated to the rural environment. This is despite well accepted concern for education in rural areas:

> The underlying educational concept should be to maximize literacy and basic education whenever it can be well used and maintained and to relate rural education to the condition of life and work. (Philips, 1975: 216)

An important limiting factor influencing rural education is the supply and training of suitable teachers. Broadly speaking, teachers are poorly paid and trained, as well as frequently not being motivated towards rural life.

Table 9.1:

The Curricular Framework of Venezuelan Basic Education

		Number of hours per week by grade								
	Grades	First stage			Second stage			Third stage		
Areas	Subjects	1	2	3	4	5	6	7	8	9
Language	Spanish lang. and literature	10	10	10	6	6	6	5	5	4
	English	-	-	-	-	-	-	4	3	3
Mathematics	Mathematics	8	8	8	6	5	4	4	4	4
Nature Sciences and Health Education	Nature study	1	1	1	2	3	4	4	-	-
	Health educ'n	1	1	1	1	2	2	1	1	1
	Biology	-	-	-	-	-	-	-	4	4
	Physics	-	-	-	-	-	-	-	2	4
	Chemistry	-	-	-	-	-	-	-	2	3
Social Studies	Venezuelan History	1	1	1	1	2	2	2	3	1
	Venezuelan Geography	1	1	1	1	2	2	2	3	-
	Citizenship	1	1	1	1	2	2	2	-	-
	World history	-	-	-	-	-	-	-	-	3
	World geog'y	-	-	-	-	-	-	-	-	3
Aesthetic Education	Plastic Arts	2	2	2	2	1	1	-	-	-
	Music	2	2	2	1	1	1	-	-	-
	Artistic Education	-	-	-	-	-	-	2	3	-
Physical Training	Physical Tr'ng and Sports	2	2	2	2	2	2	2	2	2
Education for work	Education for work	1	1	1	2	2	2	4	8*	8*
Recess		2.5	2.5	2.5	2.5	2.5	2.5	-	-	-
Planning		1	1	1	1	1	1	-	-	-

* The time will depend on the pupil's craft choice and the school's facility to offer courses (this will vary from region to region).

Source: Ministerio de Educacion, 1985c: 13

The 'programme for intercultural bilingual education' establishes the teaching of its mother tongue in its cultural context including the national language. With drama as a subject, schools also help to ensure the stability of Venezuelan society through programmes based on shared traditions which are upheld by the groups in its society. The aim is to offer all indigenous pupils the opportunity of becoming bilingual and bicultural. In fact all aspects of the study programme for each year are laid down in considerable detail, giving precise indication of the degree of maturity which is expected, as well as the objectives aimed at, the teaching strategies preferred, and the modes of assessment. This degree of detail has long been part of the Venezuelan prescriptive system. Even in 1974 a visiting Professor of Education commented:

> With several items per page thus producing a manual, for a single year, which will seem natural and valuable to a Venezuelan teacher and almost totally foreign and incomprehensible to many English speaking teachers. (Burroughs, 1974: 72)

The explanation of this is twofold. First, as the opening section of this chapter has shown, the Venezuelan educational system is highly centralized. In this kind of system, study programmes, strategies for teaching, systems of assessment, and so forth rest at the Central Ministry level, leaving only a narrow margin to heads and the personal initiative of individual teachers. As a result, many Venezuelan teachers are ill-prepared to decide by themselves what and how to teach pupils. They have come to rely absolutely on teaching guides, which they have neither the authority nor the freedom to modify. It is not surprising in these circumstances that the Ministry of Education itself has realized that: 'Teachers lack satisfactory training in relation to technical aspects such as objectives and learning processes' (Ministerio de Educacion, 1985a: 239).

The new curriculum plan of 1980 inevitably increased the need for new elements of teacher training and the Curriculum Department designed a teacher's handbook per grade and subject. These handbooks guide teachers and enable them to put into practice the study programme in a more effective way than would otherwise be the case. In general terms the handbooks broaden the methodological strategies and provide some new techniques in respect of pupil assessment. There is also a selected bibliography for further reading. The books overall provide various examples of urban, rural, and indigenous realities in order to contribute towards improving the teachers' contextual knowledge. The handbooks also provide useful ideas about planning lessons, using resources, and self-education by the teacher in order to broaden personal education (Ministerio de Educacion, 1985c). In considering the study programmes and teachers' handbooks as official documents, it is unquestionable that they define in detail all matters in relation to acceptable teacher-pupil interaction. As the Ministry of Education is therefore totally responsible, in control of every single matter related to any school, it is not surprising that teachers have little or no incentive in promoting innovation in their schools.

(b) Assessment and Evaluation:

In the area of pupil assessment there has been fundamental change. First, the elimination of the final examination at Basic and Diversified and Professional levels must be considered the most important change (Ministerio de Educacion, 1985e). Until July 1985 automatic promotion was applied to those pupils from first to fifth grade. From sixth grade and onwards, the pupil's work in each grade was assessed by means of a final annual examination in each subject. Those pupils who failed in one or more subjects had the opportunity to re-sit each in September; if they failed at this re-sit in three or more subjects they had to repeat the academic year. Since 1985 the final class mark for those pupils studying seventh grade and onwards is determined by the average obtained at the end of each period into which the school year is divided: September to December; January to April; May to July. Those pupils who do not reach the pass marks on half plus one of the studied subjects have the opportunity to be re-examined in any given subject. Those, however, who fail in two or more subjects now repeat the school year from the seventh grade onward (Ministerio de Educacion, 1985e: 37).

In addition to opening up the flow of students in this way, the greater variety of evaluation techniques now employed enable more flexibility in identifying and promoting individual capacities of pupils. For example, *formative evaluation* is used by teachers in order to determine the student's progress during the teaching and learning process. Its purpose is the feedback between the pupil and teacher about failures and successes. This kind of evaluation feeds into the work of the teacher in developing personal strategies and lesson plans to meet the stated objectives of curriculum guidelines (Ministerio de Educacion, 1985e: 29-30). Systems of self-evaluation are also now employed (Ministerio de Educacion, 1983: 30-32), as well as *co-evaluation* which is reciprocal evaluation carried out between pupils by themselves. Among other things, this enables pupils to realize their interdependence and the need for co-existence (Ministerio de Educacion, 1985: 34-37).

Throughout these various forms of evaluation a greater variety of individual skills and attributes are recorded than was possible through the old rote and recall examinations, and this goes a significant way towards reducing high rates of wastage and repeating, a trait which Venezuela, in keeping with many other Latin American countries, had been characterized by for a very long time.

(c) Pastoral Dimensions:

The 1985 Venezuelan educational reform was also very important in relation to new policies for pupils' welfare, under the office of *Asuntos Socio-Educativos* (Social Education Affairs). The whole programme covers four fields of action: social, health, children's feeding, and scholarships programmes.

The *social programme* has as its main purposes the study and prevention of social problems, which affect a considerable percentage of Venezuela's school population, and assistance in resolving them (Ministerio de Educacion, 1985f). The social worker and the specialist counsellor keep close ties between the school, family, and the community for those children who have problematic records of low achievement, behaviour, repeating and drop-out. In some cases, lectures for parents, and class parents' meetings are the basic channels through which the specialist keeps in touch with the families concerned. With younger children (seven to ten) the social programme is mainly concerned with low achievement and drop-out because, traditionally, large numbers of children who had enrolled in Venezuelan schools, indeed the majority, dropped out in the first two or three years. With older students (eleven to fifteen) social work is more related to careers guidance and vocational education, with community involvement.

With respect to the *health programme*, the approach is mainly preventive, aiming to protect student health, to achieve desirable hygienic practice, and to diagnose common diseases among Venezuelan students (Ministerio de Educacion, 1985g). Much stress is placed on the overall sanitary conditions, and special talks are arranged on hygiene for both children and parents, specially in those areas greatly handicapped by a severe lack of economic and environmental resources.

The *feeding programme* provides daily milk to those children from pre-school to sixth grade. It is important to mention that this programme has only operated in some Venezuelan deprived regions since October 1984, but in its complete form serves more than three million students. It also provides over 14,000 daily meals in the country to those children from the most marginal and rural areas.

The fourth programme related to students' welfare is concerned to offer *scholarships*. In 1985 the Ministry of Education awarded 104,000 scholarships for students from pre-school through postgraduate level. According to the Director of Social Educational Affairs, this programme is totally computerized, with specific criteria to choose the students according to their social and economic situation and study level (Larralde, 1985: 40).

All four welfare programmes are in the process of implementation throughout Venezuela and represent a major, committed, and spirited attempt to overcome the old constraints on educational experience that tended to be merely accepted. The creation of an integral nucleus of student welfare organization (Nucleos Integrales de Bienestar Estudiantil or NIBE) coordinates the work through a regional structure designed to identify need and alleviate the problem at local levels (Ministerio de Educacion, 1985h). Each NIBE is the centre for service to the individual student. It has a school doctor, dentist, social worker, psychologist, and a counsellor. As well as assisting the student, it also tries to involve parents, teachers, and other groups and institutions in seeking solutions to welfare problems. Any one NIBE may serve several schools in the same area.

Despite these innovative efforts, children's social welfare programmes still only reach a minority of the student population. Until all those in need are reached, the learning capacity of children will continue to be impaired by tiredness and malnutrition. To strengthen the base of curricular reform, more funds will have to be spent on social programmes, and this is fully recognized by educational planners in Venezuela.

(d) School Management:

Not surprisingly the 1980 educational reform also brought forward some changes in relation to the administration and management of schools. In building up the new model, the Ministry of Education worked on some fundamental reconsiderations, in particular the concept of basic education as a service, and not linked to a physical building. With basic education divided into three stages of three years' duration, each stage provides the essential component to be organized into a school. The management of the curriculum, however, has to allow integration between the different stages as the study subjects progress. In other words the authorities chose a curriculum-led rather than a structure-led model of reform (Ministerio de Educacion, 1985i: 4-5).

The management structure of each school consists of a headteacher, a deputy head, a teachers' co-ordinator to each stage, heads of academic departments, coordinators of different technical and administrative departments, and subject teachers. Within the Venezuelan system a head is an:

> innate representative of the Ministry of Education within the school and the community

> and whom conjointly with the deputy head exerts managerial functions within the institution. (Chacon, 1977: 113-114)

That is to say Venezuelan heads and deputy heads are line-officers directly responsible to the central administration and exist to carry through its directives. In this sense, the same is true for responsibility posts within the school in their relationship to the head. This is, of course, a matter of policy within a centralized system, but the lack of innovation in the structural organization and administration is also due to financial constraints. However, with such fundamental philosophical change in respect of curricular intentions there has to be change somewhere in the teacher training process.

(e) Teacher Training:

The 1980 Law, in Article 77 states that teachers' qualifications must be of higher education standard than previously (Republica de Venezuela, 1980). The threshold for primary training level had been upper secondary and for secondary training, the level moved up to post-secondary programmes in the pedagogic and higher institutions. Although the bulk of Venezuelan primary teachers are trained, they are still poorly educated and therefore unable to cope with the range of activities that the new educational reform requires of them.

In order to provide for the requirements of the reform, all pedagogical and higher education institutions and universities engaged in human resource development, revised and rationalized their curricula by adopting a common core for the whole country with some variations according to each institution and its specializations. There are two reasons for this. First a common core curriculum facilitates the horizontal and vertical mobility of students within the educational system, and secondly the decision is a means of diminishing costs, because human resources and instructional materials can be interchanged between institutions.

The experimental Pedagogic University 'Libertador' was created by the reform in order to centralize all matters arising that related to the initial and in-service training of teachers. It was injected into the system as the means of creating the necessary innovation, thus avoiding the difficult problem of inducing existing colleges to initiate the change (Universidad Pedagogica Experimental Libertador, 1985a). The teacher training curriculum design that emerged comprises the following four components: general knowledge, pedagogic studies, a specialization, and professional training (Universidad Pedagogica Experimental Libertador, 1985b). The specialization component varies according to the subject chosen by the student. The remaining components are common factors in the preparation of teaching profession throughout the country. It is a maxim that the success of any educational reform depends upon the calibre and effectiveness of the teachers. Short courses are given to teachers to enable new syllabuses and methodologies to be implanted. Five years have already passed since the Educational Law was approved and still the curriculum design of teachers' training is incomplete in practice. So serving teachers as well as initial trainees in fact still lack the preparation to face requirements that the new basic education demands of them.

. . . .

It can be seen, then, that despite genuinely radical elements and intentions towards the widening of access to education and the experience of a more dynamic curriculum, at the compulsory education level, the reform has to some extent been overtaken by inertia. However, the new basic education of Venezuela is also open to adult learners and we must now examine contemporary developments in that sector.

CONTEMPORARY ADULT EDUCATION IN VENEZUELA

Two main aspects of adult education will be considered here: the Literacy Plan (1985-1987) and the basic education design for adults.

The Illiteracy Problem

Over the past thirty or so years of Venezuelan democracy, the state has been paying special attention to the illiteracy problem due to the high, though reducing, proportion of illiterates within the country. Table 9.2 takes selected years from 1958 to 1984 and clearly illustrates the dimensions of the problem and the trend.

According to these figures, government actions seem to have been effective. One of those actions (Resolution number 10) established the Priority Literacy Programme (Andres Bello) in 1977. Another important initiative was a National Literacy Commission formed by integrating members from different official and private bodies. In the 1970s the Venezuelan government, with UNESCO's cooperation, started a pilot project on functional literacy. The aim was to run an integral programme for education to involve not just literacy, but also accelerated primary education and work training for adult people.

By the time of the 1980 reform the National Literacy Commission had extended its attention to rural and bilingual education in the Amerindian communities, with the aim of preserving their vernacular languages (Ministerio de Educacion, 1985j). Venezuela (as other Latin American countries) is a member state of UNESCO and participates in its project of literacy and adult education, whose main aim is

Table 9.2: The Trend in Illiteracy in Venezuela: 1958-1984

Year	Total population	Illiterate population	%
1958	4,272,184	2,426,463 (aged over 10)	56
1961	4,986,583	1,734,791 (aged over 10)	34.8
1971	7,331,952	1,681,630 (aged over 10)	22.9
1984	16,754,617	1,201,910 (aged over 15)	11

Source: Ministerio de Educacion, 1985j: 4-7

to erradicate illiteracy by 1999. The National Literacy Plan, established to function between 1985 and 1987 with the aim of creating no less than 600,000 newly literate people, is part of the international effort. This represents about half the illiterates remaining in Venezuela at the beginning of the project. The National Literacy Plan aims:

1. to reduce illiteracy rates throughout the country;

2. to establish and support different ways of providing basic education to people who have taken the literacy programme;

3. to provide short courses for post-literate people.

The *principles* implied in this plan are:

1. *participation*: many community bodies from the private and official sectors are called to run the planning and execution of the literacy programmes.

2. *co-ordination*: between the participative agencies to make best use of resources and agree on common targets.

3. *flexibility*: to allow each agency to administrate their own teaching resources and strategies. Each agency is free to apply its own methodology according to their adults' needs, which will depend on the environment (urban, rural, Amerindian) the age-group, and other important local characteristics.

4. *innovation and research*: programmes' evaluation processes provide elements to look for new approaches and alternatives for adult education.

The *teaching strategies* applied within the Literacy Plan are both conventional and non-conventional. The conventional or formal strategies are directed to individual instruction in order to provide the users with academic knowledge to ensure access to another educational level. Non-conventional strategies are devoted to satisfy community needs in each population group in order to link adult education with the promotion of social change. The process of popular education for adults has to be located in their own community so that favourable change can take place in their society. There is considerable flexibility here with six different bodies offering literacy programmes.

(a) The Ministry of Education:

This centralizes all planning, co-ordination, and evaluation processes. In addition, its programme includes attention to rural, urban and Amerindian areas. The methodology applied, is called 'Abajo Cadenas', and is based in the words technique which introduces a number of words at the beginning of the course with some basic sounds of the language. Those words must be related to the common language of the users. Reading and writing are simultaneously taught. Many leaflets are produced to support that learning process with reference to special topics such as health, civics, production, home economics, and other important aspects relevant to everyday life in Venezuela.

(b) The Ministry of Agriculture and the National Agrarian Institute:

This programme is called 'Literacy and Basic Education'. It includes four pamphlets, and the methodology is based in daily dialogue to ensure the client's participation. Furthermore it concentrates on solving problems related to the client's everyday needs.

(c) The National Institute of Educational Cooperation:

This has the 'A.B.C.' course, from which it is expected to read and to analyze written questions, to fill application forms, and to write short sentences. After it, users are able to carry on with, or proceed to, basic education level.

(d) Cultural Action for the Development 'Acude':

This is a privately promoted audio-visual system by which reading, writing, maths, basic economics, work techniques, health, and community life are taught. It is based on self-learning techniques devoted to adults and young people who need to use their free time for training. It includes a basic pamphlet, records and record player.

(e) Radio Station Institute 'Fe y Alegria':

This is another model which uses the ECCA media system in which the user receives a daily broadcast lesson. It also has pamphlets and exercises to complete and motivates the user to follow forthcoming lessons.

(f) The National Literacy Plan:

This is mainly taught by voluntary tutors who have attended special short courses which show them how to teach adults and to know the programmes which they will be using. Those voluntary tutors come from different organizations, such as trades unions, students, teachers, and other social groups. In this case it is important to say that in Venezuela there is no teacher training education for adult work at any level. Consequently, teachers are trained to work in pre-school, basic education or secondary school levels, and adult education teacher training programmes are attended by non- specialist teachers. The training programmes for voluntary tutors are organized by the individual agencies described above and take account of the needs of both tutors and their students.

The *evaluation process* for the Literacy Plan is very important, and it involves teaching aspects, planning, administration, tutors' effectiveness and training, statistics, execution, supervision, co-ordination among participatory agencies, and other variables.

Adult Basic Education

Adult basic education is justifiably considered a real innovation in the formal Venezuelan educational system since it provides academic knowledge and professional training to a sector of the population which has not completed or ever started basic education. It is designed according to the lifelong education approach, and is mainly characterized by:

Flexibility: allowing a continuous feedback to the planning process as a result of emerging needs as they arise; the programme must satisfy both the population's expectations and national development needs.

Participation: involving the participation of private, official, and other bodies in cooperating in the planning, development, and execution of basic adult education projects.

Innovation: including teaching techniques such as self-learning, responsibility, self-evaluation, distance courses, and other new methods emerging from related fields. Particular initiatives and individual creativity are considered important in order to satisfy social and individual needs and demands in educational terms.

Sequence: the curriculum elements are designed in such a way that clients, either by formal schooling or non-formal programmes, have the opportunity to obtain the basic education certificate. These curriculum elements must be able to ensure clients access to education at any stage. Thus a pupil who leaves daily basic education at the seventh grade can enter adult basic education at the same grade provided he or she is over 15 years of age, notwithstanding differences of syllabus and methodology.

Functionality: the planning process for adult basic education has to pay attention to regional and local needs within the country, offering different learning methods to users according to their particular characteristics.

In the 1980 Education Law, adult education is defined as a 'modality' within the system. A 'modality' is understood as the provision established by law in order to pay particular attention to specific characteristics of different sectors of basic education population. The modalities are: adult, special, military, and arts education within the education system. Administration of adult education can be provided either in school or non-school courses. Students' existing knowledge, skills and experiences are credited on their admission. Schooling and non-schooling courses are designed to respond to national, regional, local, and individual needs following lifelong curriculum patterns.

The *Curriculum Plan* is considered a technical instrument because it must guarantee the adjustment of the legal bases, syllabuses, and goals of adult education to the peculiar needs of clientele in widely differing circumstances. The plan comprises two sectors: an academic sector which involves humanities, arts, and scientific education; a technical and professional sector which involves the development of abilities and skills to improve users' job performance or to equip them with skills to enter the labour market.

Table 9.3 illustrates the Curriculum Plan through which the basic education cycle is offered to adults in Venezuela. The plan is rendered operational through a threefold system of syllabus construction.

First, the Ministry of Education designs the overall plan, deciding each course length and the user profiles. It is at this stage that syllabuses for both sectors (academic and professional) are elaborated. Second, syllabuses are complemented in cooperation with *regional* offices. Teachers, specialists and other agencies may insert a set of objectives relevant to the needs and characteristics of their particular region. Third, at the *local* level teachers are allowed to include a set of objectives and contents which they consider relevant to satisfy local and individual user needs.

In relation to time allocation for the courses length, it is well known that adult characteristics and personal capabilities are very difficult to correspond to the length of pre-fixed courses. Therefore, the basic education curriculum establishes that adult basic education may last twelve semesters (half years). Nevertheless, as a result of its flexibility, clients are able to fix their own time. It depends on their individual learning rhythm and progress. Users are invited to take examinations at any time in their learning process, but the most important innovation is that client's prior experience and knowledge are officially recognized by crediting them when they take an examination or otherwise demonstrate such skills. Clearly the imaginative way in which basic education is made available to adults contrasts somewhat with the way in which it is made to fit existing school structures at the compulsory stage.

SPECIAL EDUCATION IN VENEZUELA

The Venezuelan state assumed complete responsibility for the education of handicapped children from 1975. Before then, some institutions were wholly in the private sector (Ministerio de Educacion, 1985k). The Educational Law of 1980 considers special education as a 'modality' of the Venezuelan educational system. In other words this sector becomes integrated with the others. It is accepted that people with various handicaps are entitled to develop their potentialities in order to participate in an active life within the community.

Figures from the Ministry of Education show that enrolment of children in special education rose steadily from 1979, when 5,273 pupils attended, to 1984, when the number had risen to 14,265 (Ministerio de Educacion, 1984d). By 1985, there were 745 centres of special education throughout the country, which paid attention to children with mental retardation, visual and hearing deficiencies, speech defects and physical handicaps (Ministerio de Educacion, 1984d: 1).

The main reform within special education has been the policy of integration, by which children with visual and hearing deficiencies, but normal cognitive development, can be incorporated in a regular class. In the same way, slightly mentally retarded children are sent to regular schools in order to achieve integration with normal children (Ministerio de Educacion, 1984d: 7). The curriculum for the handicapped child has also been reformed. According to the Ministerial Special Education Directorate, experience with children within this group has revealed that a large number of children do not have real learning difficulties, but they have a poor school achievement due to other reasons, such as problems of social background and deficiencies in the *process* of teaching and learning to read. They fail to read because they are tied to mass communication systems such as TV, video and radio. In response, the Special Education Directorate has implemented a new reading programme which as a basis takes into account the cognitive process related to the act of reading, the linguistic elements, socio-cultural variables and teachers' preparation. The programme was developed with the help of UNESCO and the International Association of Reading (Ministerio de Educacion, 1984d: 44-45).

The main limitation in Venezuelan special education is a severe lack of trained teachers. By 1985 there were 2,282

Table 9.3:

The Curriculum Plan Design for Basic Education for Adults

Sectors (2)	Areas (7)	Subjects (13)
Academic	Language	Castillian Foreign language
	Mathematics	Mathematics
	Sciences	Natural sciences Biological sciences Health education Physics Chemistry
	Social Studies	Venezuelan geography Venezuelan history Universal history Family education and civics
	Aesthetics	Artistic education
Professional	Agricultural	* Subjects are chosen by users
(Education to work)*	Industrial Services	

Source: Ministerio de Educacion, 1985c: 6-7

teachers who worked with handicapped children at the ratio of eight to ten pupils per teacher. However, 50 per cent of them were not specialists, and this highlights a very critical problem, since the quality and success in teaching handicapped children in particular depends to a great extent upon the teacher's special preparation.

INTERNATIONAL COOPERATION AND VENEZUELAN EDUCATIONAL DEVELOPMENT

As no reform comes alone, a brief reference to the external cooperation with Venezuelan education reform must be made. Venezuelan educational policies have a long tradition of international cooperation leading to incorporation of suitable innovations into the educational system.

In particular, UNESCO's support of Venezuelan education reform has been very significant. Most recently, assistance for the Venezuelan Reform of 1986-1987 was sought from UNESCO at the 23rd International Conference held in Sophia in October 1985 (Carbonell, 1985). This is a two-way process whereby Venezuelan support is also offered to UNESCO programmes. At the time of writing, Venezuela is cooperating in the following UNESCO programmes:

1. *Programme II: Education for All*

2. *Programme III: Communications as a Human Service*

3. *Programme IV: Conception and Application of Educative Policies*

4. *Programme V: Education, Formation and Society*

The Organization of American States (OAS) is another body that offers external help to the development of education in Latin American and Caribbean countries. Here again, Venezuela is both a giver and receiver, being involved in at least ten OAE education programmes. Venezuela also operates bilateral educational links.

. . . .

In this chapter, it has not been the intention to describe and analyze the entire education system of Venezuela. Rather it has been to focus on an essential characteristic of contemporary Venezuelan education, namely reform and cooperation. Serious attempts have been made in the 1980s, enabled by the 1980 Education Law, to move away from the traditionally restrictive and partial system into a more open and accessible provision which any state aspiring to modernization needs. Venezuela is fortunate to have, at least for a while, profitable material resources. She also holds a key geographical position in the Caribbean region. The 1980 law, and especially its application to the wider provision of basic education, was intended to enable Venezuela to realize the potential that is undoubtedly there in both social and economic terms.

BIBLIOGRAPHICAL REFERENCES

Anzola, H. (1985) Aproximaçiones en torno a la escuela activa, **Ultimas Noticias Suplemento Cultural** 913

Burroughs, G.E.R. (1974) **Education in Venezuela** (London, Newton Abott)

Carbonell, L.M.(1985) **23a Conferencia Internacional de La Unesco** (Informe que presenta el Ministerio de Educacion en relacion con las observaciones al proyecto de programa y presupuesto de Unesco para 1986-1987, Sofia - Octubre)

Chacon, F. (1977) **Liderazgo Docente en Accion** (Caracas, Ministerio de Educacion Oficina Sectorial de Planificacion y Presupuesto, Departamento de Documentacion Bibliografica)

Constitucion de la Republica de Venezuela, (1961) No.662, Extraordinario (23 de Enero) La Torre Caracas, Venezuela 18

De Armas Chitty, J.A. (1976) Los 95 anos del Ministerio de Educacion, **Educacion** 159

Larralde, M.L.(1985) Ministerio Educacion reactiva los programas de asistencia socio-economica, **El Universal**, Domingo 6 de Octubre

Marrero, J. (1960) El bachillerato y la Educacion Media, **Educacion** 59

Marrero, J. (1964) Para una reforma del bachillerato nocturno en Venezuela, **Correo de Educacion**, Abril

Ministerio de Educacion (1982a) **Que es la Educacion Basica?** (Caracas, Oficina Sectorial de Planificacion y Presupuesto)

Ministerio de Educacion (1982b) Diseno curricular del nivel Pre-escolar **Normativo**

Ministerio de Educacion (1983) **Evaluacion Guia del Docente** (version revisada), Octubre

Ministerio de Educacion (1984a) **Innovacion Educativa y Formacion de Docentes** (Caracas, Division de estadistica)

Ministerio de Educacion (1984b) **Desarrollo de la Educacion 1981 a 1986** (Caracas, Oficina Sectorial de Planificacion y Presupuesto)

Ministerio de Educacion (1984c) **Memoria y Cuenta**, Capitulo VI, Resumen estadistico, desercion escolar en educacion basica (1o a 6o grado) (Caracas)

Ministerio de Educacion (1984d) **La Educacion Especial en Venezuela** (Caracas, Direccion de Educacion Especial)

Ministerio de Educacion (1985a) Informe preliminar de la evaluacion del proyecto educacion basica, **Curriculum** 16

Ministerio de Educacion (1985b) **Normativo de Educacion Basica** (Caracas, Oficina Sectorial de Planificacion y Presupuesto)

Ministerio de Educacion (1985c) **Plan de Estudio Educacion Basica** (Caracas, Oficina Sectorial de Planificacion y Presupuesto)

Ministerio de Educacion (1985d) **Manual del Docente** (Caracas, Division Curricula Grabados Nacionales C.A. Edo. Aragua)

Ministerio de Educacion (1985e) **Reglamento General de la Ley Organica**, Segunda version del Consejo Central, Capitulo V (Caracas)

Ministerio de Educacion (1985f) **Lineamientos del Programa Social 1985-1986** (Caracas, Oficina de Asuntos Socio-Educativos)

Ministerio de Educacion (1985g) **Programa Salud** (Caracas, Oficina de Asuntos Socio-Educativos)

Ministerio de Educacion (1985h) **Nucleos Integrales de Bienestar Estudiantil** (Caracas, Oficina de Asuntos Socio-Educativos)

Ministerio de Educacion (1985i) **Estructura Organizativa de la Escuela Basica** (Caracas, Division de Organizacion y Sistemas)

Ministerio de Educacion (1985j) **Plan Nacional de Alfabetizacion** (Caracas, Comision Nacional de Alfabetizacion)

Ministerio de Educacion (1985k) **Informe de la Direccion de Educacion Especial sobre las Acciones Cumplidas en 1984-1985** (Caracas)

Philips, H.M. (1975) **Basic Education, A World Challenge: Measures and Innovations**, (London, New York, Sydney, Toronto: John Wiley)

Republica de Venezuela (1980) **Ley Organica de Educacion Gaceta Oficial** 2635, (Extraordinario - 28 Julio) (Caracas)

Rodriguez, N. (1983) Criterios para el analisis del diseno curricular, **Cuadernos Educacion** 102: 73-86

UNESCO (1983) Declaracion de Mexico, **Curriculum** 13: 15-22

UNESCO XII Conferencia General (1965) **Educacion** 115: 73

Universidad Pedagogica Experimental Libertador (1985a) **Informe de la Comision Inter-Institucional de Evaluacion y Homologacion Curricular** (Caracas)

Universidad Pedagogica Experimental Libertador (1985b) **Proyecto de Diseno Curricular** (Caracas)

Urriola, J.S. (1973) La educacion permanente de adultos y el desarrollo, **Educacion** 148: 7-18

Zambrano, G. (1983) Educacion Basica, **Educacion** 166: 38-40

INDEX